The Letters of Paul,
Sixth Edition

The Letters of Paul, Sixth Edition

Conversations in Context

Calvin J. Roetzel

WESTMINSTER
JOHN KNOX PRESS
LOUISVILLE • KENTUCKY

Sixth edition
Published by Westminster John Knox Press
Louisville, Kentucky

16 17 18 19 20 21 22 23 24—10 9 8 7 6 5 4 3 2

Book design by Sharon Adams
Cover design by Dilu Nicholas

Library of Congress Cataloging-in-Publication Data

Roetzel, Calvin J.
    The letters of Paul : conversations in context / Calvin J. Roetzel. — Sixth edition.
       pages cm
    Includes bibliographical references and index.
    ISBN 978-0-664-23999-2 (paperback)
    1. Bible. Epistles of Paul—Textbooks. I. Title.
    BS2650.55.R64 2015
    227'.06—dc23

                                                                        2015009075

Most Westminster John Knox Press books are available at special quantity discounts when purchased in bulk by corporations, organizations, and special-interest groups. For more information, please e-mail SpecialSales@wjkbooks.com.

In loving memory of

Frank and Myrtle Roetzel, "The Poor among the Saints,"
parents

Juanita Garciagodoy,
student, colleague, friend

Ernst Käsemann,
teacher

Contents

Images

Preface to the Sixth Edition

Forty years ago I sat down to write the preface to the first edition on my office IBM typewriter. My students were struggling to make sense of Paul's letters, arguably the most important collection of letters ever, and I was trying to help. Fortunately at the same time I was a member of a seminar on the ancient letter in the Society of Biblical Literature. Those two events conspired with the endorsement of this project by Richard Ray, then chief editor of John Knox Press, to give life to the first edition of *The Letters of Paul*. It was 114 pages in length and sold for $4.95. Since that initial effort, teachers, laypersons, seminarians, pastors, and even a prison inmate have joined the readers' circle and offered suggestions for improving this book. I have read them all and am grateful for their suggestions.

While the former revisions addressed gaps and urgent issues left hanging or in need of further development, this edition seeks to be more forthright about how the field has developed and how my mind has changed since that first iteration. It includes an additional chapter on the place of the Gentiles and the Law in the Judaisms of Paul's day, an updated bibliography for further study, and other changes that note the ongoing study of Paul, the marginal Jew, and his conversations with a broadened context. I have tried to smooth lumpy phrasing, to make judicious cuts, and to add some relevant photographic material. I have also tried to underscore the brilliance of Paul's theologizing in context and to acknowledge his human struggles with doubt, the "thorn's" torture, suspicions of converts, prison experience, outsiders' harsh critique, and the heartbreak that the rejection of his own "children" of faith caused. I recognize that Paul was capable of outbursts so harsh and angry that they spawned regret and freely admit that on occasion Paul changed his mind. In his day when the Gentile aggregation of believers was a minority, Paul could hardly have been certain that his version of an inclusive Gentile gospel would survive to shape a majority movement.

Recognizing that reality will help us better appreciate the heat of Paul's defense of his "law-free" gospel and his apostolic legitimacy, while finding in those contrarieties the inspiration for a radical redefinition of power. This edition unapologetically asks more of the first time *and* experienced readers. For those who persevere, however, this edition promises rich treasure. For example, one may find in Paul's vigorous engagement with his context an eschatological vision of reconciliation so grand that it almost takes the breath away, the excitement generated by an unfinished and open future simply inspires, and an emphasis on the solidarity forged by the offering for the "poor among the saints" in Jerusalem that was pregnant with meaning.

In what is likely my last revision of this introduction, no words can express my heartfelt thanks to teachers, students, family, colleagues, friends, laity, and editors past and present who have used and supported this project for forty years. I am especially grateful to Dr. Warren Kendall for allowing me to use photographs made as he followed in some of Paul's footsteps and to Linda Brooks for her expert preparation of photos for print. To the original dedication of the book in memory of my dear parents, "the poor among the saints," this edition adds the name of Juanita Garciagodoy, student, colleague and friend who was snatched from us at a young age by cancer's greedy hand. Her wit, insight, love of texts, compassion, poetic genius, and puckish smile enlivened and enriched her world in countless ways. Of all of my students only she was in the first class at Macalester where we were trying to make sense of Paul's letters *and* with me in my last, where she sat as an auditor. She also was a dear colleague and friend.

This preface must also pay tribute to Ernst Käsemann, who welcomed my family in Tübingen, Germany, when I came to study under him in his last year of his teaching before retirement. I was just a green, aspiring student of Paul beginning my journey, and he was at the end of his distinguished career. His welcome of us as "strangers within his gates" was inspiring and initiated a relationship that continued until his death some thirty years later. His abiding influence on this book will be obvious to any serious student of Paul.

And finally to my esteemed colleagues at Macalester College, where I taught for thirty-five years; to colleagues and students at the University of Minnesota, where I taught and served for portions of eight years; and to colleagues, students, and the dean of the Divinity School of the University of Chicago, who welcomed me as a guest professor: my fragile vocabulary fails to adequately express my thanks. My debt to this great host makes clear that this work was a joint enterprise. Its errors I freely own, and its pages clearly and positively show the fingerprints for good from that great host. Last but not least, I must express my undying thanks to my family that in life's high and low tides nurtured, supported, and encouraged my fascination with Paul: my wife, Caroline; children, Lisa (Alan), Frank (Lisa Chandler), and Mary; and grandson, Anthony.

January 1, 2015
Calvin J. Roetzel,
Arnold Lowe Professor of Religious Studies,
Macalester College, Emeritus;
Sundet Professor of New Testament and Christian Studies,
University of Minnesota, Emeritus;
Visiting Professor, University of Chicago Divinity School

Introduction: Contrary Impressions

Few who know him are neutral about Paul. Some love him; others hate him. And so it has always been. Within his own churches he was worshiped by some and maligned by others, called courageous by some and scoffed as a coward by others, viewed as true by some and dismissed as an impostor by others. In some quarters he was a persona non grata, in others warmly welcomed. In the second century, Polycarp revered him as "blessed and glorious"; a Jewish Christian sect later rebuffed him as Satan incarnate. And so to this day Paul continues to provoke and excite, to challenge and antagonize.

A female student, for example, feels insulted by Paul's views of women. She is offended by the popular legend that calls Paul's "thorn in the flesh" a woman, and she is disgusted by the command in Paul's name in 1 Timothy 2:12 that no woman is "to teach or to have authority over men." Rather, it says there, women are to be silent and submissive, earning their salvation by bearing children *if* they continue in "faith and love and holiness" (2:11–15). How revolting, she says, that Paul should advise male believers "not to touch a woman" (1 Cor. 7:1), or that he should think it shameful for women to speak in church gatherings (1 Cor. 14:34). Instead, he advises them to bring their queries to their husbands in private (1 Cor. 14:35). Why, she asks, should girls grow up thinking there is something dirty or inferior about being female? Why doesn't Paul command women not to touch a man? Why must he assume that subordination of women to men is an essential part of the divine order (1 Cor. 11:3)? In order to realize her full humanity, must a woman feel she is defying the Creator? Are the Christian gospel and full humanity for women mutually exclusive?

Another student of Paul, however, argues that Paul was not a male chauvinist but a feminist. Paul, in his view, has suffered the double misfortune of being misunderstood and having bad press. At the risk of sounding defensive, he asks, "What has a late letter not written by Paul, like 1 Timothy, to do with the views of Paul?" On this issue most scholars agree that Paul did not write 1 Timothy (or 2 Timothy or Titus). In the popular mind, however, the viewpoint expressed in 1 Timothy continues to taint the interpretation of the undisputed Pauline letters. Such a passage as 1 Corinthians 14:33b–36 was most probably not Paul's work. It was probably added later by another hand to make Paul's view conform to that expressed in 1 Timothy. Scholars point out that the verses clearly interrupt Paul's discussion of prophecy, and it flatly contradicts 1 Corinthians 11:5 and following, where Paul takes the active verbal participation of women in the service for granted. Even 1 Corinthians 7:1 ("It is well for a man not to touch a woman") has its positive side. Paul prefers celibacy, not because women are "dirty" or because sex is evil, but because he feels that the special urgency of the times requires emergency measures. With the end in sight, he feels Christians should brace themselves for traumatic suffering. In the face of the impending distress (1 Cor. 7:26), normal domestic concerns must be suspended.

However, what is overlooked in this chapter is the evenhanded way Paul addressed men and women. Concerning marriage Paul said, "Each man should have his own wife and each woman her own husband" (1 Cor. 7:2). Concerning sexual intercourse Paul said, "The husband should give to his wife her conjugal rights, and likewise the wife to her husband" (1 Cor. 7:3). Concerning sexual abstinence Paul addressed the husband and wife together. Concerning divorce Paul said, "The wife should not separate from her husband . . . and . . . the husband should not divorce his wife" (1 Cor. 7:10–11). Concerning mixed marriages Paul said, "If any brother has a wife who is an unbeliever, and she consents to live with him, he should not divorce her. And if any woman has a husband who is an unbeliever, and he consents to live with her, she should not divorce him" (1 Cor. 7:12–13). So throughout the passage, Paul argued for mutual responsibility and the equality of man and woman.

The same impartial treatment is given in 1 Corinthians 11. Verse 3 is usually translated "the head of a woman is her husband." It should read, however, "the source of a woman is her husband." Paul was obviously recalling Genesis 2, where woman is made from a rib taken from Adam's side. Later, Paul notes that God makes woman the source of man (through giving birth) and thus he underscored the interdependence of man and woman (1 Cor. 11:12).

Galatians 3:28, however, best expressed Paul's view: "There is no longer Jew or Greek, there is no longer slave or free, there is no longer male and female; for all of you are one in Christ Jesus." Paul felt that "in Christ" believers already shared in God's new community of the end time. In this new age all barriers that divide the human family are removed, and all obstacles to fulfillment are torn down. Although Paul nowhere attacked prevailing customs that assign women inferior roles in society, he obviously believed they are full partners "in Christ." When one treats women as full and equal citizens in the kingdom of God, it is difficult to hold disparaging views of them. Moreover, only Paul in the entire New Testament named a woman (Junia) as an apostle (Rom. 16:7).

In response to this rejoinder, the female student may still harbor doubts. Can she be sure that 1 Corinthians 14:33b–36 was inserted later? Does it really help to say men and women are equal "in Christ" if old patterns of discrimination are endorsed in Paul's name in the culture? And in spite of this short exercise in biblical interpretation, she does not like the tone of 1 Corinthians 11:7, where Paul says man is the glory of God but woman is the glory of man. Finally, even if 1 Timothy is not Pauline, it is still in the New Testament, and she finds the view of woman expressed in that book disgusting.

Even in these days of renewed interest in religious studies, many students have a cordial dislike for Paul. In their view, whereas the teachings of Jesus are clear, simple, and basic, Paul's writings are abstract, abstruse, and complex. Where Jesus spoke of a childlike trust in the father God, Paul constructed a complicated system of belief. The death of a sparrow brings a groan from the God of Jesus (Luke 12:6); the God Paul knew cared nothing for animals (1 Cor. 9:9–10). Jesus is warm where Paul is harsh; Jesus is patient where Paul is impatient. Jesus is an unassuming, unpretentious—even unlettered— Galilean peasant with a gift of prophetic insight and empathy for the poor and social misfits. Paul the learned rabbi, on the other hand, is seen as a kind of bully, forcing his dogma on others and merciless in his attacks on opponents. In the view of Paul's critics, this apostle to the Gentiles deflected Christianity away from the path, style of life, and teachings of its founder.

Where some see Paul as a corrupter of the religion of Jesus, others see him as the greatest theologian of all time. They point to his brilliant and incisive interpretation of the gospel for the Hellenistic world. It was Paul who took a message that was Hebraic in concept and idiom and adapted it to a non-Jewish setting without dilution or compromise. It was Paul who faced the hard questions about the gospel versus Jewish law, the church versus society, believers versus competing visions of religiousness—questions that had to be answered if the Christian gospel were to remain intact. Moreover, Paul was a daring and imaginative apostle. As a great advocate for the Gentile mission, he crisscrossed Asia Minor and plunged into Europe. Tireless in his mission and undeterred by hardship or persecution, Paul pressed on. And he died with his boots on, still longing to go to Spain, the western horizon of the world he knew.

Where some portray him as a dogmatic grouch, others point to the strains of tenderness in his letters. He tried to be as "gentle as a nurse" with the Thessalonians. He seemed overwhelmed that a brother in Christ, Epaphroditus, would risk his life to serve him. He thought of his converts as his children, and he rejoiced at the restoration of a disciplined member of the congregation. His pastoral concerns surfaced time and again. Unquestionably, his gentle admonition could give way to harsh polemic. But was this because Paul was dogmatic and inflexible or because he felt the essential character of the gospel was being compromised?

Some accuse Paul of male chauvinism, and some think he diverted Christianity from its pure source in the simple religion of Jesus. Many Jews accuse Paul of being the father of anti-Semitism in the West. It was he, they claim, who uprooted the Hebraic heritage from Palestine and turned it into a rival of the synagogue. It was he who lashed out in frustration and anger when Jews resisted his gospel. It was he who warned that acceptance of circumcision meant damnation. And it was he, they believe, who was an apostate from Judaism and who misrepresented the Hebrew religion. Jews find it difficult to understand why Paul the rabbi would call observance of the law dark and joyless. Had he never read Psalm 19, which speaks of the law "reviving the soul" and "rejoicing the heart"? Was he ignorant, they ask, of the traditions of the rabbis, which spoke of the "joy of the commandments"? In their view, the acceptance of Paul means the rejection of Judaism. And all too often it has been a short step from the repudiation of Judaism to the persecution of Jews.

Some Protestants would wince at the suggestion that their theology is anti-Semitic. Nevertheless, many, perhaps most, feel that Christianity according to Paul is the exact opposite of Judaism. They question whether all Jews find delight in the law. The story of Richard Rubenstein would seem to suggest another view of Paul. Rubenstein grew up as a secular Jew and started keeping the law in his late teens. He tells of wanting a "cosmic Lawgiver" who would provide order through discipline. But Rubenstein later came to despise that Lawgiver. His hatred of that exacting Judge ran so deep he wanted to murder him. Then, while mourning the death of his son, he suddenly realized that the law could never give him what he desperately wanted, a triumph over mortality. Finally, while going through psychoanalysis, he discovered a kindred spirit in Paul. The release from the law that Paul found in Christ, Rubenstein found through his psychoanalytical experience. Paul's liberation from a troubled conscience in bondage to the law perfectly described, Rubenstein felt, his own release from deep personal anguish. Thus he came to know Paul as a "spiritual brother."[1]

1. Richard L. Rubenstein, *My Brother Paul* (New York: Harper & Row, 1972), 6ff.

According to the usual Protestant view, Paul, like Rubenstein, found the law oppressive. Through Christ, Paul learned that salvation has an "in spite of" quality. That is, God loves the individual not because of anything he or she does but in spite of his or her inability to become worthy of love. God simply accepts each person as he or she is. It was Paul's emphasis on this "grace" that was distinctive. Others get the impression that though Paul was a marginal Jew he did not break with his native faith. They note that frequently the traditional juxtapositions of Paul and Judaism have been weak. They observe that Judaism also spoke of salvation by grace. They note that the neat dichotomy between faith and works is not really a judgment against Judaism, for Jewish religion did not make that distinction. Last, and most significantly, they find no evidence that Paul ever felt oppressed by the law. Instead, Paul is viewed as a faithful Jew who came to believe that the Messiah had come. This belief did not separate him from Judaism but confirmed his place in it. Thus they feel that Paul did not reject his Jewish heritage but reinterpreted it in light of his experience of Christ. So which was Paul—a Semite turned anti-Semitic, a Christian who rejected his Judaism, or a Jewish Christian who saw his life in Christ as a fulfillment, not a rejection, of Judaism?

The impressions registered here are only a small sample of the opinions about Paul one could assemble. Most readers will bring some notion about Paul to their reading of the letters. Even seasoned biblical critics hardly come to the epistles with a blank tablet. But the honest critic is always testing preliminary impressions against the evidence and correcting them if necessary. The aim of this study is to help the novice read the letters in light of her or his social and cultural background. Through such a reading, perhaps new data will be brought to light that may require the alteration or even surrender of our first impressions. My hope is that such a change will bring our views of Paul into closer conformity with the reality of the man himself.

1

Paul and His Hellenistic World

Most might agree with second-century Polycarp, that neither he nor anyone like him was "able to follow the wisdom of the blessed and glorious Paul" (*Letter to the Philippians* 3.2). Parts of the letters are "hard to understand" (2 Pet. 3:16), and at times we might side with the great Pauline scholar Ernst Käsemann, who once complained that no one understood Paul except the heretic Marcion, and even he misunderstood him. Nevertheless, information about Paul and his world, now available, makes attempts to understand the apostle less daunting, though still difficult. While Paul's letters are understandable only in light of his genius and gospel, understanding their contexts will offer clues to their purpose. In the discussion below we shall examine the milieu of both Paul and his readers for hints of the dynamic of the letters, the refinement of Paul's theologizing and fiery rhetoric that helped shape the Jesus movement.

As Acts suggests, Paul probably grew up in Tarsus, an important commercial, intellectual, administrative, and cultural center on the southeast coast of Asia Minor, modern Turkey (Acts 9:11; 21:39; 22:3). As the Roman provincial capital of Cilicia, Tarsus rivaled Alexandria, Corinth, and Athens in importance. There Paul would have learned his first language. There he would have studied the Septuagint (LXX), the Hebrew Scriptures in Greek translation. There he would have learned to read, to write, and to imitate Greek literary and rhetorical forms. There he would have received his Latinized Greek name *Paulos* (Paul), rather than the Hebrew *Shaul* (Saul, Acts 13:9). There he would have been introduced to a vibrant Hellenistic culture—its anthropology, its political and religious institutions, its cosmology, its sports, and its universalism. There he doubtless would have had both Jewish and non-Jewish friends and playmates. And that rich, multifaceted experience would have lingered to influence his messianist thinking and his worldly experience. Some sense of the interplay of these multiple factors is fundamental for a serious and discerning reading of the letters.

SELECTED WAYS LANGUAGE CREATED A WORLD

The great philosopher of language Ludwig Wittgenstein has taught us that a whole mythology is embedded in our language. Similarly the blind, deaf, and speechless Helen Keller once wrote that the power of language to create and affirm identity is magical. Language, we now know, is no mere passive mirror of the world or a mute tool, to be discarded after world construction is complete. Rather, language shapes one's worldview, one's sense of self, and one's understanding of ultimate reality, history, community, family; and it identifies such mundane things as color, smells, and sacramental meaning. Paul also gained his understanding of life, death, fate, freedom, sin, piety, and community through his native language. Within his Diaspora community Paul became what Adolf Deissmann almost a century ago called a "Septuagint-Jew."[1] But before turning to consider his Greek Scriptures, let us first survey the Hellenistic world bequeathed to him.

While the Septuagint was central to Paul's theology, much of his language and important religious expressions came from the wider Hellenistic culture. The Greek word for "conscience" (*syneidēsis*), for example, commonly appeared in the writings of the Stoic philosophers but is missing entirely from Jewish Scriptures. Even allowing that the thing may exist when the word does not, "conscience," as used by Paul, resembled its Hellenistic parent even when sharing a family likeness with its Jewish genealogy. The apostle appropriated the word to defend himself against charges of insincerity (1 Cor. 4:2), and he asked the Corinthians to acknowledge the truth of his apostolic claim (2 Cor. 5:11). In the first reference Paul allowed that conscience was culturally conditioned, and thus partially flawed, for he argued there that even though no charge was brought against him by his conscience, he was not, therefore, necessarily innocent. For he recognized that he would ultimately have to stand before the divine tribunal ("I am not aware of anything against myself, but I am not thereby acquitted. It is the Lord who judges me," 1 Cor. 4:4). Elsewhere, however, he spoke of the important function of the conscience for the Gentile unbeliever (Rom. 2:15) as well as the "weak" (1 Cor. 8:7, 10, 12). So

---

1. Adolf Deissmann, *Paulus*, 2nd ed. (Tübingen: Mohr [Siebeck], 1925), 69. Eng. trans.: *Paul: A Study in Social and Religious History*, trans. William E. Wilson, 2nd ed. (New York: Harper & Bros., 1927), 90.

Paul's understanding embraced both concepts—conscience that served as an inner critical voice that he recognized as culturally shaped, and conscience as an awareness of the ultimate accountability to the one God. The two stand in tension in Paul's thought, even though both play important roles.

Elsewhere Paul drew on the tradition of the Hellenistic church that predated him. But even if Paul borrowed these traditions, they were no less his own, for in adopting and using the traditions of others Paul shared the views expressed, even if he did not author them. In the closing admonition of his letter to the Philippians, for example, he cited a tradition packed with language from his Hellenistic milieu. There he wrote, "Whatever is true (*alēthē*) is honorable (*semna*), whatever is just (*dikaia*), whatever is pure (*hagna*), whatever is pleasing (*prosphilē*), whatever is commendable (*euphēma*), if there is any excellence (*aretē*), and if there is anything worthy of praise (*epainos*), think about these things" (Phil. 4:8). A survey reveals ways this passage mirrored a world quite apart from that of the Hebrew parent. For example, *alēthēs*, the "true, truthful, or honest," *and semnos*, that which is "august, sacred, or worthy of honor," are hardly intelligible apart from their Hellenistic origin. Anything judged more important—for example, the majesty of the king's throne, gorgeous dress, eloquent speech, beautiful music, or graceful motion—shared that same world. *Hagnos*, much used in Hellenistic circles to refer to the sanctuary, and *prosphiles*, that is, the "lovely, pleasing, or agreeable," likewise are of Hellenistic parentage. *Euphēmos*, what is "auspicious, praiseworthy, attractive, or appealing," and *aretē*, a prominent word in Greek philosophy and literature, referred to excellence of achievement or mastery of a field; it may even signify valor. Also special merit, honor, good fortune, success, and fame likewise had a Hellenistic genealogy. *Epainos*, "recognition, approval, or praise," similarly shared the Hellenistic world of the words above.

The alert reader will recognize the nonbiblical character of other materials in the Pauline epistles. Scholars recognize, for instance, that the virtue and vice lists that interlarded Hellenistic writings shared the world of Paul's letters. Galatians 5:19–23, for example, lists "works of the flesh"—"fornication, impurity, licentiousness, idolatry, sorcery, enmities, strife, jealousy, anger, quarrels, dissensions, factions, envy, drunkenness, carousing and things like these"—to admonish readers to produce the "fruit of the Spirit": "love, joy, peace, patience, kindness, generosity, faithfulness, gentleness, and self-control."[2] Such lists came to Paul from his Hellenized Judaism, and more than an emphasis on works of the law were the focus of his native faith framed by the Hellenistic world. Except for "love," his list of virtues contains nothing

2. For a survey of the literature, see Hans Dieter Betz, *Galatians: A Commentary on Paul's Letter to the Churches in Galatia* (Philadelphia: Fortress Press, 1979), 281–83.

that would have appeared as strange or unusual in conventional Greek ethical writings. The eschatological tone of those lists came from Paul. The very use to which Paul put these lists demonstrates how fully he inhabited his Hellenistic Jewish world.

Paul also made copious use of metaphors from his Greek milieu. While not literally true, the metaphor aimed to provoke thought and to engage the hearer as an imaginative partner in conversation. If one should say, "Sam Jackson is a horse," or "Stephanie Grant is a gazelle," the hearer would know those expressions are not to be taken literally, but at some level they are true.

So also Paul's letters use metaphors from sports, politics, nature, and religion to provoke thought. In 1 Corinthians 9:24–27, for example, Paul used a boxing metaphor to describe his discipline of the body to make it serve his mission. While boxers try to defeat opponents in a slugfest, Paul pummeled his body to bring it into submission to Christ (see also Phil. 3:12–15). This statement offered believers an optic through which they might view their world afresh. Similarly, when Paul bestowed citizenship in heaven's colony (*politeuma*) on Philippian converts (Phil. 3:20), he invited them to ponder the fateful difference between this world and another. Likewise, he admonished fractious Corinthians to ponder their place in the "body of Christ" (1 Cor. 12:27). With sharp irony Paul invited them to reflect on a conversation between the ear and the eye. How silly for the ear to say, "Because I am not an eye, I do not belong to the body" (12:16). Designed to puncture inflated pretensions, these metaphors aimed to move believers from a self-absorbed, individualistic, puffed-up spirituality into a concern for the welfare of the whole church. Similarly, his metaphorical statement that among the Thessalonians he was "gentle . . . like a nurse" (1 Thess. 2:7) aimed to assure a cell of converts of his tender care for them.[3] While all of these metaphors spring from a Greek context, they depend on the familiarity of converts with their place in the "new creation" and on their ability to translate those images into their religious experience. Note how elsewhere also Paul used metaphor to advance his mission, to educate his churches, and to instruct his converts in the gospel's imperative.

Paul's play with metaphor often signaled a crucial turn or a struggle with a seemingly insolvable problem. In Romans 9:30–33 and 11:11, for example, he sketched a scenario in which Israel, while running a race, comically (or tragically) tripped on a rock placed on the track by *God*, only to be beaten to the finish by Gentiles who were not even competing. After its introduction

3. Abraham J. Malherbe, *The Cynic Epistles: A Study Edition* (Missoula, MT: Scholars Press, 1977).

in 9:30–33, this farcical construction ferments for more than a chapter before resurfacing in 11:11. There Paul asks, "Have they [i.e., the Israelites] stumbled so as to fall?"[4] Then he snorted, "No, no, absolutely not!"

In an aha moment, the racing metaphor provoked new thought even in the apostle himself. Paul opined that this race was unlike other races in which winners require losers; this race, he argued, was to have only winners. Jews who ran the Torah race and Gentiles who did not would both be victorious. When we come to discuss Romans 9–11 and Paul's response to the question, "Now in turning to the Gentiles, has God reneged on promises made to Israel?" we shall see how this metaphor worked to advance thought about a difficult question.

Mixed with the language drawn from his Hellenistic environment were also metaphorical expressions that were unmistakably Jewish in origin. For example, Paul called the church "God's temple" (1 Cor. 3:16–17) and thus used a powerful religious symbol to bolster the identity of Christ people. He also referred to Philippian believers as "the circumcision" (Phil. 3:3),[5] and he invited the Romans to present their bodies as a "living sacrifice, holy and acceptable to God" (Rom. 12:1). All such metaphors bore the unmistakable fingerprints of a vital Jewish legacy. Inasmuch as Paul's background contained a dynamic blend of Jewish and Hellenistic elements, it is no surprise to find a mix of those elements in nonmetaphorical language as well. That complex mix may account in part for Paul's success in preaching a Jewish gospel to a Hellenistic audience. Sensitivity to the interplay of Hellenistic and Jewish language worlds will offer the curious reader clues to the dynamic of the exchanges between Paul and his churches.

METHODS OF ARGUMENTATION

Rudolf Bultmann once noted how Paul used a form of Hellenistic philosophical argumentation, the diatribe, to respond to those contesting his gospel.[6] Used as a tool of Stoic and Cynic argumentation from the third century BCE onward, the diatribe enjoyed broad popular use in Jewish circles as well. The diatribe was an argument form that placed sharp questions on the lips of hypothetical objectors as an entry to blunt responses.

---

4. Victor C. Pfitzner, *Paul and the Agon Motif: Traditional Athletic Imagery in the Pauline Literature* (New York: Humanities Press, 1967), and Calvin Roetzel, *Paul: The Man and the Myth* (Minneapolis: Fortress Press, 1999), 129–31.

5. Not *"true* circumcision" as in RSV. AE.

6. Rudolf Bultmann, *Der Stil der paulinischen Predigt und die kynisch-stoische Diatribe* (Göttingen: Vandenhoeck & Ruprecht, 1910).

In reading Romans in particular, you will recognize how cleverly Paul used the form to respond to opponents. For example, sensitive to the slanderous charge that his gospel of salvation by grace actually encouraged immorality, the apostle offered the hypothetical question: "Should we continue in sin in order that grace may abound?" (Rom. 6:1), which opened the door to strong denial, (Gk. *mē genoito*) "No! No! Never." Answering those who charge that his gospel is antinomian, that is, antilaw, Paul introduced his sharp reaction with the question, "What then should we say? That the law is sin?" (7:7). Elsewhere, when he was accused of denying God's promises to Israel to offer a gospel to Gentiles, the question, "Is there injustice on God's part?" (9:14) introduced his strong denial. Although the questions were all hypothetical, they were rooted in real-life experience. Thus Paul made the diatribe respond to the charge against his gospel that it encouraged immorality and that it implied that a good gift of God—the law—was evil. Critics charged that in offering salvation to Gentiles, Paul implied that God had reneged on promises to Israel.[7]

Recently critics have shown that Paul used methods of oral argument from Hellenistic rhetoric to persuade his audience. The expense of learning and developing these rhetorical skills, either in schools of rhetoric or from private tutors, was prohibitive for all except the most privileged. Designed to equip persons for service in law or politics, rhetoric also took literary form in the apologetic letter. Hans Dieter Betz, for example, has argued that Paul's letter to the Galatian churches followed such a strategy, and Betz even offered an outline of the letter drawn from rhetorical speech.[8] Recognizing its popularity in Roman circles, Betz employed the Latin structure of rhetorical speech in a letter analysis:

    I. Epistolary prescript (Gal. 1:1–5)
    II. *Exordium,* or statement of the cause of the letter (l:6–11)
    III. *Narratio,* or autobiographical support for the cause (1:12–2:14)
    IV. *Propositio,* or points of agreement and disagreement (2:15–21)
    V. *Probatio,* or evidential arguments from Scripture, experience, Torah, Christian tradition, friendship, and allegory (3:1–4:31)
    VI. *Exhortatio,* or warnings and recommendations (5:1–6:10)
    VII. *Conclusio,* or attack on the opposition (6:11–18)

Although Betz's work provides a welcome fresh look at Galatians, scholars have expressed reservations about the degree of Paul's reliance on classical

---

7. See Stanley Stowers, *The Diatribe and Paul's Letter to the Romans* (Chico, CA: Scholars Press, 1981) for an excellent treatment of this phenomenon.

8. See Hans Dieter Betz, *Galatians, a Commentary on Paul's Letter to the Churches in Galatia* (Philadelphia: Fortress Press, 1979), 14–23.

rhetoric.[9] Paul, for example, did not enjoy the privilege required to finance such an education. Moreover, classical rhetoric as practiced by Cicero, a first-century rhetorician of note, was primarily an oral vehicle. Some scholars have doubted that Paul and others adapted classical oral, rhetorical strategies of persuasion to letter writing. Others have objected that while a consideration of strategy may be important, the truth of Paul's gospel, not his political acumen as a persuader, was invariably his primary concern.

While questions about rhetorical criticism will continue to be raised, and confusion will continue, the serious student of Paul cannot dismiss the concerns of rhetorical criticism: its interest in the arrangement of an argument and persuasion throws light on the foreground of the text. Such a focus on the politics of persuasion draws attention to the foreground rather than exclusively to the background of the text and rightfully brings the reader into the text's context.[10]

As we shall see, Paul's method of Scripture interpretation owed much to his Pharisaism. However, in Galatians 4:21–5:1, with its allegory of Sarah and Hagar, we have an example of a popular Hellenistic method of text interpretation. Allegory was seen as a veiled presentation of meaning, usually in the form of a story, where each part of the story stood for a deeper truth. Unlike metaphor, allegory was self-enclosed, carrying its own explanation and leaving less room for the creative role of the listener (see Mark 4:14–20).

First used by the Greeks responding to the unseemly and even immoral actions of the gods of the classical myths, allegory was employed by the Stoics to rationalize those actions by seeking in them a deeper meaning. An instance of the use of allegory appears in the explanation of the adulterous relationship between Aphrodite and Ares. Aphrodite invited Ares, "Come and lie down, my darling, and be happy! Hephaistos [my husband] is no longer here but gone" (Homer, *Odyssey* 292–93). But their tryst ended abruptly when the suspicious husband, Hephaistos, returned to find them out and snared them in his net. Using an allegorical approach, the Greek philosopher Heraclitus found in this text not just a description of a bawdy affair but of a harmonious relationship between love and conflict (*Homeric Questions* 69). Allegory thus became the key that unlocked the treasure of texts dealing with gods at war, deceit, and treachery.

While instances of allegory appear in the Old Testament and the Qumran texts, and apocalyptic allegory was present in Jewish pseudepigraphy, it

9. Hans Hübner's review, "Der Galaterbrief und das Verhältnis von antiker Rhetorik und Epistolographie," *Theologische Literaturzeitung* 109 (1984): 241–50.

10. See Wilhelm Wuellner, "Where Is Rhetorical Criticism Taking Us?" *Catholic Biblical Quarterly* 49 (1987): 448–63 offers a positive assessment of this approach and a helpful bibliography.

was the literature of Diaspora Judaism that exploited the allegorical method to the fullest. One of the most skillful writers in this use was Philo of Alexandria. Like the Greeks, Philo believed that the literal meaning of a text was only its superficial meaning and that the literal text pointed beyond itself to a deeper reality. Philo expressed contempt for unimaginative literalists, calling them "slow-witted" (*On Flight and Finding*, 179), "obstinate" and "rigid" (*On Dreams*, 2.301), and he noted that it was silly to think God literally planted a garden of "soulless" plants. The reference to God's planting a garden in Genesis 2:8, Philo argued, was not to literal trees and herbs but to divine plants that have virtue, insight, and wisdom to distinguish between the ugly and the beautiful (*On the Creation* 154). Similarly, since no botanist knows of a "tree of life" (Gen. 2:9), Philo suggested that the image expressed "reverence toward God . . . by means of which the soul attains to immortality" (*On the Creation* 154). When we later discuss Paul's use of allegory (e.g., the story of Sarah and Hagar in Galatians 4:21–5:1), Philo's use of allegorical interpretation will be helpful. Although Paul never knew Philo, he grew up in a Diaspora community (probably Tarsus) that in some ways resembled that of Philo, and for that reason a consideration of Philo's writings is useful.

HELLENISTIC RELIGION AND PHILOSOPHY

In the Hellenistic world the line between religion and philosophy was a blur. The philosopher's search for wisdom was often informed by religious piety, and even when philosophers were self-consciously atheistic, as were some Sophists, they vigorously engaged religious issues. Even the Epicureans from the third century BCE did not, as some suggest, deny the existence of the gods. They asserted instead that it was useless to solicit their aid in prayer or to propitiate them with sacrifice, for they were either indifferent to human concerns or chose not to intervene in them. Conversely, major religious figures of the day like Apollonius of Tyana and Philo of Alexandria worked in the current philosophical idiom. We are being faithful to the spirit of the time, therefore, when we link religion and philosophy in this treatment. Both were vital parts of Paul's world and that of his churches.

Any suggestion that Paul's hearers had no religious practice before baptism is erroneous. Although Gentiles made up a great part of Paul's congregations,[11] some had at least a nodding acquaintance with Jewish traditions, institutions, philosophy, and Scriptures. As God-fearers, sympathetic or even

---

11. Here I follow Johannes Munck, *Paul and the Salvation of Mankind*, trans. Frank Clarke (Richmond: John Knox Press, 1959).

partial to Judaism but not yet converts, some of Paul's hearers might have been more receptive to Paul's Jewish gospel. Others, however, worshiped the popular deities of the Greek and Roman worlds. Aware of their participation in Hellenistic religious rites, Paul reminded them that they had "turned to God from idols" (1 Thess. 1:9) and warned them against any lingering reverence for old religious rites associated with "pagan"[12] devotion. He urged the Corinthians to "flee from the worship of idols" (1 Cor. 10:14) and warned that idolaters (i.e., converts still clinging to old religious rites) would not inherit the kingdom of God (Gal. 5:20).

But sometimes the divide between life in the new age and the previous existence was indistinct and moved Paul to forbid participation in local cults, even while he allowed the consumption of idol meat. (In the entire New Testament such behavior is endorsed only by Paul; cf. 1 Cor. 8:1–13 and 10:14–22.) Paul's gospel, therefore, did not address a religious vacuum but contended with other religions in a highly pluralistic setting. Sparked off by the conquests of Alexander in the third century BCE, which opened up the whole eastern Mediterranean to a dynamic exchange of ideas, the older religions[13] competed with the new for converts. But all were affected by a disenchantment that characterized the Hellenistic world.

The causes of that first-century malaise go back to the third century BCE, a period of severe economic depression, civil war, infanticide and depopulation, the decline of the city-state, and a serious weakening of the judicial system that worsened the suffering. Infanticide of female infants was common; but two sons were kept, for it was assumed that one would die in a war, leaving only one to maintain the family legacy. The decline of social institutions and the rise of religious doubt profoundly influenced the old religions. To be sure, certain primitive forms of religion remained. But even though people still stood in awe of the power and mystery of certain primal forces, devotion to the old gods—Zeus, Aphrodite, Apollo, and others—was in decline.

With the decline of traditional religions, Hellenistic piety assumed new forms. In some cases the old corporate theology gave way to a type of individualistic piety fixed on some particular god or even foreign deity. In other cases belief in an impersonal divine force present in the world (e.g., in Stoicism) replaced the venerable old tradition. In still other instances many felt no kinship with any divine principle that gave the cosmos any semblance

---

12. The word "pagan" used here hardly refers to a religionless people but instead to a people outside the orbit of the Abrahamic religion.

13. I recognize the falsity of the phrase "older religions," but I use it nevertheless for the sake of convenience.

of order. The feeling was pervasive that an oppressive, blind, impersonal, cosmic force called *heimarmenē* controlled the world. That dark necessity that ruled was a stranger to love, and many felt like reeds at the mercy of a capricious wind.

This shift in mood and darkness of spirit cast menacing shadows over the Hellenistic landscape, and the great dream of one world, free of barbarism and corruption, soured. Any hope that a political power could deliver the good life evaporated. As Professor Helmut Koester noted,

> In Athens, the city in which the most magnificent cultic buildings were erected, the visible presence of splendid temples did little but create the impression that this city was only a museum of classical greatness. The more the old traditions received support and were subsidized by the government, the more the cultic activities of the temples were estranged from the religious consciousness of the majority of the population.[14]

This eclipse of the old had far-reaching implications. For example, in place of the earlier Greek fascination with the body and appreciation for beauty and order in the universe, there appeared a devaluation of the world and the body. The Greek word for "athlete" (*askētēs*) came to mean "ascetic."[15] Gilbert Murray once characterized the period thus:

> This sense of failure, this progressive loss of hope in the world, in sober calculation, and in organized human effort, threw the later Greek back upon his own soul, upon the pursuit of personal holiness, upon emotions, mysteries and revelations, upon the comparative neglect of this transitory and imperfect world for the sake of some dream-world far off, which shall subsist without sin or corruption, the same yesterday, today and forever.[16]

Even granting this decline of traditional religions, their wasting away hardly left a landscape barren of religious expression. Fertility cults remained viable in the rural areas; the mystery religions enjoyed a resurgence in the cities; the healing cult of Asclepius became increasingly popular everywhere; and religious movements from the east grew in favor in the cosmopolitan west. Because of the urban character of Paul's mission, the latter three are of special interest to us here.

---

14. Helmut Koester, *Introduction to the New Testament, History, Culture and Religion in the Hellenistic Age* (Garden City, NY: Doubleday, 1955), 1:4.

15. Martin P. Nilsson, *Greek Piety* (Oxford: Clarendon Press, 1948), 188.

16. Gilbert Murray, *Five Stages of Greek Religion* (Garden City, NY: Doubleday & Co., 1955), 4.

The Mystery Religions

Perhaps because of their success in guarding their secrets, we know little about the mystery religions in first-century Greece.[17] What we do know harmonizes well with the spirit of the time. Although participation in the mysteries was most often corporate, the central concern of the mysteries was salvation through direct identification with the deity. This knowledge was less intellectual than mystical, less rational than relational. Through the prescribed rites the participants received more than a vision; they experienced solidarity with the god. Preparation included elaborate cleansing rites (lustrations or baptisms), and in some of the mysteries sexual union in a cultic setting offered ecstatic union. Through ritual mergers with the deity, initiates experienced a state of blessedness: the terror of history was overcome, release from the corruption of this world was achieved, and immortality became a present reality.

The Eleusinian Mystery

The dying and rising god or goddess at the center of the mystery cult normally had his or her first home in agriculture, with its vital interest in the turning of the seasons. In that context the deity's life and death had practical issue for the renewal of crops. Eventually, however, under the influence of the mystery religions, the ancient fertility rites changed focus from the renewal of crops to the renewal of life after death.[18] In the words of Firmicus Maximus we see how the fate of the god became the fate of the initiate: "Take courage, ye initiates! As the god was saved, so too for us comes salvation from suffering."[19]

---

17. The term "mystery religion," though problematic, is used here for the sake of convenience. No definition of the mysteries is without objection. For example, if one defines the mysteries as religions of secret rites, one can place Christianity in this category, while excluding the cult of Dionysus, with its public rites and festivals. If one uses the term to refer to religions whose rites brought its devotees into a mystical union with the god, one may note the Christian union with Christ. If one thinks of the mysteries as those promising to their initiates esoteric wisdom that sets them apart from the masses, and offering a new life or conversion that transcends human limit, mortality, or culpability, then the definition is so broad that it fits almost all religious movements and is, therefore, useless. Here we accept the self-description of the movements themselves—that is, as those that are privy to the divine mysteries and as such can offer deliverance from this mortal web of fate, matter, mortality.

18. See Frederick C. Grant, ed., *Ancient Roman Religion* (New York: Bobbs-Merrill Co., 1957), xxiv. For materials ascribed to the mystery religions, see Charles K. Barrett, ed., *The New Testament Background: Selected Documents* (New York: Macmillan Co., 1957), 92–104.

19. Rudolf Bultmann, *Primitive Christianity in Its Contemporary Setting*, trans. R. H. Fuller (New York: World Publishing Co., 1947), 159.

Most typical of this pattern was the Eleusinian mystery, based on a myth in which Hades-Pluto kidnaped Kore-Persephone, the beautiful young goddess of fertility, carrying her off to the underworld to rape her. In her absence Demeter, her mother, mourned, the earth languished, and the grain wilted. Demeter's desperate search for her daughter met success only after her persistent appeal persuaded Zeus to intervene and rescue the people from starvation and death. As a result, Kore-Persephone spent eight months of every year on earth and four months in the underworld. (The four months were the hot, dry summer months, when the grain lay dormant.)

Though little is known of the rituals marking these seasonal passages, surely rites of mourning and celebration existed. But evidence from the Roman period proves that the Eleusinian mysteries had a reach far beyond their immediate agricultural home. Cicero, one of the most important Roman jurists and philosophers of the Roman period, was an Eleusinian initiate and spoke of the power of the mystery to enable believers to "live with joy . . . and die with a better hope."[20] A number of emperors accepted initiation into the cult (Augustus, Hadrian, Marcus Aurelius, and others), but the expense of the initiation discouraged participation by the poor and slaves. The attention given in the mystery to ties with the dead heightened its appeal. Yet there was no community of Eleusinian initiates, and the mystery's individualistic character separated it radically from the early Christian community.

Isis and Osiris Myth (or Serapis Cult)

One of the most popular mysteries of the first century was the Isis-Osiris (or Serapis) cult, a transplant from Egypt that flourished in the cities ringing the Mediterranean. In this rite Isis was ritually recalled as an Egyptian goddess, the consort of Osiris, who was murdered by his brother Seth and departed to become lord of the netherworld. Though linked to the realm of the dead, Osiris held the secret to the powers of life and fructification. He brought the benevolent Nile floods that caused the delta to bloom. He caused the wine to ferment, the bread to rise, and the crops to yield their fruit. Osiris's green face, still evident in tomb drawings from the second century BCE, symbolized his intimate association with verdant nature's abundance.

Although the history of the Osiris myth informing the first-century mystery is complex, the basic outline of the sacred story is known. Both born of the sun god Ra, Seth, the older, jealous rival sibling, murdered Osiris, dismembered him, and heaved the mutilated carcass fragments into the Nile. Stricken with grief, Isis, Osiris's consort, scoured the land in search of her lover. Eventually, she located the fragments of his body, reassembled them,

20. Cicero, *De leg.* 2.38.

breathed life into the reassembled corpse, and consummated her love. From this sexual union issued Horus, Osiris's heir to the throne and the pharaoh of upper and lower Egypt. Later interred by the jackal-headed Anubis, Osiris returned to the netherworld to become lord of the Nile, which caused it to flood, thus assuring abundant harvests. Meanwhile, Horus, his son, ruled the land from a throne shaped like the lap of his mother Isis.

Depicted often as a black or Apis bull, a powerful symbol of fecundity, Osiris became the guarantor of life after death and the god with whom Egyptian women and men identified as they faced their own mortality.[21] Through their participation in this myth, they expressed their hope someday to join the great god Osiris and thus be absorbed in the great rhythm of the universe.[22] The name Osiris, when combined with the name Apis, the name of the beautiful, virile black bull in which he was manifest, produced Serapis, the Greek version of the Egyptian cult that became highly popular well into the Roman period. In the translation into the Greek experience by Alexander's successors, the Ptolemies, however, it was Isis, not Osiris, who became the dominant figure.

So this primal myth, so deeply rooted in Egypt's fertile cultural landscape, promised victory over mortality to its initiates and became influential with the masses in the great urban centers of the Greco-Roman world. To establish its importance it is unnecessary to see parallels, as does Koester.[23] Nevertheless, Paul's account of dying and rising with Christ (Rom. 6:3–5) and the rite of participation in the Isis initiation may have resonated with many in Paul's congregations who were aware of the cult and may have even been attracted to its wondrous vision of Isis:

> The mother of the universe,
> The mistress of all the elements,
> The first offspring of time,
> The highest of the deities,
> The queen of the dead.[24]

Sketches of Mary later betray the influence of the Isis myth on the Jesus tradition and thus reveal the continuing appeal of this mystery religion. But most would have recognized the profound differences between Paul's gospel and the message of Isis. Whereas the Isis cult promised a triumph over

21. An old but still highly instructive work on Egyptian religion is Henri Frankfort, *Ancient Egyptian Religion* (New York: Columbia University Press, 1948). On Isis and Osiris, see esp. 104–23.

22. Ibid., 106.

23. Koester, *Introduction*, 191.

24. Apuleius, *Metamorphoses* 11.5.1.

death in the present, the triumph over the power of death for Paul remained a future prospect. And, of course, although both begin with the story of a tragic murder (Jesus and Osiris), Paul's gospel had a historical dimension that the Isis-Osiris myth lacked and a radical monotheism that would have been totally alien to the Isis-Osiris mystery.

The Mystery of Dionysus

No sketch of the mysteries would be adequate without some reference to Dionysus, the most popular Greek mystery of the Hellenistic age. Although Dionysus is a venerable god of distant antiquity, his land of origin is disputed.[25] However that dispute turned, all who recognized and revered Dionysus before the sixth century BCE would have still venerated him in the first.

Dionysus's myth of origin recalled that he was conceived in a tryst between the god Zeus and the mortal Semele, the daughter of Cadmus the king of Thebes. His birth, like his conception, stood outside the order of nature. Jealous of Semele's success with Zeus, Hera tricked Semele into begging Zeus to reveal his full splendor to her. After initially resisting, Zeus reluctantly agreed, but in the theophany Semele was struck down, consumed by a bolt of lightning. Dionysus, the foetus, was rescued from the dying Semele (birth #1) and carried to full term by Zeus in his thigh (perhaps a euphemism for abdomen). From there he eventually emerged (birth #2). Devotees, identifying with Dionysus, spoke of themselves as "born again" or recipients of a "second birth." Once grown, Dionysus descended to Hades to rescue his mother, Semele, and return her to Mount Olympus to live with the gods. In addition to presiding over a cult of rebirth, he was best known as the bringer of wine and as the victor over death symbolized by a green ivy headband.

Vase paintings from the sixth and fifth centuries BCE depict maenads, or female worshipers, in wild, ecstatic nocturnal and highly erotic dances. Under the power of Dionysus they broke free of onerous work at looms. Other sources describe the feast of *sparagmos*, in which ecstatic women tore flesh from living animals and devoured it raw in a reckless act of divine possession. Since many believed that Dionysus was somehow present in both the wine and the wild animals, to eat the sacred flesh and drink the wine became the mythical basis for enthusiasm (literally, having "god within"). Given the prominence of both the bloody sacrifice and wine from the crushed grape, the symbolic association of blood and wine as living sacrifice was natural.

25. Martin P. Nilsson, *The Dionysiac Mysteries of the Hellenistic Roman Age* (Lund: C. W. K. Gleerup, 1957), followed by Koester, traces Dionysus's origins back to Thrace and Phrygia. Walter Friedrich Otto, *Dionysus, Myth and Cult* (Bloomington: Indiana University Press, 1965), 58, disputes Nilsson's claim, arguing that Dionysus was always thought to be of Greek origin.

Whether the church's association of blood and wine in the Eucharist was influenced by the Dionysiac mysteries is uncertain. What is certain, however, is that the command to drink the wine as Jesus' blood, so repulsive to Jews, would have sounded entirely natural to converts familiar with the mystery. Men also worshiped Dionysus, though their adulation was usually segregated from that of women. In their stag parties they drank copious amounts of the wine symbolically containing the spirit of the god. Only in the spring festival apparently did women and men join together in one joyous act of celebration. But whether segregated or integrated, men and women throughout Greece, the islands, and onto the coast of Asia Minor hailed Dionysus in intoxication and dance as the "'Raw-Eater,' 'Man-smasher,' 'Great Hunter,' 'Steer,' 'Roarer,' 'the-one-with-the-black-goatskin,' 'Erect,' 'Tree-like,' 'Flowerer,' 'Liberator.'"[26]

These metaphors associated with Dionysus reveal some of the complexity and irreconcilable polarity of this god. He stood for blood and gore, as well as rescue and salvation. His dark side touched on bloodshed and pollution, his light side on liberation and freedom. His savagery and destructiveness linked him with death; his rescue of his mother from Hades established him as giver of life. His association with life and death, light and darkness, the world above and the world below, and the wild and the tamed inevitably tied him to contradictions many felt.

From the third century BCE to the first, however, the gravity and complexity of the earlier Dionysus gave way to a vision of the god much more in tune with Hellenistic ideals. Now more a symbol of the sophisticated, refined lifestyle of the Hellenistic period and an advocate of the ecumenical vision of the one civilized world, Dionysus was increasingly used by rulers to reinforce political agendas. Nevertheless, Dionysus did not lose touch with the common lot. His gospel promised strength to endure life's trials and offered rescue from death in the world to come. His association with wine, dance, and drama remained unshakable, and his powers remained to be implored by emperor and slave alike. His tolerance for excess made it easy for followers to identify with him.[27] His affirmation of the physical legitimated the sensual element in the human experience and offered release from the mundane. Caroline Houser aptly summarizes the basis of Dionysus's appeal: Dionysus "is a realist who knows the dark and frightening side of nature as well as

26. Albert Henrichs, "Greek and Roman Glimpses of Dionysus," in *Dionysos and His Circle, Ancient through Modern*, ed. Caroline Houser (Cambridge, MA: Fogg Art Museum, Harvard University, 1979), 6.

27. Nilsson, *Dionysiac Mysteries*, 143–47, usefully summarized the Dionysiac mystery religion; however, he overemphasized its elitist appeal to the rich and cultured conservatives. Caroline Houser's estimation is more convincing.

the light and joyful side. He promises transcendence or metamorphosis, not annihilation."[28]

In sum, one might say that the primary emphasis of the Dionysiac mystery was on the struggle between life and death. The emphasis on the life-giving power of the phallus must be seen against an awareness of death as the one great absolute. As early as the fifth century BCE the mystery was concerned with the terror and bliss of the afterlife. This emphasis on funereal elements continued well into the Roman period. Yet the Roman version of the worship of Bacchus (Latin for Dionysus) differed in the way it exaggerated certain elements in the Greek version. Devotees of Bacchus, for example, were much more direct in their pursuit of erotic pleasure, and the Roman maenads, or female devotees, were much more provocative than their Greek counterparts. Although Paul's warnings against drunkenness and lust may not have been specifically aimed at the devotees of Dionysus, surely the context required such warnings, for Paul would have been acutely aware of the hold of this mystery on some of his followers.

The Healing Cult of Asclepius

Due to the short life span common in the first-century world and the pervasiveness of illness and epidemics, no ancient was a stranger to illness, and that human extremity often prompted an appeal to the gods for help. In the Hellenistic world, that request most frequently was lifted up to Asclepius, the god of healing. Son of the god Apollo and the mortal Coronis, according to one account, Asclepius was born at Epidaurus, which later became the location of an impressive sanctuary in his honor. According to the myth, Asclepius died as a mortal but returned to earth as a god to live and serve humanity as the compassionate god of healing. Devoted primarily but not exclusively to the poor and disadvantaged, Asclepius was known as the kind, compassionate god.

Seeking relief from sickness at any one of more than three hundred sanctuaries dedicated to him at Epidaurus, Athens, Corinth, Pergamum, the island of Cos, and other places, the masses came. There were 160 rooms for guests at Epidaurus alone. As precursors of modern holistic medicine, these centers ministered to the mind and spirit as well as the body. Like that at Epidaurus, for example, these centers included libraries, gymnasia, theaters, baths, clinics for physicians, and a holy place (*abaton*) where the ill slept, hoping for a healing encounter with the merciful god, Asclepius. For example, we read that at Epidaurus, a young girl was visited by Asclepius as she slept in the *abaton*.

---

28. Caroline Houser, "Changing Views of Dionysos," in *Dionysos and His Circle*, 24.

Healing God of Asklepios (Courtesy of Warren
Kendall; used by permission)

"The god appeared before her [Ambrosia], telling her that she would be cured
and that she had to dedicate a pig made of silver as a token of her gratitude.
Having said this he cut out the bad eye and immersed it in medicine. She
awoke at dawn, cured."[29]

While no such centers of healing existed in Jewish or early Jesus circles,
there was, nevertheless, as the Gospels show, a profound interest in the powers of charismatic healers. One difference, however, was that the emphasis
on healing in the Asclepius cult was individualistic, whereas the corporate

29. *Inscriptiones Graece* (Berlin, 1902), vol. 4, no. 951, 11:36, cited in Frederick C.
Grant, ed., *Hellenistic Religions: The Age of Syncretism* (New York: Liberal Art Press,
1953), 57; see also 49–59. See also Howard C. Kee, *Medicine, Miracle and Magic in
New Testament Times* (Cambridge, MA: Harvard University Press, 1986), and E. J. and
L. Edelstein, *Asclepius: A Collection and Interpretation of the Testimonies,* 2 vols. (Balti-
more: Johns Hopkins Press, 1945).

Theater of Epidaurus (Courtesy of Warren Kendall; used by permission)

dimension of Jewish and Christian healing stories is unmistakable. Although Paul's addressees, like all people of the time, and he himself suffered many illnesses and physical handicaps, except for 2 Corinthians 12:7–12, the letters themselves record no single healing he performed. He did note that he was able to perform mighty works (Gal. 3:5) and that he suffered from various afflictions, but he more strongly emphasized God's strength made manifest in his weakness (2 Cor. 12:9), in contrast to those who displayed their miracle-working powers as proof of the truth of their gospel. Yet healing cults were very much a part of the environment in which Paul proclaimed his gospel and may have influenced his hearers more than we know.

Stoicism

The personal agony and social upheaval of the third century BCE provided the ingredients for the formation of Stoicism. With the shaking of the foundations that came with the collapse of Alexander's empire, questions about the gods' concern were raised in the sharpest possible way. Social upheaval, civil war, famine, corruption, infanticide, and tyranny prompted the questions: If the gods care about the plight of humanity, why do they fail to redress the wrongs inflicted by this hostile world? If Providence favors justice and fairness, then why is life so unfair?

The Stoics answered by affirming rather than denying a divine presence in the world. "God" for the Stoics was less a divine personality engaged in human affairs than a divine principle (*logos* or divine reason) that pervaded and governed the universe. As Edwyn Bevan noted, for the Stoic "the whole universe was only one Substance, one *physis*, in various states" and "that one Substance was Reason, [and] was God."[30] Like humans, the world, the Stoics held, had a soul that directed its affairs, and existence was deemed fundamentally rational. Even natural disasters such as floods, earthquakes, or famine advanced the divine purpose in ways beyond human comprehension; perhaps they controlled population or served hidden purposes. In this spirit, Chrysippus once remarked that even the lowly bed bug was an instrument of the divine reason, because it kept people from sleeping too much or too long. The humble pig, likewise, mirrored this divine reason, for its "soul of salt" allowed its flesh to be preserved for eating, and its tendency to fatness made its meat delicious and nourishing.

Chrysippus had the rather optimistic view that if the world could have been better arranged, the divine reason would have made it so. In the third century BCE, the famous Stoic Cleanthes well articulated this vision in his hymn to Zeus:

> For nought is done on earth apart from thee,
> Nor in the earth nor in the sea,
> But skill to make the crooked straight is thine,
> To turn disorder to a fair design
> Ungracious things are gracious in thy sight
> For ill and good thy power doth so combine.[31]

Once a person understood the universe to be fundamentally rational, he or she could accept whatever happened with equanimity (or *apatheia*). *Apatheia* was no mere resignation to fate (as its English cognate "apathy" suggests) but a source of strength based on the conviction that a divine will controlled and directed all things. *Apatheia*, therefore, was the gateway to true freedom, for the truly disinterested person was untrammeled by the cares of the world. In the Stoic view, a kind of self-sufficiency or spiritual autonomy characterized the life of the truly liberated person. Though

---

30. Edwyn Bevan, *Stoics and Skeptics* (Oxford: Clarendon Press, 1913), 41.
31. AChrysippus, as cited by Edward Vernon Arnold, *Roman Stoicism* (Freeport, NY: Books for Libraries, 1971), 86.

Stoicism was pantheistic (i.e., the universe was infused with divine soul, *logos*), it was no mystery religion.

Its emphasis on the inner life and personal initiative, however, did give it an individualistic character. Its stress on personal detachment and the orderliness of the cosmos undermined any interest in history. Since the world moved in ways predetermined by cosmic reason, it minimized the importance of either a past or a future.

As Bultmann once said, "The Stoic believes that it is possible to escape from his involvement in time. By detaching himself from the world he detaches himself from time. The essential part of man is the Logos, and the Logos is timeless."[32] One can easily translate this statement to make it gender neutral without violating Bultmann's intent.

Paul's early years were probably spent in Tarsus, a center of Stoic teaching. Certainly his letters show signs of Stoic influence. His use of the diatribe to argue his case in Romans and his creative appropriation of the allegorical method of Scripture interpretation both owe something to the Stoics. His tendency to view believers as citizens of heaven (Phil. 3:20) rather than of the city (*polis*) strongly resembles a Stoic vision. Possibly even the scope of Paul's vision embracing the whole world may owe something to a Stoic cosmopolitanism (Rom. 10:18).

At points, however, Paul's worldview differed markedly from that of his Stoic contemporaries. His gospel's emphasis on history departed from the Stoic outlook. Paul's gospel was rooted in a historical event, was based on a historical person, and anticipated fulfillment in a historical (real) future, which separated his vision from that of the Stoics. Unlike the Stoic view of freedom as spiritual autonomy, freedom for Paul meant liberation from hostile cosmic powers (e.g., King Death, or Satanic Sin) for service to Christ. The Stoic was confident that individuals could win freedom through their own dedication; Paul took freedom to be an eschatological gift of God. And whereas the Stoic's concern centered on freedom, and thus on the individual, Paul's emphasis was corporate, implying a positive interaction of persons in a common bond. We see, therefore, that while Paul used the Stoic idiom, he normally subordinated it to his gospel and in the process transformed it. But what was true of Paul was not always true for his converts, who were often inclined to familiar and even natural compromises that led to sharp exchanges with the apostle. While strictly speaking Stoicism was no mystery religion, with the call for identification with the divine logos there was a mystical element.

---

32. Bultmann, *Primitive Christianity*, 159.

Cynic Philosophy

The Cynics were less philosophers than advocates of a lifestyle and method of teaching; but since their contemporaries called them philosophers, they deserve our attention. The word "Cynic," from the Greek for dog (*kyōn*), was an epithet hung on them by the culture critics of the day. Tracing their lineage back to Diogenes of Sinope (fourth century BCE), their presence in cities of Paul's day was significant. Claiming to live by nature (*physis*), they expressed their contempt for the well dressed by wearing rags; they registered their disdain for the wealthy by begging. They gave voice to their repudiation of the politically powerful with sarcasm. As keen observers of nature, they modeled their lives by its rules. Living as naturally and comfortably as possible, they, like animals, defecated in public places and had sexual intercourse wherever they felt the urge. Like animals they sought to reduce life to its barest simplicity. So impressed was Diogenes, for example, by a child's drinking from cupped hands that he discarded his cup, saying, "A child has beaten me in the plainness of living."[33] Boldness of speech they claimed for themselves as a freedom usually reserved for citizens in the assembly. Reportedly, so overawed was he by Diogenes's example that Alexander the Great told the philosopher, "Ask me any boon you like."[34] To which Diogenes allegedly replied, "Stand out of my light."

Paul, like the Cynics, spoke of having boldness "in our God to declare to you the gospel of God in spite of great opposition" (1 Thess. 2:2). Although they were not atheistic, Cynics found religious language discomfiting;[35] they viewed such language as an expression of popular religion, which they criticized as an endorsement of the status quo.

Understandably, many found the Cynics' ragged, dirty clothing, smelly hair, matted and unkempt beards, surly manner, and disgusting personal contempt for normal habits of behavior to be revolting. Writing in the middle of the first century, Seneca scoffed at their behavior and at their "repellent attire, unkempt hair, sloven beard, open scorn of silver dishes, a couch on the bare earth and . . . other perverted forms of self-display."[36]

In spite of popular disdain for them, Cynics, nevertheless did at points influence New Testament writings. Paul's use of the diatribe came at least indirectly from Cynics *and* Stoics. Some of his language (e.g., "boldness of

---

33. Diogenes Laertius, "Diogenes," in *Lives of Eminent Philosophers*, trans. R. D. Hicks (London: William Heinemann, 1925), 4.39.
34. Ibid., 6:41.
35. Bultmann, *Primitive Christianity*, 159.
36. Seneca, *Ad Lucilium Epistulae Morales*, trans. Richard M. Gummere, Loeb Classical Library (Cambridge, MA: Harvard University Press, 1979), 5:21.

speech") shows some debt to the Cynic philosophers. The lists of hardships that he notes in 2 Corinthians 11:23–29 closely follow a Cynic pattern. Paul's own understanding of the radical character of his wandering mission may have owed something to the Cynic practice. At other points, Paul emphatically distanced himself from wandering popular preachers whom many deemed hucksters preying on simple souls. Paul's letters reveal little inclination to engage in a radical critique of society. Why should they? He was convinced that the form of this world was passing away and would soon be replaced by a new creation. And he, much more than any Cynic preacher, saw the necessity of religious institutions and the importance of corporate support for the life of radical obedience to God (e.g., the offering for the church in Jerusalem).

So, being aware of this vibrant conceptual context in which Paul preached, we must also exercise caution, for conceptual parallels may not mean or suggest agreement. It is important to see that Paul based his critique of the world and his readers on the gospel he preached, which was significantly different from the Cynic philosophy and ethos.

Neo-Pythagoreanism

Because of its ability to synthesize diverse traditions, Pythagoreanism enjoyed a widespread revival in the first century BCE. With the venerated name of Pythagoras to legitimate their teachings, the neo-Pythagoreans forged a union of philosophy and religious piety that had genuine popular appeal. Far from being just an exercise in speculation, this philosophy concerned itself with cultivating a sensitivity to the divine element within. The axiom that "like seeks like" was a fundamental of neo-Pythagorean thought of the first century. This meant that humans, like the movie character E.T., constantly sought to return home to their cosmic divine source; the aim of life was to strip off the body to allow the spirit to rejoin the divine source. Naturally this loyalty to one's higher nature required repudiation of the flesh, because it was by flesh, they believed, that the spirit was tethered to this world. This emphasis on liberation from the body often led to a repression or a sublimation of sex (i.e., body) and to a life of poverty, free from earth's trappings. Sometimes a vow of silence was taken to stifle traffic with this world and afford fuller contemplation of the world of spirit.

Since the soul was divine, and the divine eternal, neo-Pythagoreans firmly believed the soul was immortal, and this led to a belief in transmigration. Soul was not the exclusive property of human life: the divine element went beyond the human family to include animals. This belief formed the basis of the conviction that the divine ether was present in animals and led neo-Pythagoreans to ban the eating of meat and to forbid the wearing of clothes made from animal pelts or wool.

A strong mystical current ran through neo-Pythagoreanism. Like the god-intoxicated worshipers of the mysteries, they called themselves *entheoi* ("those with god within") or *ekstatikoi* ("those possessed or beside themselves" with the spirit).

This enthusiasm (literally, "infusion with god") often manifested itself in miraculous works. In some circles miracles were thought to reveal the divine within of the one performing them. In this view, charismatic male figures, or "god men," performed divine or miraculous deeds as authenticating signs.

For some neo-Pythagoreans, numbers held significance beyond their numeric value as abstract ciphers. Apparently this reverence for numbers sprang from the conviction that harmony was the essence of divine nature. The precise rhythm of the cosmos, as well as the delicate and perfect balance between odds and evens, between the one and the many, and between finitude and infinity, suggested a divine principle holding opposites in harmony. Between the one and the many they saw a fundamental reality that manifested itself in the division between male and female, light and darkness, good and evil, and so on. Although their interest in astrology and numbers did prompt the neo-Pythagoreans to an accurate reading of the movements of the heavenly bodies, their aim was religious. The heavenly spheres were more than an expression of divine order; they were its source. The astral bodies were in some sense divine, and the will of the gods could be learned from their movements.

Knowing that divine will was important, because those bodies were thought to fix the destiny of the world. The goal of knowledge was to penetrate to the very heart of the cosmos and to find truth "as something at once beatific and comforting." This philosophy "presents the human being as cradled in a universal harmony."[37] The saving quality of this knowledge was especially precious in the first century BCE because of the decline of social structures and the loss of faith. Neo-Pythagoreans sought comfort in a belief that there was some connection between the heavenly "fixed glare of alien power and necessity"[38] and the destiny of the world. In the view of some, neo-Pythagoreanism was a degenerate philosophy. The movement did address itself, however, to a major concern of the time. Increasingly, many felt ruled by powers they

37. For still the best treatment, see Walter Burkert, *Lore and Science in Ancient Pythagoreanism*, trans. Edwin L. Minar Jr. (Cambridge, MA: Harvard University Press, 1972), 482.

38. Hans Jonas, *Gnostic Religion: The Message of the Alien God and the Beginnings of Christianity*, 2nd ed. (Boston: Beacon Press, 1963), 328. Although meant to describe an existential dimension in Gnosticism, it applies equally well to a developing mood shared by neo-Pythagoreans.

could not pretend to comprehend or understand. Life seemed capricious and unfair; the only certainty was uncertainty. The elder Pliny well articulated that feeling, a feeling that was widespread in the cities of his day, when he said, "We are so much at the mercy of chance that Chance herself, by whom God is proved uncertain, takes the place of God."[39]

Added to this sense of helplessness before those powerful forces was a growing suspicion that the powers were careless. Many felt as though they were mere playthings of Fate (*moira*), Chance (*tychē*), or Necessity (*anankē*). Life, they believed, was determined by forces that were fundamentally blind to and heedless of moral distinctions. Although neo-Pythagoreanism did not elevate reason, it did offer an alternative to surrender to Fate. It promised desperate men and women a way out of this world.

By touching the divine within, believers could anticipate liberation of the divine spark from its fleshly prison and a reunion of it with the source of all being and truth. Freed from the tyranny of capricious, irrational powers, life assumed meaning and purpose that made it tolerable.

The character of first-century neo-Pythagorean thought was perhaps best exhibited in the life of Apollonius of Tyana. Although his highly romanticized biography was not commissioned until 216 CE, over a century after his death,[40] the piety reflected in it conforms rather well to Apollonius's actual first-century outlook noted by historians. Renouncing wine, meat, and marriage, Apollonius wandered about barefoot and was clad only in an "earthwool" (linen) that spared animals. Through gifts to the poor he rid himself of the burden of wealth, and through a vow of silence that reputedly lasted for five years he screened out this world to concentrate on the divine. His travels carried him eastward to India, south to Egypt, and west to Rome. He conferred with the sages in Nepal, preached and performed miracles through Asia Minor and Greece, visited naked sages on the upper Nile, and advised public officials in Rome. His preaching emphasized a strong link between salvation and self-knowledge.

Inasmuch as knowing the self meant an existential or deep religious knowing of the divine within the self, he claimed self-knowledge to be synonymous

39. Pliny, *Natural History*, trans. Harris Rackham, Loeb Classical Library (Cambridge, MA: Harvard University Press, 1938), 2.5.22.

40. Philostratus, *The Life of Apollonius of Tyana*, trans. F. C. Conybeare, Loeb Classical Library (Cambridge, MA: Harvard University Press, 1960), 135–46; E. R. Dodds, *The Greeks and the Irrational* (Boston: Beacon Press, 1951), 135–46, shows how interest grew in philosophic miracle workers; David L. Tiede, *The Charismatic Figure as Miracle Worker* (Missoula, MT: Society of Biblical Literature, 1972), 16ff., saw the tension between traditions that viewed Pythagoras as a divine philosopher and those that remembered him as a miracle worker.

with becoming god. Consequently, to know oneself is to know all things, since the gods know everything. Moreover, the truly good person is divine, that is, one whose actions reflect what one essentially is. These divine acts reach beyond high moral concerns to include miraculous deeds. In the biographical account, for example, Apollonius not only denounced Roman tyranny, repudiated gladiatorial combat, exhorted the common people to improve their morals, and admonished all to be responsible citizens; he also reportedly predicted a plague, raised a dead girl, healed a boy bitten by a mad dog, exorcised demons, and quelled riots. There is little cause for wonder that when Nero asked Apollonius at his trial, "Why do people call you god?" he reputedly answered: "Every man believed to be good is honored with the title god."[41] Persecuted under Nero for his "meddlesome business," he was apparently martyred under Domitian near the end of the first century. One tradition, however, speaks of an end befitting an immortal: his mysterious disappearance and ascension before his execution.

Although the biography of Apollonius is late, his activity as a wonder worker, wise man, lawgiver, and patron of the mysteries is in tune with the spirit of the age. Whereas the literary portrait of Apollonius, broadly stroked by Philostratus, reflects some later concerns, the basic outline of his sketch closely resembles the portrait of first-century neo-Pythagorean philosophy presented by others.[42] Given the spiritual hunger of the fatalism many felt, the hopeful emphases of neo-Pythagoreanism were popular. It enjoyed success among rich and poor, privileged and slave, literate and illiterate. Considering its broad popular appeal, the likelihood is great it influenced some of Paul's hearers, perhaps rather significantly.

Gnosticism

Gnosticism (from Gk. *gnōsis*, "knowledge") was important in the experience of the early church. Although the background of Gnosticism is extraordinarily complex, it is likely that the spirit of the Hellenistic age played some role in its genesis and formation. While it is unlikely that Gnosticism was merely an acute Hellenization of early Christianity, as Harnack claimed generations ago, it surely was at home and flourished in a deeply disenchanted age.

Whether Gnosticism antedated Christianity is much disputed, but gnostic materials with sources that go back to the second century CE were discovered at Nag Hammadi in Egypt in 1945. Now published, these materials

41. Philostratus, *Apollonius of Tyana* 8.7; vol. 2, 315.
42. Holger Thesleff, *An Introduction to the Pythagorean Writings of the Hellenistic Period* (Abo: [Turku] Finland, Abo Akademi, 1961).

assist in sketching the contours of thought in this movement.[43] The polemical description of Gnosticism by the church fathers in the late second century was formerly discounted; but read in light of the Nag Hammadi collection, that description has proven not to be the caricature some thought it to be. Since our earliest secure historical evidence for second-century Gnosticism is second century, it is not always applicable to Paul, but certain features of the second-century version reflected those of the first.

While the presence of the divine *logos* in the natural world allowed the Stoic to view his environment positively, the devoted Gnostic viewed the world as evil. If the creation is evil, they reasoned, then the creator also must be evil. Thus the god of this world became an antigod or demonic figure. This radical dualism between the god above and the god below, between matter and spirit, between light and darkness, between knowledge and ignorance, formed the core of gnostic thought.

The denigration of matter profoundly influenced gnostic anthropology. The product of an evil being, imprisoned in a demonic world, unconscious of the divine within, humans wander aimlessly in perpetual stupor. Were it not for the great high god who took pity and sent a redeemer to remind them of their true origin and destiny, all would be hopelessly lost. But once awakened from the ignorance of one's divine origin, gnostics experienced salvation fully here and now. The knowledge of divine origin was no mere intellectual exercise but a signifier of a relationship. Liberated from the bodily prison, the "spiritual" person realized absolute freedom, a freedom that embraced both stringent asceticism and voluptuary license. In the repudiation of the flesh (asceticism), gnostics exhibited their freedom over the body. In their indulgence, gnostics demonstrated their freedom from the body, because what is done in the body does not affect the real self. Moreover, since the fallen god, YHWH, gave the laws, law breaking became a signifier of freedom from the clutches of that god.

The Corinthian correspondence opens a window onto a community with some of those tendencies. But those links are hardly iron clad, for it is anachronistic to argue for a second-century movement in the first. It is likely, however, that pre-gnostic emphases on wisdom (*gnōsis*), libertinism, devaluaton of the creation, a realized eschatology or spiritual elitism, and even an ascription of evil to the god of this world (2 Cor. 4:4) were shared by some of Paul's converts. Those early gnostic tendencies received fuller development a century later in certain Egyptian and Syrian churches. Certain Pauline texts like

---

43. Most of these documents included in *The Nag Hammadi Library*, ed. James M. Robinson (San Francisco: Harper & Row, 1977). For an older account needing correction, see Hans Jonas, *Gnostic Religion*.

1 Corinthians 15:50—"flesh and blood cannot inherit the kingdom of God"—
when taken out of context could be made to support a gnostic tendency.[44]

THE GREEK TRANSLATION OF PAUL'S BIBLE

As an important feature of Paul's Diaspora Judaism, the Septuagint was the
Bible of the common people. It was fully intelligible even to the illiterate person hearing it read in a synagogue meeting. It also was the focus of study and
commentary by Jewish intellectuals like Philo of Alexandria and Aristobolus,
and it inspired romantic legends like Joseph and Aseneth, a tale about Joseph's
marriage to a beautiful, privileged, powerful Egyptian woman whose conversion offered permission for such inevitable unions in the Diaspora.

Moreover a popular legend, the *Letter of Aristeas*, lent the Septuagint a communal authority. According to that fanciful tale, the then-pharaoh brought
seventy-two Hebrew scribes fluent in Greek to Alexandria from Jerusalem for
the translation of Torah. Sequestered on an island in total isolation from one
another, each of those scribes completed his translation in exactly seventy-two
days, and when their translations were compared they were found to be identical. The end product completed the holdings of the "world famous" library of
Pharaoh Ptolemy II Philadelphus (287–284 BCE) in Alexandria[45] and became
the Bible of Greek-speaking Diaspora Jews. (This weird combination of sev-
enties led to naming the book the Septuagint, or LXX, the Roman numeral
for seventy.) In reality, the translation evolved over more than two centuries,
and its faithfulness to the Hebrew varies greatly from book to book. Nevertheless, it provided guidance and instruction for minority Jewish communities
living in a powerful, alluring, Hellenistic majority culture.

Once accepted and revered by the Greek-speaking Diaspora community,
a vast body of commentary arose, lending an authority to the Septuagint.
Philo of Alexandria, a first-century Jew, devoted most of his multiple volumes
to commentary on the Septuagint. Even earlier, in the second century BCE,
the Jewish scholar Aristobolus sought to render the anthropomorphic references of the Septuagint to God and make them acceptable to sophisticated,
educated Jews of the Diaspora.[46] The later commentary on the romantic tale
noted above had enduring relevance for a community in which intermarriage

44. A fuller development of these ties may be seen in Elaine Pagels, *The Gnostic
Paul: Gnostic Exegesis of the Pauline Letters* (Philadelphia: Fortress Press, 1975).
    45. "The Letter of Aristeas," trans. R. J. H. Shutt, in *Old Testament Pseudepigrapha*,
ed. James H. Charlesworth (Garden City, NY: Doubleday & Co., 1985), 2:177–201.
    46. "Aristobolus," trans. A. Yarbro Collins, in *Old Testament Pseudepigrapha*,
2:831–42.

became more common.[47] These works and others lent authority to the Septuagint as God's preeminent vehicle of revelation. Annual festivities celebrated its origin, and weekly synagogue readings gave it a status that rivaled or even surpassed that of the Hebrew master texts.

More than a text generating interpretation, however, the Septuagint itself was an interpretation. From different periods, from many hands, and scribed in the vernacular Greek of the day, the Septuagint offered an interpretation of the Old Testament in Greek while seeking to remain true to the spirit of the Hebrew. The Greek translation inevitably, however, made adjustments in three important areas.

First, the Septuagint's view of God contained a Hellenistic bias. Especially noteworthy was the disappearance of Hebraic personal names for God. The proper nouns *YHWH* and *Elohim* of the Hebrew became a generic *theos* ("god"). The common Hebrew proper names *El Shaddai* and *YHWH Sabaoth* became *pantokratōr* ("almighty"). Likewise, *Adonai*, which implied a relationship between deity and worshiper, became *kyrios* ("sovereign lord").

That trend toward abstraction surfaces in Exodus 3:1–14, where Moses cleverly attempts to worm the secret, powerful divine name out of God. Elohim answers the impertinent Moses with "'I AM WHO I AM. . . . Thus you shall say to the Israelites, 'I AM has sent me.'" In order for the wordplay to work, a knowledge of the Hebrew verb "to be," from which the word *YHWH* is formed, is required. The wordplay, however, is missing entirely from the Septuagint. The Greek translation has instead, "I am The Being. . . . say to the children, 'The Being (*ho ōn*) has sent me.'" With that move, God is depicted as the Self-Existent One, the absolute, cosmic divine being of the Greek philosophers.

In a pluralistic setting with many gods and daily contact with non-Jewish peoples, some level of tolerance was required to allow for tolerable working relationships. Aware of that need, translators made a clever move. Where Exodus 22:28 has the command "You shall not revile *Elohim*," the Greek translator(s) took the Hebrew plural form literally, whereas in its original the plural suggested a level of holy "otherness" that the Greek plural form did not capture. The Septuagint has instead, "You shall not revile the gods." Whereas the Hebrew commandment centered on the one holy God to the exclusion of all others, the Greek translation encouraged some level of tolerance for different forms of religious piety. While the worship of foreign gods was forbidden, a tolerance of other religious expressions was commanded. While

47. "Joseph and Aseneth," trans. C. Burchard, in *Old Testament Pseudepigrapha*, 2:177–201.

Paul himself may have resisted such a broad tolerance, his converts were more open to the spirit of the age than he.

Second, the Septuagintal word "faith" (*pistis*) shaped Paul's thought in important ways. The Septuagintal word *pistis* was used to translate the Hebrew *'emet*, which referred to firmness, stability, and/or reliability. When the Hebrew text intended to speak of trust in someone or something as reliable, most commonly the verb form was used. We see, therefore, that the Hebrew distinguished between reliability (or faithfulness) and faith or trust in that which was reliable. The Septuagintal word "faith" (*pistis*) was ambiguous enough to sometimes allow for both uses.

While this point may sound trivial, it does have relevance for understanding complex passages like Romans 1:17: "the righteousness of God is revealed through faith for faith; as it is written, 'The one who is righteous will live by faith.'" The Hebrew is clear and should be translated "the righteous live by *their* faith," but Paul's Septuagint has, "the righteous shall live by *my* [i.e., God's] faithfulness" (AE). Did Paul refer to faith as "belief [i.e., trust] in" God's work in Christ (i.e., Septuagint, hereafter LXX), or did he intend faith to refer to the fidelity of the righteous (i.e., as LXX suggests)? Or did he deliberately use Greek that was ambiguous to allow both meanings?[48] The scholarly debate has produced no consensus on this issue. In any case, the point is that the passage is so notoriously difficult at least in part because of the ambiguity of the language that Paul used.[49]

While this point may sound trivial, it has come to have relevance for the church in the centuries past. Martin Luther once deemed that verse the most important in the Bible. And his early lectures on the Psalms used it to guide his reading of that vast collection.

Third, the Septuagint's interpretation of law shaped Paul's understanding in ways that require the fuller discussion in the following chapter. Here we pause only to note that the Septuagint almost always translated the Hebrew word *torah* with the Greek *nomos*. Rather than the multivalent Hebrew that could refer to Israel's sacred story, and rules and customs governing communal life within the covenant community, the translated Greek usually denoted the code guiding individual or community behavior, and cosmic principles like gravity, the turning of seasons, and parental protection of vulnerable offspring. The influence of these Septuagintal tendencies best accounts for Paul's use of phrases like "law of my mind" (Rom. 7:23), or "law of works,"

48. See C. H. Dodd, *The Bible and the Greeks* (London: Hodder & Stoughton, 1935), 65–99. The most complete bibliography of *relevant* studies appears in Robert Jewett, *Romans*, Hermeneia (Minneapolis: Fortress Press, 2007), 141–45, footnotes.

49. See Robert Jewett, *Romans, A Commentary*, Hermeneia (Minneapolis: Fortress Press, 2007), 145–47.

opposing the "law of faith" (Rom. 3:27) best rendered as "principle." For a fuller treatment, see chapter 2.

In the following sample passages we can see how the Hellenistic spirit of the Septuagint intruded into the Hebrew text at points. While that intrusion may not have compromised the basic character of the Hebrew religion, it is inaccurate to claim that no change in emphasis occurred.

Translation of Hebrew Texts	Translation of Septuagint*
Who has known the Spirit of the Lord . . . (Isa. 40:13)*	Who has comprehended the mind of the Lord . . . (cf. 1 Cor. 2:16)
He bore the sin of many, and made intercession for the transgressors. (Isa. 53:12)	[He] bore away the sins of many, and on account of their lawlessness was he handed over. (cf. Rom. 4:25)
The rabble among them had a strong craving. (Num. 11:4)	And the people who were among them had an eager desire . . . (cf. 1 Cor. 10:6)
The righteous shall live by their faith. (Hab. 2:4)	The righteous shall live by my [i.e. God's] faithfulness . . . (cf. Rom. 1:17)
By you all the families of the earth shall bless themselves. (Gen. 12:3, RSV)	In you shall all the peoples [i.e. Gentiles] of the earth be blessed. (cf. Gal. 3:8)
Moses went up to God (Exod. 19:3)	Moses ascended to the mount of God
And they [i.e. Moses and the elders] saw the God of Israel. (Exod. 24:10)	And they saw the place on which the God of Israel stood.
[Isaiah said to Ahaz,] "Look, *the young woman* is with child and shall bear a son, And shall name him Immanuel." (Isa. 7:14)	"Behold, a *virgin* shall conceive and bear a son, and shall call his name Immanuel." (cf. Gal. 4:4)
Elohim said to Moses, "I AM WHO I AM." (Exod. 3:14)	And the God spoke to Moses saying, "I am The Being."
You shall not revile Elohim (Exod. 22:28)	You shall not make light of the gods.
YHWH is a man of war (Exod. 15:3)	The Lord causes wars to cease.

* = author's translation,
italics = emphasis added

COMPARISON OF TRANSLATIONS OF HEBREW AND GREEK TEXTS

While no comprehensive treatment of tendencies of the Septuagint is available, scholars recognize that certain viewpoints of Paul's native Greek translation influenced his religious outlook. Heard in the home, memorized in the school, read and discussed in the synagogue, the Septuagint was in Paul's blood as much as the King James translation was in the blood of Milton or my pious mother. Lodged in Paul's soul, the language of the Septuagint informed his views of such great issues as sin and justification, law and liberty, his Gentile mission, and his understanding of faith. Its language defined his world and informed his gospel. Paul indeed was a Septuagintal Jew. One must hasten to add his identity and the worldview of his Scriptures were also dramatically shaped by his encounter with Messiah Jesus, whose life, death, and resurrection he was convinced inaugurated history's final, dramatic, revolutionary episode.

SUMMARY

Each of the elements of the Hellenistic world described above was in some ways peculiarly its own, but in other ways they were fully representative of the spirit of the age. Apart from these elements, what had previously been central to Hellenism continued, namely, openness to other cultures and to the surprises that came from engagement with other religious views. Although such cross-fertilization could be and often was fruitful, the risk was great that the gods of the Hellenistic world and its habits of being would radically alter or even supplant the religious views of the Christ community.

One other important motif from that Hellenistic world survived—its sense of community or *sympatheia*[50] with the divine. By the first century the heroic period of Hellenism had faded, but if the traditional gods of classical Greece had lost their power to save, in subtle ways they remained in the architecture and in fresh incarnations. Almost all felt related to a divine principle that bound all together and erased artificial distinctions between man and woman, barbarian and Greek, slave and free. Moreover, it was the godly ether shared by the animals that linked them with humanity through *sympatheia*.

A significant development in the Hellenistic period, however, was the emerging split between the celestial and terrestrial worlds, which revealed a terrifying rupture between flesh and spirit, between the world below and the world above, and between the gods of this world and of the world beyond. Whether this dualism was homegrown or imported is unclear. What is clear, however, is that it found conditions favorable for growth in Hellenistic soil. Even if many of Paul's readers had never read or heard of any of the philosophers, they would have been influenced by the spirit of the age.

---

50. *Sympatheia* stands behind the English word "sympathy," meaning to suffer with someone. Here, however, the word is taken to mean feel with or acknowledge kinship or relationship to all things, so that what affects one affects the whole.

Once we realize that Paul's gospel ran counter to that zeitgeist, we can begin to locate the point where his readers would have found it difficult to understand or accept his message without explanation or adjustment. Undoubtedly, Paul's gospel was a source of joy and hope to many, but the acceptance of his kerygma did not change cherished ideas overnight. Only reluctantly did Paul's converts surrender their views that matter was evil, that salvation was an individual not a corporate experience, that history was circular, or that God could be apprehended directly without the need of historical media like Scripture or apostles (1 Cor. 4:1–4:5). Over these and other habits of being, Paul and his converts often clashed. Once these points of friction are recognized, one can better read the letters as real conversations over real concerns.

In the discussion above we have seen important elements of the social, cultural, and spiritual environment inhabited by Paul and his churches. Their Greek Bible inevitably contained Hellenistic idioms. The mythology embedded in that language shaped their understanding of the human condition and the Christian gospel. For that reason, in their dynamic interaction with a rich Hellenistic, cultural legacy Paul's letters offered flashes of insight that generated new symbols, inspired new visions of the present and the future, destabilized patterns of religiosity that were taken for granted, and infused existing structures with ferment and even protest. This dynamic interaction was profoundly influenced by the Hellenistic Jewish home environment of Paul's formative years. To other important dimensions of that Jewish legacy we now turn.

2

Paul and His Jewish World

The separation of the treatment of Paul's Hellenistic and Jewish worlds is artificial, but useful for discussion purposes. In the first century there was no Judaism untouched by Hellenistic sway and no Hellenism totally isolated from a Jewish influence. Paul's letters are an amalgam of Jewish and Hellenistic forces. Paul spent his formative years in a bustling, cosmopolitan trade center with an energetic Stoic school; his first language was Greek; and his Bible was the LXX. So it is hardly surprising that traces of that past appear in the letters. But was that Hellenistic influence dominant? John Knox was so convinced of such a dominant motif that he wondered if Paul ever studied in Jerusalem, as Acts once claimed (22:3).

But given the pervasive reach of Hellenistic culture and the fact that there was no Judaism in the first century that was not Hellenized, there is no need to know, if ever we *could* know, whether Hellenism or Judaism dominated Paul's thought. Given the reach of the Hellenistic culture in Paul's day, Knox's dichotomy was false. What is clear is that Paul skillfully appropriated literary forms and devices, expressions, methods of rhetorical argumentation, and concepts from his Hellenistic world. As we noted above, the special language and outlook of his Greek Bible, the creeds, hymns, and language of the Hellenistic church and/or the Diaspora synagogue, as well as a host of influences from the culture at large, all informed Paul's thought. Yet, in spite of his openness to the Hellenistic world, Paul was proud of and loyal to his Israelite heritage until the end of his life. He was born a Jew, lived as a Jew, and eventually died as a Jew, albeit a Jew on the margin of the Judaisms of his day. In the discussion below we shall note important aspects of that Jewish legacy and its influence on the letters of the apostle.

PAUL THE PHARISEE

In Philippians 3:5–6 Paul refers to himself as "circumcised on the eighth day, of the people Israel, of the tribe of Benjamin, a Hebrew born of Hebrews; as to the law, a Pharisee; . . . as to righteousness under the law, blameless." Acts also attested to Paul's Pharisaism. Going beyond what Paul himself reported in his letters, Luke's Acts later suggested that Paul remained a loyal Pharisee until his death. Given the unflattering picture of the Pharisees in the Gospels, Luke's positive assessment of Paul's Pharisaism may surprise some.[1] But the harsh polemic against the Pharisees in Matthew's Gospel reflects the struggle between church and synagogue in a post-Pauline period and should not be read as an objective description of the Pharisees of Jesus' or Paul's day. A brief consideration of some recent scholarship on the period should facilitate our study.

In Philippians 3:4–6, the apostle offers us a brief and rare glimpse into an earlier time in his life. Responding angrily to Jewish Christian missionaries whom he scorned as "dogs" (3:1), Paul fumed, "If anyone else has reason to be confident in the flesh, I have more: circumcised on the eighth day, a member of the people of Israel, of the tribe of Benjamin, a Hebrew born of Hebrews; *as to the law a Pharisee*; as to zeal, a persecutor of the church; as the law, blameless" (AE). Some critics wonder if it would have been possible for Paul to be a strict Pharisee outside of Palestine. But caution is in order, for Paul only claims an interpretation of the law that was Pharisaic. Might the phrase "according to the law a Pharisee" suggest only that he agreed with the Pharisaic interpretation of the law? While some hold that Pharisees could remain loyal Pharisees in the Holy Land only, we now know that there was more variety in first-century Pharisaism than we usually allow and that writers of the period, like Josephus in Rome and Philo in Alexandria, shared Pharisaic inclinations, even though strictly speaking they were not Pharisees. So can we know what was the nature of the Pharisaism of Paul's day?

One must warn against using the ugly polemics of the Gospels to define first-century Pharisaism. Those documents fulminate against the Pharisees as "vipers," "hypocrites," "blind guides," "whitewashed tombs," and "murderers of the prophets of old" (e.g., Matt. 3:7; 12:34; 23:16–33). Similarly, attempts to define first-century Pharisaism by reading views of late Jewish documents like the Mishnah (200 CE) or Talmud (fifth and sixth centuries)

---

1. In the Gospel of Matthew, for instance, the Pharisees are scorned as "viper[s]" (3:7; 12:34; 23:33), "hypocrites" (23:27), "blind guides" (23:16), keepers of the minutiae of the law who neglect "justice, and mercy and faith" (23:33), murderers of the prophets (23:30), and "white-washed tombs" (23:27); but when this description is read as one side of a vicious quarrel between church and synagogue, it sounds less like an objective historical description than a bitter competition.

back onto the first century are also unhistorical.[2] Jacob Neusner's definition of first-century Pharisaism as apolitical and focusing primarily on the observance of the laws of purity has been enormously influential but was criticized by Rivkin, who argued that the Pharisees of Paul's day were indeed politically active and hardly limited their concerns to issues of ritual purity.[3] But Rivkin's dependence on late rabbinic materials to "disprove" Neusner's thesis was flawed. More recently, the late and revered Anthony J. Saldarini offered a more reliable thesis that combined both views. He suggested that while observing the laws of purity as the Gospels claim, first-century Pharisees were both ritually observant and politically active.[4] Without a political patron they were less politically active in Paul's formative years; nevertheless, they did seek to influence figures with access to power.

Did Paul continue in the way of the Pharisees after his apostolic call? Certainly Paul's letters bear traces of a Pharisaic inclination. His view that the resurrection of the just comes at the end of the age, his concepts of predestination *and* human responsibility, his estimate of what was Scripture, his involvement in the workaday world, his spiritualization of religious language and practice (e.g., sacrifice in Rom. 12:1–2), and his method of scriptural exegesis all reflect Pharisaic tendencies.

But there is evidence on the other side as well. Paul's free association with Gentiles, his casual attitude toward the laws of purity, his view of Jesus as the Messiah whose life, death, and resurrection signaled the beginning of the end time, and his interpretation of the law in the messianic age all separate him from Pharisaic traditions. Certainly, by the strictest interpretation, Paul compromised his Pharisaic tradition, but to say that he rejected it outright is going too far. It is better to say that his letters offer a fresh and radical reappraisal of those traditions, rather than that Paul rejected them.

PAUL'S JEWISH METHODS OF SCRIPTURE INTERPRETATION

The apostle's ties to his Jewish heritage are also evident in his methods of Scripture interpretation. First, it must be noted that his Scriptures were exclusively and emphatically Jewish. Greek ideas did intrude through the

2. Jacob Neusner, *Rabbinic Traditions about the Pharisees before 70*, 3 vols. (Leiden: E. J. Brill, 1971), 3:177, 244–47.

3. Ellis Rivkin, *A Hidden Revolution: The Pharisees' Search for the Kingdom Within* (Nashville: Abingdon Press, 1978), 72–75.

4. Anthony J. Saldarini, *Pharisees, Scribes and Sadducees in Palestinian Society* (Wilmington, DE: Michael Glazier, 1988), 79–143.

Greek language of his Scriptures, but the biblical story for Paul was fundamentally a Jewish story about God's covenant with the Hebrew people and
the responsibilities that went with that relationship. In the full light of that
grand narrative, Paul crafted his gospel. His various methods of interpretation aimed to show how Messiah Jesus, crucified and risen, fulfilled the hopes
and expectations of that script.

Many of those methods Paul probably learned from his Jewish teachers.
His use of midrash (sacred story interpretation), his appeal to Jewish legend,
his use of Scripture to interpret Scripture, his collection of random texts clus-
tered around a common theme, his reading of the prophets as seers predicting
the end time, his reasoning from the lesser to the greater, and his attempt to
draw analogies through link words are all methods of exegesis that Paul shared
with the learned interpreters of his day.

One important method of Scripture interpretation used by the rabbis was
midrash, an interpretation that sought to find in a text its inner significance,
to discover principles or laws for living, or to reveal the authentic or true.
Note Paul's use of such a method in 1 Corinthians 10. Drawing on Israel's wilderness experience, he found instruction for a church in which some viewed
the sacraments as a guarantee of salvation. Paul cautioned against such a magical practice and reminded his readers that their life as a sacramental community was prefigured in Israel's wilderness wandering. Israel too ate sacred
food (manna) and Israel also drank the supernatural drink (water from the
rock). Yet, Paul warned, Israel's status as a sacramental community in no way
exempted it from accountability. Its murmuring brought death, and idolatry
brought the fall of more than 20,000 in a single day. From this Paul drew a
lesson for a wayward church.

Other Pauline images came from legends related to but not specifically
mentioned in his Scriptures. In Galatians 3:19 he spoke of the role the angels
played in the giving of the law. In 1 Corinthians 10:4 he referred to the moving rock in the wilderness, and in 1 Corinthians 11:10 he noted a command
given to women to cover their heads in the service of worship "because of the
angels." At the very least, Paul's willingness to cite these legendary materials
reveals the breadth of his understanding of the sacred tradition.

Paul also followed the practice of his Jewish community in using one text
to interpret another. In 2 Corinthians 3:16–17 we can observe him contrast-
ing the covenant made with Moses with that forecast by Jeremiah: "The
letter kills, but the Spirit gives life" (2 Cor. 3:6). Then he told the old,
familiar story of the giving of the law to Moses "chiseled in letters on stone
tablets" (2 Cor. 3:7). Because Moses' face reflected that brilliant splendor,
the patriarch veiled his face to shield the people from the blinding light. Paul
suggested in allegorical fashion that, like Moses' face, the true meaning of the

Torah, veiled up to now, has become known. The Christ event surpassed that glory associated with the giving of the law as the sun surpasses the moon. Paul then quoted Isaiah, which forged a link between this glory of Christ and the outpouring of the Spirit to come at the end time: "Now the Lord is the Spirit, and where the Spirit of the Lord is, there is freedom" (2 Cor. 3:17).

Another instance of the interpretation of one passage by another may be seen in Galatians 3. While discussing the promise given to Abraham, Paul quoted Genesis 12:3: "In you shall all the peoples of the earth be blessed" (LXX). In another version of the same account the expression "in you" he changed to "in your seed [or offspring]" (Gen. 22:18). After taking the phrase "in your seed" to refer to "in you," Paul made a rather dramatic interpretive leap. Reading "seed" as singular, he took "seed" to refer not to Abraham's many descendants (plural) but to one descendant (singular): Christ. Thus Paul interpreted Genesis 12:3, by way of Genesis 22:18, to mean, "All the Gentiles shall be blessed in you [i.e., Christ]" (Gal. 3:8).

While such exegesis may strike the modern reader as arbitrary or even dishonest, Joachim Jeremias was correct when he wrote that Paul was using a method of Scripture interpretation commonly utilized by the rabbis.[5] Paul's collection of random texts around a common theme echoes a method of interpretation used in Jewish circles also. Romans 3:10b–18, for example, interlaced six quotations to underscore his point. Held together by a theme that Paul emphasized, these citations addressed a common topic, the universality of human sin. The cumulative effect of such clustering was to underscore a central point, namely, to establish culpability that allowed no excuse or special pleading, and the need of all people, Gentile and Jew, for the gracious righteous benefit bestowed by Christ.

In another instance, Paul read the prophets as if they were forecasters of the eschatological future of the apostle's present. Paul either alluded to or quoted the prophets more than ninety times,[6] and almost all of those references refer to Paul's present or near future. The prophets, he believed, predicted the dawning eschatological age (Rom. 1:2; 3:21; 16:26; etc.). They foresaw the rejection of Jesus by most Jews and the inclusion of Gentiles in God's elect (Rom. 3:29; 9:25–26; 10:20; 15:12). They anticipated the laying of the new cornerstone in Israel in the person of Jesus (Rom. 9:33), they foresaw the covenant being established in his own day (2 Cor. 3:14–18),

5. Joachim Jeremias, "Paulus als Hillelit," in *Neotestamentica et Semitic Studies in Honour of Principal Matthew Black*, ed. E. E. Ellis and Max Wilcox (Edinburgh: T. & T. Clark, 1969), 88–94.

6. For a list of these passages, see Calvin Roetzel, *Judgment in the Community: A Study of the Relationship between Eschatology and Ecclesiology in Paul* (Leiden: E. J. Brill, 1972), 153–54.

and they predicted the present manifestation of God's righteousness (Rom. 3:21) in the death of Jesus (1 Thess. 2:15). This use of the prophets reveals Paul's preoccupation with the end time, which colored the way he read all biblical texts.

Paul was hardly alone in such a reading of biblical texts. Qumran texts contain the selfsame tendency to read the prophets as seers whose predictions focused on the "day of the Lord." The Qumran sectarians believed that the secrets (Heb. *razin*) of Scripture heretofore unknown were revealed to their leader, the Teacher of Righteousness, and after his death to the members of the community. Selected members of the community studied those texts day and night to divine their secrets and to read themselves into the text. While Paul's focus on Jesus as the Christ was different from the Qumran-inspired exegesis, his conviction that Scripture contained eschatological secrets about the future was the same.

With the benefit of historical criticism we now know that the prophets spoke to their own time and that their predictions had a limited horizon. Yet to say that Paul and the sectarians of the Dead Sea community were simply mistaken is to impose on them unfairly our canons of historical-critical interpretation. More important than whether they misread Scripture is how the sacred texts functioned for them. For Paul the Scriptures did more than rehearse a sacred story of a venerable past. They also anticipated a future linking the storied past with the community's present. In that dynamic, the past was no dead past, but it provided the key that unlocked the future, and the future provided the optic for viewing the past. For Paul the Scriptures legitimated the proclamation of the early church and anchored the gospel in the history of Israel. By attending to the ways the Scriptures came to life for Paul and how they functioned in the letters, we should gain a clearer idea not only of how the apostle's argument unfolded but also of how the past, far from being a dead past, remained alive for him.

Jeremias (and Michel before him) found evidence in the letters that the apostle followed the rabbis in other ways.[7] The first rule of Hillel involved the reasoning from the lesser to the greater. Similarly, in Romans 5:15, 17 Paul tried to show how one person's act affected human destiny. After citing as a negative example Adam, whose disobedience brought death, Paul argued that many may participate in the obedience of the one man, Jesus, and live. But the comparison, Paul continued, was inapt, in that the grace

---

7. See Jeremias, "Paulus als Hillelit," as well as Otto Michel, *Paulus und Seine Bibel* (Gütersloh: C. Bertelsmann, 1929). See Geza Vermes, *The Complete Dead Sea Scrolls in English* (New York: The Penguin Group, 1997).

experienced "in Christ" was more efficacious than the power of sin experienced "in Adam."

The development of Paul's argument thus moved from the lesser (Adam) to the greater (Christ) and in so doing followed a pattern of argument practiced by the famous rabbi Hillel and even Hellenistic peers.

The second guide of Hillel involved drawing analogies through catchwords. In Romans 4:1–12 Paul quoted Genesis that "Abraham believed [trusted] God, and it was *reckoned* [counted] to him as righteousness" (Rom. 4:3 AE). That Abraham received the promise through grace rather than through works was corroborated, Paul held, by Psalm 32:2, where forgiveness was taken by the psalmist to mean that "the LORD will not *reckon* [count] his sin" (AT, AE). Finally, we are told that just as righteousness was reckoned (counted) to Abraham because of faith rather than works, so also Gentiles who believe in God because of Christ's faithfulness will be reckoned (counted) as righteous (4:22–23). Thus we see how Paul used the word "reckon" to link the faith of Abraham with the inclusion of Gentiles in the eschatological community. Although the content Paul gave this argument from the lesser to the greater reflected his commitment to Messiah Jesus, the method he used in making his point came from Jewish interpreters.

PAUL AND JEWISH APOCALYPTICISM

While recognizing that Paul's views on eschatology completely suffused his interpretation of Scripture, we note the relationship of Paul's eschatological outlook to his Jewish apocalyptic traditions.[8] Such terms as "wrath" (*orgē*), the

---

8. The word "eschatology," signifying thinking or reasoning about the end, has come to refer to God's decisive conclusion to the "end time." Apocalyptic literature is normally the literature of an oppressed people dealing literally with God's revelation. Usually apocalyptic ideology is eschatological in character, but not all eschatological writings are apocalyptic in character. More highly imaginative and more volatile, apocalypticism allows for anything the imagination can conjure—for example, seven-headed beasts, astral pyrotechnics, depictions of brutal and bloody vengeance, and victory for those who persevere. Jesus' proclamation, "The rule of God is at hand," is eschatological; the depiction of the Anti-Christ as Nero Redivivus with the number 666 is apocalyptic. For an excellent discussion of apocalypticism, see the treatment by John J. Collins in the *Interpreter's Dictionary of the Bible* (Nashville: Abingdon Press, 1962), 1:157–61, now treated afresh in the *New Interpreter's Dictionary of the Bible*, vol. 1. A vast literature on the nature and development of apocalyptic literature is now available. See John J. Collins, *The Apocalyptic Imagination An Introduction to the Jewish Matrix of Christianity* (New York: Crossroad, 1984). For an outline of issues facing the interpreter of apocalyptic literature and a useful guide for further consideration, see Klaus Koch, *The Rediscovery of Apocalyptic* (Naperville, IL: Alec R. Allenson, 1970).

"day" (*hēmera*), "death" (*thanatos*), "righteousness" (*dikaiosynē*), "judgment" (*krisis*), and the distinction between the two ages (*aiōn*) are intelligible only within their Jewish homeground and the view of the eschatology they share. Both are dominated by a longing for a taste of the end time. An intensity that came from living on the boundary between two worlds—one dying and the other being born—burned in both. Both shared a link with Israel's past, and both hoped for the imminent fulfillment of God's promises. Although Paul's understanding of Jesus as the beginning of God's future age differs from the ideas in his native Jewish apocalypticism, he shared the conviction that his present generation was to be the last. That heightened awareness of the impending end influenced everything Paul said to the churches. Everything he wrote concerning marriage (1 Cor. 7:26), regarding mediating disputes in the church (Rom. 14:10–12), relating to the celebration of the Eucharist (1 Cor. 11:32), and his own mission is hardly intelligible apart from his conviction that his was the last chapter of the story.

No discovery has more revolutionized biblical studies than the 1947 discovery of the Qumran scrolls by Muhammad ed-Dib, a Bedouin boy searching for a lost sheep. Stored in jars and hidden in caves on the northwest corner of the Dead Sea, in anticipation of the arrival of a Roman legion on the march (ca. 68 ce), now after more than 1,800 years the scrolls have emerged to reveal much about the life and religion of an intense apocalyptic sect that had withdrawn from priestly service at the temple in Jerusalem. Convinced that the ruler Jonathan the Maccabee of the Hasmonean ruling family had polluted the temple by taking over the high-priestly office, these rebellious priests abandoned this holy place to follow the injunction of Isaiah 40:3: "In the wilderness prepare the way of the LORD."

Archaeological excavations have shown the Qumran site to be an impressive establishment. Built around a system of reservoirs and canals for catching and delivering water for daily needs and ritual bathing, these facilities included a large assembly hall, a scriptorium for transcribing sacred texts, a kitchen, a bakery, a pantry, a watchtower, a kiln for baking pottery, and even a laundry and stable. Scholars judge that at its peak the site may have supported approximately two hundred members. These impressive facilities supported a community that was chiefly (though not exclusively) celibate for almost two hundred years, all the while living in feverish expectancy of God's final visitation.

The apocalyptic tone of their writings is unmistakable, and though there is no evidence for a direct link between the Qumran community and Paul, indirect influence is evident. Like the Qumran community, Paul divided humanity into two camps, the children of light and the children of darkness (1 Thess. 5:4). Like the sectarians, he trumpeted his generation as the last. Like the Qumran

Wadi Qumran (Courtesy of Calvin J. Roetzel;
used by permission)

Qumran Cave 4 (Courtesy of Calvin J. Roetzel;
used by permission)

community, he associated God's righteousness with the redemption of the
elect, and like that company, he discouraged (though he did not forbid) marriage, in anticipation of the final eschatological crisis (1 Cor. 7:26, 32–35).
Like the Qumran community, he insisted on purity in the community, in anticipation of the final judgment (1 Thess. 3:13, 4:7–8). Finally, like the Qumraners,
Paul believed the raging cosmic conflict between God and "the ruler of this
world" was replicated in microcosm in the life of every believer, and that by
God's grace that believer would triumph.

Though abundant precedent exists in Jewish circles for apocalyptic tendencies resembling those of Paul, differences existed as well. Paul and the early
church held that in Jesus' death and resurrection the end time had already

begun. Whereas the Qumran community retreated to the wilderness to prepare for the end, Paul encouraged no such isolation. The priestly community at Qumran expected God to inaugurate a purified cult in Jerusalem, but Paul harbored no such expectation. The members of the Qumran community had fantasies about fighting in God's final battle for control of the world, but no such hope was voiced in the Pauline letters. We see, therefore, that Paul's apocalypticism hardly originated with him or even the church before him, but was deeply rooted in Jewish traditions. Yet in important ways it was different, and Paul played a role in reshaping the Jewish and Christian apocalyptic myth that he inherited.[9]

In all the ways noted above—Paul's views of the resurrection and predestination, his liberal assessment of what was scriptural, his uses of traditional methods of scriptural interpretation, and his extensive use of imagery from Jewish apocalyptic thought—the Hebrew tradition informed Paul's thought. Hans Joachim Schoeps quite properly once stated that Paul's argument is obscure if not altogether incomprehensible, apart from its relationship to Old Testament traditions and his belief that his was the last generation of humankind.[10]

In the discussion above we have seen that Paul was deeply influenced by both the Hellenistic and Jewish texts and traditions of his day. Yet the combination of Hellenistic and Jewish elements hardly originated with Paul. It came at least partly prepackaged in the Jewish tradition he knew and the Christ tradition he came to embrace. In the Asia Minor of Paul's youth the Jews had already accommodated themselves to their Greek environment in many ways. Philo noted how they attended the theater, took part in sports, gave their children Greek or Latin names, intermarried with Gentiles, and decorated their tombs with Greek art. This accommodation, however, was an uneasy one, fraught with surprise and fear of the loss of identity.

The Jews of the Asia Minor of Paul's youth were well integrated into the community. They were good citizens up to a point. But at that point, where they believed the claims of Gentile society eclipsed those of Torah, community solidarity was reaffirmed, a solidarity firmly rooted in the great Scriptures and traditions of Israel. Judging by the archaeological evidence, even Palestinian Judaism had been Hellenized to a degree. E. R. Goodenough drew our attention to numerous Greek inscriptions found in Jerusalem

9. See Calvin Roetzel, "Paul as Organic Intellectual: The Shaper of Apocalyptic Myth," in *Common Life in the Early Church, Essays Honoring Graydon F. Snyder*, ed. Julian V. Hills et al. (Harrisburg, PA: Trinity Press Int., 1998), 221–43.

10. Hans Joachim Schoeps, *Paul: The Theology of the Apostle in the Light of Jewish Religious History*, trans. Harold Knight (Philadelphia: Westminster Press, 1961), 38.

itself.[11] A Greek word, "Sanhedrin" (*synedrion*), designated the most significant judging body in Palestine, and astonishingly a few Greek manuscripts were found among the scrolls from the Qumran sect. We see, therefore, to quote the revered W. D. Davies, that "the traditional convenient dichotomy between Judaism and Hellenism was largely false. In the fusions of the first century, the boundaries between these were very fluid."[12] That hardly means, however, that they were nonexistent.

Using different information, Martin Hengel came to substantially the same conclusion in his well-documented study.[13] Therefore, to attempt to understand Paul exclusively in light of his Hellenistic or Jewish background is to misunderstand him. For example, Philippians 2:6–11, a pre-Pauline Christian hymn that Paul edited to serve his epistolary interests, offered a smooth blending of those worlds. Whether the background of the hymn was basically Jewish or Hellenistic has been hotly debated. The issue is made more complex by the presence of both Jewish and Hellenistic elements in it. The opening line of the hymn transports the reader into the heavenly realm, the primary abode of Jesus, who humbled himself, took the part of a "slave" in human form, and descended to earth. Obedient unto death, he was exalted to assume the place he once occupied with God and then will receive the praises of all humankind. The hymn ends with a paean of praise: "At the name of Jesus every knee should bend . . . and every tongue should confess that Jesus Christ is Lord." Scholars have taught us that this closing doxology is an echo of Isaiah 45:23: "To me every knee shall bow, every tongue shall swear." In this echo of Isaiah, and probably also in the allusion to the role of the "slave" assumed by Jesus, we may have vestiges of the Hebrew scriptural tradition. But in the references to the world above as Jesus' first habitation and the world below as the locus of his ministry, as well as in the descent-ascent motif (i.e., Jesus' coming down to death and ascending to his former home), and in the cosmic lordship bestowed on the glorified Christ, to whom all powers "in heaven and on earth and under the earth" (Phil. 2:10) will do obeisance, we have evidence of Hellenistic influence. We see, therefore, that the riddle of the hymn's background finds its solution in neither the Jewish tradition nor the Hellenistic milieu alone. What we see in this pre-Pauline hymn is a synthesis of Jewish and Hellenistic

11. E. R. Goodenough, *Jewish Symbols in the Greco-Roman Period* (New York: Pantheon Books, 1953), 1:61ff.

12. W. D. Davies, "Paul and the Dead Sea Scrolls: Flesh and Spirit," in *The Scrolls and the New Testament*, ed. Krister Stendahl (New York: Harper & Bros., 1957), 157.

13. Martin Hengel, *Judentum und Hellenismus* (Tübingen: J. C. B. Mohr [Paul Siebeck], 1969), 453–68; Eng. trans.: *Judaism and Hellenism* (Philadelphia: Fortress Press, 1974).

elements. Traces of a Jewish heritage remain, but these have coalesced with a Hellenistic cosmology (view of the world) and Jewish soteriology (understanding of salvation).[14]

Some have claimed to see Hellenistic influence as dominant in Paul's messianism. Others are just as firmly convinced of the overriding importance of Judaism in Paul's thinking. But there is no need to know, if ever we could know, whether either exclusively dominated Paul's thought. What is clear is that he employed certain literary forms and devices, expressions, methods of argumentation, and concepts from his Hellenistic tradition. The special language and outlook of his Greek Bible, the creeds, hymns, and language of the Hellenistic church, and the Diaspora synagogue, as well as influences from the culture at large, all informed Paul's thought to a significant degree. Nevertheless, in spite of his openness to the Hellenistic world, his Jewish heritage was the dominant feature of Paul's religious world.

The burden of translating a Jewish gospel for a Hellenistic world did not rest on Paul's shoulders alone. Given the presence of Jews in all the major cities of the Mediterranean world (Acts 15:21), we must assume Gentiles learned about Judaism from direct contact with individual Jews and synagogue congregations. Salo Baron's estimate that every tenth Roman was a Jew and that 20 percent of the population of the empire east of Italy was Jewish sounds incredibly high;[15] nevertheless, it is widely granted that the Jewish minority exercised an influence on the Hellenistic world out of all proportion to its size. Paul, for example, could assume that his predominantly Gentile congregations knew about Jewish Scripture. It is unlikely that that familiarity with Scripture was grounded in Paul's preaching alone.

The archaeological evidence suggests that many cities in the Mediterranean world had at least one synagogue. We know of nine synagogues in Rome, and the largest building in first-century Sardis was the synagogue. A post-Pauline synagogue in Corinth was strategically located near the heart of the city. The number, size, and location of these buildings show that the Jewish presence could not be ignored. Moreover, although many Gentile "God-fearers" (Gk. *sebomenoi*) did not convert to Judaism, they attended synagogue and were strongly attracted. It was not uncommon for such a person to abstain from eating pork, to observe the Sabbath, to study Torah, and to

14. See Ralph Philip Martin, *Carmen Christi: Philippians ii.5–11 in Recent Interpretation and in the Setting of Early Christian Worship* (Cambridge: Cambridge University Press, 1967) for a dated but still excellent survey of the problems associated with this passage and the scholarly opinion regarding it.

15. Salo W. Baron, *A Social and Religious History of the Jews* (New York: Columbia University Press, 1952), 1:171.

have a son circumcised while still holding back from conversion. Through active but not necessarily organized proselytizing, Jews influenced, if they did not convert, their Gentile neighbors. And considering the commerce of the Mediterranean world, recognition of the Torah and its teachings was hardly limited to a single Jewish community.[16]

As important as the Hellenistic world and Jewish tradition were in shaping Paul's thinking, the most formative item in Paul's experience was his meeting with the risen Lord (1 Cor. 9:1; 15:8). Scholars have frequently called that experience of Paul a conversion, but more than a generation ago Johannes Munck argued that Paul's own description of that meeting resembled less a conversion than an Old Testament prophetic call. Like Jeremiah of old, Paul claimed that God "set me apart before I was born" (Gal. 1:15), and he described himself as "called . . . set apart for the gospel of God, which he promised beforehand through his prophets" (Rom. 1:1–2). That Paul viewed himself as a latter-day Jeremiah is unlikely. But it is almost certain that Paul regarded his critical turn as a call, like that of Jeremiah or Isaiah, and not just a psychological change.

In the view of some scholars the Acts account of Paul's Damascus road encounter (Acts 9:1–30; 22:3–21; 26:4–20) does denote a sudden conversion experience. Increasingly, however, others caution against making the views expressed in the later Acts normative for understanding Paul. Whereas the term "conversion" suggests a radical break with the past, Paul's Damascus experience produced no such repudiation. Although he did turn from persecuting the church to nurturing it, he linked the church (or its gospel) with God's promises to Israel (e.g., Rom. 9:4–5). His conviction that the Messiah had come distinguished Paul from the Jewish majority, but it did not divorce him from his Jewish tradition. Paul's relationship to Christ was central, but it was not exhaustive. Any emphasis on his relationship to Christ that excludes consideration of his Hellenistic and Jewish habitat, or any stress on the habitat to the exclusion of his gospel, distorts our view of Paul and the gospel he preached. It is important, therefore, while reading the letters, to remember that Paul was many things at once—a Hebrew of the Hebrews, a Pharisee, a member of the tribe of Benjamin, a Hellenistic Jew, an apostle of Christ, and a missionary to the Gentiles. Though these differing aspects of his life did not all hold equal place in Paul's theology, each of them contributed something. Alertness to the way these forces worked on Paul should give a fuller appreciation of the range, complexity, richness, and subtlety of his epistles.

16. See Baron, *Social and Religious History*, 171.

GENTILE INCLUSION WITHOUT JEWISH EXCLUSION

The Jewish apocalyptic thought informing Paul's grand vision was in the very air he breathed. Historically, it had given voice to war's victims, comfort to despairing captives, consolation to those grieving over land lost or temple destroyed, and hope to those straining to be free of the grip of dark, sinister, crushing evil powers. That apocalyptic medium conjured a future reversal when the oppressed would rule and victims would become victors. It proclaimed a future when justice delayed would no longer be justice denied. Apocalyptic material promised hope to the hopeless and consolation to the despairing.

A great sage/seer wrote Daniel to strengthen, encourage, and console victims of the ugly Hellenistic brutality unleashed to crush the Maccabean Revolt (167–164 BCE). Similarly, scribes of the Dead Sea community (or Qumran) of Paul's day combined multiple traditions to create and sustain an apocalyptic mind-set. How Paul parsed that Jewish apocalyptic mind-set to frame his gospel, to defend the legitimacy of his apostolic mission, and to define his Gentile message was hugely influential, if not brilliant. Jesus' resurrection, he held, was the first stroke of the end time's midnight hour, signaling the approaching end of the tyranny of the "principalities and powers" (Rom. 8:38), a triumph over the hegemony of celestial powers like King Sin, Lord Death (Rom. 6; 1 Cor. 15), and other sinister, dark satanic personages. Though not the first to preach a gospel that expanded the reach of that dawning eschatological deliverance to embrace non-Jews, the apostle Paul was its most eloquent defender.[17]

That apocalyptic vision literally consumed Paul. It imbued his mission with urgency, conjured a vision of a mission reaching to the edge of the world he knew, gave his letters practical issue, and construed believing cells of converts as a surrogate family. He felt himself a partner and herald of God's triumphal eschatological moment (2 Cor. 2:14–17). What was new in that claim was his aggressive and eloquent apology for the inclusion of outsiders on terms that did not first require law observance and conversion to the Israelite religion.

That bold—and some thought outrageously novel—vision found symbolic expression in the offering he promoted among the pagan converts for the "poor among the saints" in Jerusalem. It sought to incarnate the prophetic vision of history's final, climactic eschatological moment. Echoing Isaiah 2:2–3 and 60:5, which had Gentiles (pagans) streaming up to Zion in the last

17. For fuller discussion, see Calvin Roetzel, "Paul as Organic Intellectual, The Shaper of Apocalyptic Myths," cited in note 9.

days to make offering to Israel's God, Paul conjured a breathtaking scene. Echoing the Septuagint of Isaiah 23:14–24:1 in 2 Corinthians 9, he imagined his Gentile converts in Jerusalem witnessing the procession of Gentile believers with the offering and blending their voices with those of Jewish believers in a mighty chorus of praise and thanksgiving. That overwhelming prospect evoked Paul's spontaneous outburst: "Thanks be to God for his inexpressible gift" (2 Cor. 9:15 KJV).[18]

The Meaning of Paul's Word "Gentile"

The word "Gentile" was a favorite of Paul, appearing in the undisputed letters more than thirty-five times. Stemming from the Latin *gens* (pl. *gentes*) and in translation rendered by the Hebrew *goi* and the Greek *ethnos*, the oft-used translations "nation" and "race" are inadequate. They come from the post-Renaissance era and the emergence of nationalism, or out of a cultural legacy that assigned the word "race" to the other. Nineteenth-century anthropological debates showed that the term "race" signifies a culturally conditioned state and that use of the word to denote an immutable physical trait is incorrect.[19] Given that fairly recent history, it is best to avoid those terms and limit our use of "Gentile" to denote a tribe, people (*genus*), clan, ethnicity, extended ethnic group or corporal collection. The Latin *gens*, I recognize, was nuanced and also could signify hierarchical rank, status, nuclear family, extended family, or social location. Those possibilities all combine to give Paul's use a mix of both the subtle and the complex. To a consideration of the Scriptures, Jewish traditions, Hellenistic and Roman usage, and Diaspora adaptations that shaped Paul's understanding we now turn.

Some Sources of Paul's Vision

In almost every culture, fearful, threatening circumstances may encourage a xenophobia that pits "us" against "them" or that separates the humane, rational, righteous "us" from the subhuman, immoral, base "them." In ancient Israel as well as the modern West, such walls of separation met contrary views that resisted simplistic social constructions. For example, scholars recognize that Israel's early settlement stories contain unflattering characterizations of resident Canaanites as subhuman, idolatrous, immoral "other," with whom

18. For fuller discussion see Calvin Roetzel, *2 Corinthians*, Abingdon New Testament Commentaries (Nashville: Abingdon Press, 2007), 152–54.
19. See Calvin Roetzel, "No 'Race of Israel' in Paul," in *Putting Body and Soul Together: Essays in Honor of Robin Scroggs*, ed. Virginia Wiles, Alexandra Brown, and Graydon F. Snyder (Valley Forge, PA: Trinity Press Int., 1997), 230–44.

no negotiation of difference or enrichment from interaction was allowed.[20] But other early writings traced descent from outsiders—for example, "A wandering Aramean was my father" (Deut. 26:5 RSV). Some early traditions also urged special protections for the outsiders—the "sojourner," the orphan, the widow, and the slave, for "remember that you were [once] a slave" (Deut. 24:17–18 RSV).

Shermayahu Talmon has taught us how one set of such contrary views developed. He showed how rules forged by Judean Babylonian captives were retained after their return to the homeland to frame identities and order that restored world. He noted how the habits and rules forged in captivity remained to separate returnees from those who were allowed to remain in the homeland during the exile (as "second class"). Those people of the land (Heb. *'am ha-'aretz*), Samaritans, Edomites, Galilean Arabs, and even Israelite Greeks and Syrians were assigned a rank they did not choose, and after them in third place, in this ranking, stood the foreigners and pagan aliens.[21] Schwartz showed how the resulting temple-state hegemony endured for centuries and expanded under the Maccabeans (167–135 BCE) into Galilee and Syria to encompass an area rivaling that of King David.[22]

Similarly, later Qumran sectarians claimed to be the true Judah (*Yehuda*). They also used a similar strategy of identity maintenance to castigate Jerusalem priests, to demean Pharisees as the "seekers of smooth things," to assign lineage to Sadducees as descendants of Ephraim and Manasseh, scorned patriarchs of northern tribes, and to label outsiders as Kittim or "other."[23] The book of *Jubilees* similarly underscored separateness by castigating Gentiles as heartless and forbidding Jews to share their mealtimes (22:16–19). Similarly the Apocalypse of Weeks (*1 En.* 91–107) marked Gentiles as "sinners." But this pattern of separation was by no means uniform or consistent in Jewish writings.

20. The most useful discussion I know distinguishing these two categories is that of J. Z. Smith, "Differential Equations: On Constructing the 'Other,'" in a lecture printed and distributed by the Arizona State University, Department of Religious Studies, March 5, 1992. Reissued in *Relating Religion, Essays in the Study of Religion* (Chicago: University of Chicago Press, 2004), 230–50.

21. S. Talmon, "The Emergence of Jewish Sectarianism in the Early Second Temple Period," in *Ancient Israelite Religion. Essays in Honor of Frank Moore Cross*, ed. Patrick D. Miller Jr., Paul D. Hanson, S. Dean McBride (Philadelphia: Fortress Press, 1987), 583–616.

22. Seth Schwartz, *Imperialism and Jewish Society, 200 B.C.E.–640 C.E.* (Princeton, NJ: Princeton University Press, 2001), chap. 2.

23. Daniel Boyarin, "The IOUDAIOI in John and the Prehistory of 'Judaism,'" in *Pauline Conversations in Context: Essays in Honor of Calvin J. Roetzel*, ed. Janice Capel Anderson, Philip Sellew, and Claudia Setzer (Sheffield: Sheffield Academic Press, 2002), 230.

For example, the *Letter of Aristeas*, written from Egypt shortly before 200 BCE, offered contradictory advice. On the one hand, there was the exhortation in verses 139–42 against mixing:

> In his wisdom the legislator [i.e., Moses], . . . being endowed by God for the knowledge of universal truths, surrounded us with unbroken palisades and iron walls to prevent mixing with any of the other peoples in any matter, being thus kept pure in body and soul, preserved from false beliefs, and worshipping the only God omnipotent of all creation. . . . He hedged us in on all sides with strict observances connected with meat and drink and touch and hearing and sight, after the manner of the Law.[24]

But the selfsame writing drew on Greek philosophical traditions to praise tolerance, generosity, fairness, equanimity, prudence, justice, temperance, and moderation, all staple emphases of the Greek *Paideia*.[25] Diaspora Jews like Philo of Alexandria were acutely sensitive to the ambiguity imposed by the Diaspora. There both danger and reward inevitably plagued Jews intent on identity maintenance, but the promise of a fruitful engagement with an alluring, majority Hellenistic culture was near irresistible and inevitably attenuated the admonition to separate and loosened ties to temple, land, and covenant. Daily encounters with Gentiles in the marketplace, in business transactions, at the games, and in other cultural venues required a negotiation of competing claims to guard against the twin dangers of assimilation and segregation.

Absent the specter of episodic violence, the accommodations to the majority culture were nigh irresistible. Philo reminded his Jewish peers that they shared the Stoic vision of world citizenship and urged tolerance even when marginalized (*Special Laws* I, 308). Openly critical of his Jewish peers for mistreating Gentile converts to Judaism, he offered counsel that still resonates with tenderness:

> [T]hey have left . . . their country, their kinfolk and their friends for the sake of virtue and religion. Let them not be denied another citizenship or other ties of family and friendship, and let them find places of shelter standing ready for refugees to the camp of piety. (*Spec. Laws* I, 51)

---

24. From *Old Testament Pseudepigrapha*, ed. James H. Charlesworth, trans. R. J. H. Shutt (Garden City, NY: Doubleday & Co., 1985), 2:32.

25. Calvin Roetzel, "Ambivalence and Ambiguity on the Margins: *Oikoumene* and the Limits of Pluralism," in *Paul, A Jew on the Margins* (Louisville, KY: Westminster John Knox Press, 2003), 57.

Philo's engagement strategy well illustrates the tension between engagement and isolation. So the counsel to separateness and the characterization of Gentile as "other" was balanced by the admonition to positive engagement and openness. In those cases law was less a fence shielding the community from attenuation (*Letter of Aristeas* 141) and more a protocol guiding positive interaction. Gates in the metaphorical fence opened out to an engagement with the majority culture that was full of surprises.

Added to these sources were centuries-old testimonies that protested harsh strictures of isolation. The books of Jonah and Ruth, in particular, offered satirical, ironic, comical, and stinging critiques of strategies of separation. The former portrayed the Ninevites, that is, descendants of earlier hated Assyrian invaders, as objects of God's mercy. YHWH's commission to Jonah sent him against his will to preach to the Ninevites (!), residents of the capital of the Assyrian Empire and traditional enemies of Israel. With a blatant satire, the author shows how the comical (if not pathetic) Jonah unwittingly became a vehicle of God's mercy, a mercy that transgressed traditional boundaries of separation from the alien, uncivilized, subhuman, bestial, unclean, and demonized Ninevites. But after Jonah's warning of coming destruction, the population *and their animals* repented in sackcloth and ashes (Jonah 3:8), and God relented and spared the city.

The final scene has Jonah on a hill overlooking Nineveh, eagerly awaiting God's destruction of the hated "other." Jonah's disgust at God for granting the Ninevites mercy, and his despair as his shade, the *qiqayon* plant, wilted, exposing him to unbearable heat, are indeed comical. The story ends with a question. YHWH asked Jonah if he was really angry over the loss of his shade (4:9); when Jonah replied that he had a legitimate right to be angry, YHWH then asked: "You pity the plant for which you did not labor, nor did you make it grow. . . . [S]hould I not pity Nineveh, that great city, in which there are more than a hundred and twenty thousand persons who do not know their right hand from their left, and also much cattle?" (4:10–11 RSV). This critique of strategies of identity construction and maintenance that rely on the fabrication of a falsified, subhuman "other" was brilliant enough to assume one day the status of sacred Scripture. Surely Paul was aware of this funny story.

The book of Ruth, on the other hand, elevated an alien Moabite to heroic status. Israelites long held the Moabites in contempt as children of incest (literally, "from the father"). The story casts the alien Ruth as fiercely loyal to her Jewish widowed mother-in-law, whose deceased sons had wed Moabite women. With those marital ties severed, Naomi released her Moabite daughters-in-law and announced plans to go home. But the stubbornly loyal Ruth, professing undying loyalty ("Whither thou goest, I will go," Ruth 1:16

KJV), rejected Naomi's admonition to remain in Moab. Once in Judah and under Naomi's tutelage, Ruth wooed, seduced, and married Boaz and by him bore Obed, grandfather of the revered king David (Ruth 4:13–17). Thus, like Jonah, this tale mocked traditional religious constructions of the "other," while affirming a "difference" that remained open to surprise and a glorious conclusion.

The complex positions outlined in these materials clearly show that the old moniker pinned on Israel as focused on its exceptional and particularistic status is erroneous. Our brief survey shows how Israel's narrative contained elements of both the particular *and* the universal.[26] The complexity of that narrative stands as a cautionary tale against the tendency to juxtapose the universalist Paul against a narrow, particularist Judaism. As we read the letters, it will be helpful to attend to the way the contexts bring both into conversation.

UNIVERSALISM AND PARTICULARISM IN PAUL

One might speculate that Paul's gospel of inclusion of the excluded would have met with an enthusiastic embrace in the church, but at best, the terms of that embrace were debated. To many, Paul's inclusion of Gentiles in the people of God, on the basis of trust in the faithfulness of God shown in Christ, made him a pariah. The letters offer stark accounts of the opposition to him and his gospel.

Hints of that gainsaying surfaced in rumors with wings that reached churches in Rome before he did (Rom. 3:8). In the letter to those churches Paul complained, "Why am I still being condemned as a sinner?" (3:7). The rumor that his inclusion of Gentiles ("pagans") by grace was antinomian, and thus encouraged immorality, sparked an outburst: "And why not say (as some people slander us by saying that we say), 'Let us do evil so that good may come'? Their condemnation is deserved" (3:8).

We know little of the rival, unnamed apostles provoking his disclaimer in Corinth. We know nothing about the alternative gospel they preached, the spirit they claimed, or the Jesus they preached (2 Cor. 11:4–5). We do

26. The emphases on particularism and universalism in the *Letter of Aristeas* well illustrate the point made here. Attention to the context of a letter or its individual parts may reveal some of the tensions noted here. Beth A. Berkowitz has offered a useful qualification of the scholarly paradigm juxtaposing Jewish particularism against Christian universalism. See her "The Afterlives of the Torah's Ethnic Language: The Sifra and Clement on Leviticus 18.1–5," in *Jews, Christians, and the Roman Empire: The Poetics of Power in Late Antiquity*, ed. Natalie B. Dohrmann and Annette Yoshiko Reed (Philadelphia: University of Pennsylvania Press, 2013), 29–42.

know they scorned Paul as "weak" (i.e., womanish), dangerous, uncharismatic (2 Cor. 3:1–15), untrustworthy (2 Cor. 1:15–2:4), and as a preacher of "cheap grace" and a fraud (2 Cor. 10:1–13:12; Gal. 1:6–9; Phil. 3:1). With the proximity of Corinth to Rome across the Adriatic, one can easily imagine how criticisms of Paul might join other malicious rumors to poison his promised visit.

Jewish Christians in Rome who may have heard of Paul's starkly negative remarks in Galatia about the law might quite properly have been offended. The apostle's double, angry curse laid on Galatian Judaizers (Gal. 1:8–9) surely would have raised their hackles. Paul's fit of rage unleashed on those imposing Torah's protocols on Gentile converts might have offended those law-observant believers. His fuming remark that "through the law I died to the law" (Gal. 2:19) might have legitimately sounded like a repudiation of law, when stripped of context. Paul's ugly pun about circumcision, that those accepting it would be *cut off* from Christ (Gal. 5:4), would have sounded crude. Moreover, rumors of factional quarrels between Roman Jewish and Gentile Christians, had they reached Paul, would have alarmed him, for such a divided church could hardly welcome one who was a persona non grata from the east, nor could they support his Spanish mission with enthusiasm.

Such a dim prospect may help explain Paul's rhetoric in Romans. Embedded in that rhetoric are clues to Paul's view of law in the messianic age, to his defense of his gospel, to his response to slanderous charges about his gospel, to his defense of his apostolic legitimacy, and to his careful negotiation of differences between particularistic and universalistic elements in his gospel.

The purpose of Romans was at least in part to mediate the conflict between Jewish believers and Gentile converts. The tension between those Roman factions noted above may go back to the edict of Claudius that expelled Jews from Rome about 49 CE.[27] Absent the leadership of expelled Jewish Christ believers, Gentile converts would have filled the vacuum and lived with little or no engagement with the memory or practice of the Jewish Jesus people or the law. So when Emperor Nero lifted Claudius's ban in 54 CE, the returning Jewish Christian refugees faced an uncertain welcome of the Gentile majority (Rom. 15:7).[28] News of the resulting intramural squabbles would surely have

27. Rome jealously guarded the *Pax Romana* in the homeland, even when war raged in the hinterlands; thus local disturbances often met harsh reprisals. See Suetonius, "Tiberius Claudius Drusus Caesar 25," in *The Lives of the Twelve Caesars* (London: Wordsworth, 1997). Some of Paul's coworkers in Corinth and Ephesus were likely victims of the edict.

28. Romans 16 names Jewish believers who once assisted Paul in the east but were then in Rome.

troubled Paul and would have jeopardized their endorsement and support for his Spanish mission (Rom. 15:29).[29]

Paul's prayer request in Romans 15:30 that the offering from Gentile converts might be acceptable to the Jerusalem "poor" may strike the modern reader as a non sequitur. As disconnected as those emphases may sound, the prayer request may have been brilliant (Rom. 15:30–31). That request inserted its readers into a grand narrative of the end time, when Gentiles would process across the Palestinian plains to Zion to affirm Israel's God and blend their voices with a chorus of Israelites in one mighty chorus. The promise that imagined grand finale held for a triumphant union of Jew and Gentile in one people of God is hard to overestimate. Its relevance for mediating the tensions of the interim is obvious.

That best description of that grand finale appears in 2 Corinthians 9:12–15, where the apostle wrote with a full heart about the offering presentation. He conjured a Jerusalem eschatological scene so grand it almost takes the breath away. In that passage, his mind raced ahead without filling the gaps to project an offering pilgrimage such as the prophets could only dream of, when Gentiles would stream up to Zion in the last days to offer gifts and to learn the ways of Israel's God. Paul's Septuagint text of Isaiah 23:14–24:1 projected a future when Gentile gifts from Tyre would be offered and accepted as "holy" and acceptable to God. See also the glorious end time anticipated in Isaiah 2:2–3 and 60:5, bringing Jew and Gentile together (see also Isa. 45:14; 60:1–22; Mic. 4:1–2; 4:13).

In ancient societies, no less than in our own, gift giving was a transaction pregnant with meaning. The rule of reciprocity was absolute, requiring a gift in return.[30] Such exchanges signified a solidarity to which Paul now appealed to encourage the reconciliation of Jewish and Gentile believers. The stunning reconciliation Paul sketched earlier in 2 Corinthians 5:19 provoked in him a spontaneous outburst in 2 Corinthians 9:15 (RSV): "Thanks be to God for his inexpressible gift!"

As part of this formula of gift and reciprocity, Paul urged Gentiles who received "spiritual blessings" from Jews to reciprocate with the "material blessings" for the Jerusalem "poor among the saints" (Rom. 15:26–27). Any

---

29. For a full treatment of this intramural dispute, see Mark Reasoner, *The Strong and the Weak, Romans 14.1–15.13* (Cambridge: Cambridge University Press, 1999).

30. Marcel Mauss, *The Gift: The Form and Reason for Exchange in Archaic Societies*, trans. W. D. Halls, foreword by Mary Douglas (1st Eng. trans., London: Routledge, 1990; New York: W. W. Norton, 2000). This small book explores the economic, moral, religious, and aesthetic aspects of giving in archaic societies. Aspects of the gift transaction extended into nonarchaic societies of the ancient Greco-Roman world, and vestiges of it still remain.

compromise of that formulaic transaction, any failure to reciprocate, and any refusal of the gift by the intended recipient, Paul assumed, would heap shame on shame on the giver, and the insult would mean, "I want nothing to do with you"—a flat repudiation of solidarity or kin.

Although in Romans Paul sided psychologically with the "the strong," his advocacy for an integrated family of God was well known. Earlier in Galatians 3:28 he had recited a baptismal creed underscoring the solidarity of God's people. "In Christ," he recited, "there is neither Jew nor Greek [i.e., Gentile]; . . . for all of you are one in Christ Jesus." Given that foreground, Paul most earnestly counseled both the Jewish believers prone to self-righteousness and the Gentile converts inclined to arrogance (Rom. 11:17–22) to affirm their solidarity in Christ. The stormy, dark clouds of those sectarian disputes held frightening implications for Paul's vision of the union of Jew and Gentile in God's end time and the Spanish mission.

Please note, Paul's gospel promising Gentiles access to the company of God's elect was not universal salvation in the classic sense. Only believing Gentiles, that is, non-Jews, who believed that, in the death and resurrection of Messiah Jesus, God was in the process of liberating them from the clutches of King Sin, out to control the world. While those believers, however, were not of the world, they were still immersed in it, struggled against it, and expected to observe God's command to love both insiders and outsiders.[31] The recognition that an imperative was linked to God's indicative leads into the following discussion of Paul and *nomos* ("law").

PAUL AND LAW IN THE MESSIANIC AGE

The challenges noted above forced a defense of Paul's gospel (Rom. 1:1–4:25), a categorical rejection of the charge that its inclusion of "Gentile sinners" in the elect either encouraged immorality (Rom. 6:1–7:5) or repudiated the law as God's gift (9:1–11:36). That defense stretched toward universalism while vigorously defending God's venerable particularistic promise to Israel, he claimed (i.e., Rom. 11:26). An end-time protocol, Paul hoped, would make Gentile converts "honorary members"[32] of God's elect. Note especially Paul's emphatic assertion made without qualification that "the gifts and calling of God [to Israel] are irrevocable" (Rom. 11:29) and that "all Israel will be saved" (Rom. 11:26).

31. Victor Paul Furnish makes this point well in his article "Inside Looking Out," in *Pauline Conversations in Context: Essays in Honor of Calvin J. Roetzel*, 104–24.

32. Krister Stendahl's phrase offered in conversation.

Any persuasion of Jewish believers in Rome to embrace the Gentile mission to "outsiders" in faraway Spain (Rom. 14:1–15:29) required a positive treatment of law in the messianic age. The following summary of selected aspects of Paul's view of law aims to assist in understanding the conversation between Paul and readers, most of whom he had never seen and did not know.

Multifaceted Law

The Greek word for "law" (*nomos*) was pluri-significant for Paul *and* his readers. It could refer to Torah or the Pentateuch, to Israel's great story, to the Ten Commandments, to the 613 commands of the Pentateuch, to the love commandments from Leviticus (19:18; Rom. 13:8–9), to the end-time "law of the spirit" (Rom. 8:1), to the "law of Christ" (Gal. 6:2), to the unwritten (Rom. 2:29) or written law, to the law of nature, to purity laws, to revisions of Jewish law inspired by the messianic age, and to statutes and ordinances ordering civic life. Awareness of that pluri-significance will assist the reading of Romans as a conversation between Paul and churches in Rome.

The Septuagint offered a view of law that Paul shared. A prominent feature of postexilic Judaism (i.e., after 537 BCE) was its concern with Torah. The root meaning of *torah*'s verb form was "to direct" or "to instruct." *Torah* could refer to a teacher's instruction, YHWH's direction, prophetic appeal, or lessons embedded in Israel's rich and varied story. In the Septuagint, some of those nuances were lost as *torah* almost always appeared there as *nomos*. The Septuagint translators usually took *nomos* as a code that governed community or individual life. In some cases *nomos* referred to a natural principle like gravity or morality, shadings more resembling the Greek understanding of natural law than the Hebrew *torah*. For example, in Romans 8:2 Paul referred to being "set free from the law of sin and death," an echo of Genesis 3:1–3 that predicted death as punishment for disobedience of the divine command not to eat of the tree.

Paul nowhere equated *torah* with sin and death. On the contrary, shortly before, he had called the law "holy" and the commandment "holy and just and good" (Rom. 7:12). And mindful of the Genesis legend that death originated when Adam and Eve disobeyed the divine command not to eat of the tree (Gen. 2:16–17), Paul in Romans 8:2 evidently suggested that the "law of the Spirit of life in Christ Jesus" liberated the believer from the age-old *principle* that death follows sin. Similarly, the "law of my mind" in Romans 7:23 and the "law of works" opposite the "law of faith" in Romans 3:27 are best translated "principle" rather than "law."

This small sample of alternative meanings offers a cautionary tale against restricting Paul's usage of law to a single meaning. As the subtitle of this book,

"Conversations in Context," suggests, strict attention to context can greatly assist in deciphering Paul's exchanges with his readers.

Qumran as Game-changer

A backward glance of the interpretation of Paul's view of law may be helpful. In 1952 a young scholar, the late great Pauline interpreter W. D. Davies, published a little bombshell (ninety-nine pages!) called *Torah in the Messianic Age and/or Age to Come*.[33] It held up third-century-CE Jewish rabbinic materials as the background for Paul's view of law. Its neglect of the role Paul's more immediate Hellenistic Diaspora Judaism may have played in shaping his view provoked a devastating review by Morton Smith, an esteemed scholar of the Hellenistic world. The pain of that deservedly sharp critique lingered, prompting Davies to abandon his early thesis for decades.[34] Nevertheless, the idea lingered and near the end of Davies's life resurfaced in an obscure footnote. In 1998, just three years before his death, Davies returned to the topic: "[T]he whole question [of Torah in the Messianic Age] needs to be reopened in the light of [the Qumran document] 11Qtemple." Davies was aware of scholarly work that drew the drapes aside to reveal the Qumran belief that in the end times God would commission a prophet to offer a new Torah (law). That awareness convinced Davies that the time was ripe to reconsider his maligned and neglected thesis.[35]

Recent studies of Qumran scholars give Davies's thesis real substance. For example, Professor Wacholder has shown how the Qumran community believed that in the end time a Teacher of Righteousness would arise and offer a new Torah.[36] He has shown how texts from the Manual of Discipline (1QS) contain the pledge to govern by "the first ordinances . . . until the coming of the Prophet and the Anointed [Messiahs] of Aaron [priestly] and Israel [royal]" (1QS IX, 10–11).[37] The reference to *"first* ordinances [Torah]" suggested to Wacholder that *"last* ordinances" would be forthcoming in the

---

33. W. D. Davies, *Torah in the Messianic Age and/or Age to Come* (Philadelphia: Society of Biblical Literature, 1952). Morton Smith's unflattering review came soon thereafter in the *Journal of Biblical Literature*.

34. See Morton Smith's review in *Journal of Biblical Literature*, 72/3 (1953): 192–94.

35. W. D. Davies and D. C. Allison Jr., *Matthew 1–7: A Critical and Exegetical Commentary on the Gospel according to Saint* Matthew, ICC (Grand Rapids: Eerdmans, 1998), 493n28. The identity of the prophet here announced may have been the "Teacher of Righteousness," the oft-supposed founder of the community.

36. B. Z. Wacholder, *The Dawn of Qumran: The Sectarian Torah and the Teacher of Righteousness* (Cincinnati: Hebrew Union College Press, 1983), 1–32.

37. From the translation of Geza Vermes, see note 7.

eschatological age. While those "last ordinances" would not totally replace the "first," they would revise them.[38]

More recently, a junior Qumran scholar, Alex Jassen, has given Wacholder's thesis support. Jassen shows how the Qumran sectarians recognized that the prophet of the end time would provide *new* laws.[39] Although the narrative of God's gift of the law to Moses in the Sinai desert (Exod. 20:1–32:16) was etched in Israel's corporate memory, it was linked to the denial of Moses' entry into the "promised land." Jassen has shown how the scrolls coupled God's promise to Moses of commandments, statutes, and ordinances (Deut. 5:23–31) to the promise of new laws and ordinances after entry into the promised land.

There, Jassen notes, the scrolls report that God promised in the end time to raise up a *"prophet like you"* and to "put my words in his mouth." Thus Qumran documents 4Q175 Testimonia and 1QS 9.11 conjured a messianic age in which a "new law" would be offered by the prophet yet to come.[40] This study also well supports Davies's note that the time is now ripe for a reconsideration of Paul's view of law.[41] That Paul envisioned a similar radical revision or even new law in the messianic age is hardly to suggest that Paul was a Qumran sectarian, but to locate him in a vital apocalyptic tradition in some ways resembling that of Qumran. That recognition will help us recognize points at which Paul revised traditional understandings of Torah.

Prophets for Inclusion

Not only the Qumran eschatological vision but also that of the prophets likely informed Paul's view of law in the messianic age (Rom. 8:1; 1:19–29; 2:29). Especially apt was Jeremiah's promise of God's eschatological gift of an unwritten, internal law. Note Paul's appeal to the prophet Jeremiah to authorize his mission to the Gentiles and to inform his understanding of law in the end time:

> Behold, *the days are coming*, says the Lord, and I will make a *new cov-enant* with the house of Israel, and with the house of Judah. . . . *I will surely put my laws into their mind, and I will write them on their heart,*

38. Note also the explicit connection of the first and last ordinances in the *Testament of Judah*, XXIV, 3 and also the *Damascus Document B*, II, 8–9.

39. A. P. Jassen, *Mediating the Divine: Prophecy and Revelation in the Dead Sea Scrolls and Second Temple Judaism* (Leiden: E. J. Brill, 2007), 160–75.

40. Ibid., 160, 175.

41. For a fuller discussion of varieties of first-century interpretation see Calvin Roetzel, "Paul and the Law: Whence and Whither?" in *Currents in Research: Biblical Studies* 3 (1995): 249–75.

and I will be God to them, and they shall be my people. (Jer. LXX
38:31–36 LXX, AT, AE)

Given the normal gap between a spoken command and the almost instinc-
tive human inclination to resist, this text envisioned a future when commands
written on the heart would make obedience automatic. Did either Jeremiah
or Paul know of the child's inclination to put beans up his or her nose when a
parent has forbidden it? Thus, in Paul's spiritualized view that pagans have the
law "written on their hearts" (Rom. 2:15) we may hear an echo of Jeremiah's
vision of law in the end time.[42]

Law in the Diaspora

Monotheism, the repudiation of idols, and the divine demand for sexual
purity were core values of Diaspora religion. The disembodied written
law, while important, was hardly the sole or even primary guide to piety
there. Instead, it received its divine valence through its incarnation in the
flesh of venerable figures like Abraham and Moses. This unwritten, internal, incarnate law assumed supreme value in the Diaspora, and figures like
Philo specifically described Abraham as "a law and an unwritten statute"
(*Abraham* 276) and Moses as a "reasonable and living impersonation of law"
(*On Moses* I.162). While the people of the covenant did enjoy pride of place
in Diaspora literature, a Gentile presence was also welcomed without first
requiring circumcision or law observance as a prerequisite for their redemption.[43] If one allows for an influence of such a Diaspora legacy on Paul, it
is easier to understand his casual references to the "law of Christ" and the
"law of the Spirit" (e.g., Rom. 8:1; Gal. 6:2) and to appreciate the umbrage
he takes when Christ Judaizers would require that his Galatian converts add
circumcision and law observance as prerequisites for their acceptance into
God's elect.

Similarly, in the last century, Albert Schweitzer observed that an "in Christ
mysticism" permeated Paul's thought and influenced his understanding of
law. He noted that

> Paul is convinced . . . that the Law can only remain in force up to
> the beginning of the Messianic Kingdom. And since he holds that the
> elect, so soon as they are 'in Christ,' no longer belong the natural,
> but henceforth to the Messianic world, he is necessarily led to the

---

42. See Roetzel, "Paul and Nomos in the Messianic Age," 121–25.
43. Please note John J. Collins, *Between Athens and Jerusalem: Jewish Identity in the
Hellenistic Diaspora* (New York: Crossroad, 1983), 167–68.

conclusion that they are no longer under the Law [as Judaizers in Galatians claimed]. . . . Paul sacrificed the Law to eschatology.[44]

With the benefit of hindsight, it appears that Schweitzer was only half right. Paul hardly sacrificed law but rather adapted it to a new reality. In Romans he emphatically denied the charge that his gospel was antilaw and encouraged immorality. Far from encouraging immorality, he argued, God's adoption of "Gentile sinners" into the elect family (Rom. 8:15) and their obedience to the "law of the Spirit" went beyond "the just requirement of the law" (Rom. 8:1, 4–5). Their entry into the people of God was not by law observance, but once in, they were obligated to observe the law to stay.[45] The righteousness under the Spirit's guidance that Paul espoused for those "in Christ" was in fact higher than that previously required. As noted in 1 Corinthians 13, the highest of all end-time gifts was love, and in Romans 13:8–10 Paul invoked the commandment of Leviticus 19:18 to "love your neighbor as yourself" as a summary of his gospel's imperative.

Nowhere does Paul suggest or even imply that such an imperative was impossible to fulfill. Older views portrayed the early Paul as a guilt-ridden Pharisee unable to keep the law, no matter how hard he tried. Weighed down by the guilt heaped on him by that failure, his "conversion" freed him from that burden. That earlier construction of Paul, however, was a historical fiction.[46] On the contrary, Paul claimed to have been "blameless" under the law (Phil. 3:8). The complex mix of Jewish apocalypticism, a Hellenistic worldview, Septuagintal texts, and a Diaspora vulnerability to absorption by a powerful, alluring Hellenistic culture that required innovative constructs to secure identity, all conspired to destabilize established views and to lend to Paul's messianism a dynamic, fresh, and multisemic quality.

Some Aspects of Law and Grace in Paul

No one questions the Pauline emphasis on grace. A good concordance will record more than twenty references to grace (*charis*) in Romans alone. There Paul wrote of "grace" in which believers stand (Rom. 5:2), of justification

44. Albert Schweitzer, *The Mysticism of Paul the Apostle*, trans. W. Montgomery (1st Eng. ed. 1931; London: Adam & Charles Black, 1967), 192. Here I side with E. P. Sanders, *Paul, the Law, and the Jewish People* (Philadelphia: Fortress, Press, 1983), 183–99.

45. See E. P. Sanders, *Paul, the Law, and the Jewish People* (Philadelphia: Fortress Press, 1983), 143–99

46. See discussion in last chapter below on "The Relationship of Paul to His Native Judaism."

by grace (3:24), of grace as God's gift (5:15), of salvation by grace not works (11:6), and of being not under law but under grace (6:14, 15). Moreover, Paul opened and closed all of his letters with grace pronouncements (Rom. 1:7; 16:20; 1 Cor. 1:3; 16:23; 2 Cor. 1:2; 13:14; Gal. 1:3; 6:18; Phil. 1:2; 4:23; and 1 Thess. 1:1; 6:21). That emphasis may explain how grace came to be pitted against law by Paul interpreters as early as the second century by Marcion, who held Judaism to be a religion of Old Testament law, opposing a New Testament religion of grace.[47] The latter, he held, focused on salvation as a gift and the earlier on salvation as a reward for human effort; one claimed to be God centered, the other was human focused. As popular as that juxtaposition is, it is historically false and even dangerous. Note especially the coupling of grace and the law's imperative by the Jewish community at Qumran:

> And if I stagger, God's mercies are my salvation forever;
> and if I stumble because of the sin of my flesh,
> my justification is in the righteousness of God which exists forever. . . .
> He has caused me to approach by His Mercy
> and by His favours He will bring my justification. . . .
> He has justified me by His true justice
> and by His immense goodness He will pardon all my iniquities.
>
> (1QS XI: 12–14)

A more careful, comprehensive reading of Paul's letters in context also complicates the juxtaposition of law and grace,[48] and Paul was hypersensitive to the charge that his Gentile gospel of inclusion in the elect by grace fostered or encouraged immorality. Paul himself was so sensitive to the charge that his gospel was antinomian (or antilaw) that he rhetorically posed the question "Is the law sin?" and then answered: "No, no, no absolutely not!" (Rom. 7:7 AT) Shortly after, he asserted that the "law is holy, and the commandment is holy and just and good" (Rom. 7:12). The problem, Paul noted, was not in the law but in the human heart: "For we know that the law is spiritual," he affirmed in Romans 7:14. The norm for the eschatological revolution underway was, he noted, the "law of the Spirit of life in Christ Jesus" (Rom. 8:2). With heat and even divine curses Paul inveighed against Judaizers out to impose circumcision and/or law observance on Paul's Gentile converts as a precondition for admission into God's elect. Paul understood that strategy as a challenge to the sufficiency of his Gentile gospel. Once converts were within the elect of God,

---

47. It appears that the terms *Old* Testament and *New* Testament originally came from Marcion, whom church fathers later called a heretic.

48. See the work of Marilyn J. Salmon, *Preaching without Contempt: Overcoming Unintended Anti-Judaism* (Minneapolis: Fortress Press, 2006).

however, he expected them to keep that law and its messianic intensification in the law of Christ.

Paul's Spiritualization of Law

A vestige of Paul's Pharisaic inclination to spiritualize the law lingered to influence his apostolic counsel. Philo, who had Pharisaic sympathies, claimed self-offering as the best sacrifice (*Spec. Leg.* I, 293), and Paul urged his Roman readers to "present [their] bodies as a living sacrifice, holy and acceptable to God" (Rom. 12:1). While this spiritualizing tendency may be most obvious in Paul's cultic language, his letters make a similar move with regard to the law. For example, the apostle noted that "real circumcision is a matter of the heart—it is spiritual and not literal" (Rom. 2:29). Similarly, he gave the purity law concerning leaven a spiritualized nuance in 1 Corinthians 5:6, 7, and 8 and Galatians 5:9 (cf. Phil. 4:8 and Rom. 14:20; Philo *Spec. Leg.* I, 293, advice against being "puffed up" as one approaches the altar).

To be clear, Paul did claim some rather radical revisions of the law brought about by the messianic age. The faithfulness of Christ made it possible for Gentiles to become members of the people of God without first converting to Judaism, and that messianic devotion did allow converts to disregard certain purity rules, but that freedom nevertheless required respect for Jesus people committed to a fastidious observance of the rules of purity (Rom. 14:1–15:6).

SUMMARY

In sum, Paul's eschatology, that is, his conviction that the death and resurrection of Messiah Jesus, accompanied by the Spirit's outpouring of the end time, signaled history's final, triumphant moment, reshaped and transformed his understanding of law, and informed his Jewish legacy. With that conviction came the belief that a new or revised law befitting the age was in play for members of the reconstituted elect. With that belief came another, that the external, written law was provisional, or a preparation for the coming of Christ. Furthermore, the law of the end time was written on the heart and was more demanding, not less. An essential piece of this reconfigured law opened the door to the elect for believing Gentiles, without requiring the usual protocol for conversion to the Hebrew religion. Finally, Paul's Pharisaic inclinations and Diaspora upbringing and education conspired to add subtle nuances to his apocalyptic revision of some interpretations, and attention to those differing emphases offers useful clues to Paul's rhetorical agenda. The two letters that offer the most extensive treatment of Paul's view of law are Galatians and Romans. These letters presume contextual issues that are quite different and will require close attention from the reader. The treatments of Paul's view of Gentiles and law above, it is hoped, when combined with a summary of important features of Paul's Jewish world, will assist in the reading of Paul's letters.

3

The Anatomy of the Letters

The earliest writings of the New Testament are the seven undisputed letters of Paul, and no letters have more profoundly influenced Western history than have these. These letters offer a window through which we can view at a distance the conflicted personality of Paul—Paul the sickly, weak apostle; Paul the proud and assertive emissary of Christ; Paul the gentle one; and Paul the blustery, threatening presence—and a troubled young church, struggling to understand itself as God's elect of the newly arriving last days but still prone to old habits.

A casual glance at these writings will reveal that they were real letters dealing with life-and-death matters and not merely abstract dogmatic treatises. Even though in Paul's time there was no postal service for public use, and even though writing materials were expensive and the delivery of letters uncertain, the Hellenistic period of Paul and his readers was quintessentially the period of the letter. Handbooks on letter writing were circulated, and a whole class of professional scribes sprang up to serve the government bureaucracy, to assist wealthy patrons in need of their reading and writing skills, and to read and write letters for the illiterate for a fee.

As in the American colonial period, in Paul's day receiving a letter was a major event. Those letters substituted presence for absence, bridged distance between recipient and sender, served as a vehicle for instruction, exhortation, praise or blame; they offered consolation and encouragement, and they often were instruments of self-defense. It is understandable, therefore, that twenty-one of the twenty-seven "books" of the New Testament are letters or letter facsimiles.

While personal letters are becoming less common in the age of e-mail and digital messaging, they still carry special significance. Our experience in pondering the messaging of those letters will assist in the analysis of the Pauline epistles.

This chapter will examine the anatomy of the Hellenistic letter, looking for clues to the writer's intent. Because the letter structure was such an important part of the ancient letter, a comparison of the key elements of the Hellenistic letter with those in Paul's Philemon (RSV) may be illuminating (see table).

Although the anatomy of the Pauline letters may be unfamiliar to us at first glance, examination of their structure may offer clues to their purpose. The discussion below will treat both the form and the function of those main elements and offer assistance in deciphering them. Our purpose is to show the working of the separate parts, not to offer an exhaustive discussion of each member. Before turning to our survey, let us take note of a typical Greek papyrus letter to guide our study. From such a model the basic skeleton of the letter will become clear, and we shall better understand how Paul duplicated and altered letter-writing patterns to serve his epistolary interests and to participate in a lively conversation with his churches.

All conversations have a structure. A "Hi" and a "See you later" bracket an exchange between friends. A "Hello" and a "Good-bye" frame a telephone conversation. A "Dear Jane" and a "Yours sincerely" mark the boundaries of a personal letter; even e-mail exchanges may contain conventions of meeting and parting. Those conventions provide a framework for conversation and serve as doorways through which a graceful entry or a smooth exit from the conversational circle takes place. However habitual this litany of meeting and parting may be, it is a vital part of sharing another's presence.

All conversations do have a structure, but not all structured conversations are letters. A telegram, an announcement, an e-mail, a text, and a letter all rely on a medium for delivery. All are instruments of communication between separated persons. Yet the differences among them are instantly apparent to even the most casual reader. It is the structure as well as the content that identifies the letter as a letter. It begins, continues, and ends in a predictable way. We all learned early that the sender's return address, date, greeting, body, and conclusion form the skeleton of a personal letter, and that all letters have this same structure, more or less. But the skeleton of the letter provides a medium through which information is shared and concerns expressed. Thus letters, like people, share a common frame; yet each is distinct.

Paul's letters, like our own, have a structure. Fortunately, the discovery of thousands of Greek papyrus letters from ancient times has helped us define more precisely the shape of the letter in Paul's day. Study of those papyri has identified the parts of the ancient letter, as well as the function of each part.[1] We

1. Summarizing this topic is William Doty, *Letters in Primitive Christianity* (Philadelphia: Fortress Press, 1973). An excellent survey of recent scholarship and the emerging consensus is available in John L. White, *Light from Ancient Letters* (Philadelphia: Fortress Press, 1986). Stanley K. Stowers, "Greek and Latin Letters," in

now know that the use of the letter-writing conventions of Paul's day was just as natural (or even unconscious) for Paul as for us. Nevertheless, his use of those conventions was hardly mechanical, for Paul, like writers today, altered the traditional epistolary forms to suit his purposes. And it is the alterations he made that tell us most about Paul's self-understanding, his intentions, and his theologizing.

However complex such an analysis may sound, each reader will recall how carefully he or she pondered the structure of an important letter. The letter from a boyfriend, or girlfriend, for example, may begin, "Dear Sue" or "Sam," which in and of itself may seem insignificant. But suppose the previous letter began, "My Dearest." Then the new form of the greeting may raise a host of questions: Is he/she losing interest? Is there another? Is he/she taking me for granted? On and on, the reader goes, combing the letter for clues in the structure of the letter to the writer's deep and true intent. So, although the anatomy of the Pauline letter may be unfamiliar, we are sensitive to the nuances that structural alterations encode.

Before turning to our survey of the separate elements of the Pauline letter, let us take note of the Greek papyrus letter below. From this model the basic skeleton of the letter will become clear, and we shall better understand how Paul copied and exploited it for multiple uses.

A Typical Greek Papyrus Letter

Irenaeus to Apollinarius his dearest brother	SALUTATION
many greetings. I pray continually for your	PRAYER
health, and I myself am well. I wish you to	
know that I reached land on the sixth of the	
month Epeiph and we unloaded our cargo	BODY
on the eighteenth of the same month. I went	
up to Rome on the twenty-fifth of the same	
month and the place welcomed us as the	
god willed, and we are daily expecting our	
discharge, it so being that up till today	
nobody in the corn fleet has been released.	
Many salutations to your wife and to	CONCLUSION
Serenus and to all who love	(Greetings, final wish, date)
you, each by name. Goodbye. Mesare 9[2]	

The Anchor Bible Dictionary, ed. David Noel Freedman (New York: Doubleday & Co., 1992), 4:290–93, and *Letter Writing in Greco-Roman Antiquity* (Philadelphia: Fortress Press, 1986), thinks Paul was influenced by the philosophical letter-writing tradition. Of late see the brilliant Hans-Josef Klauck, *Ancient Letters and the New Testament: A Guide to Context and Exegesis* (Waco, TX: Baylor University Press, 2006).

2. B. G. U. 27 (H.E. 113) as cited by C. K. Barrett, *New Testament Background: Selected Documents* (New York: Macmillan Co., 1957), 29.

A comparison of the key elements in this letter with those of Philemon, Paul's shortest letter (RSV), may be illuminating:

	Papyrus Letter	Pauline Letter
I. Salutation		
A. Sender	Irenaeus	Paul, a prisoner for Christ Jesus and Timothy our brother
B. Recipient	to Apollonarius his dearest brother	To Philemon our beloved fellow worker and Apphia our sister and Archippus our fellow soldier, and the church in your house
C. Greeting	many greetings	Grace to you and peace from God, our father and the Lord Jesus Christ
II. Thanksgiving	I pray continually for your health and I myself am well	I thank my God always when I remember you in my prayers
III. Body	[Information about his arrival on the grain boat from Egypt]	[Discussion of his return of Onesimus the slave]
IV. Closing	[absent here but . . . present elsewhere]	receive him. . . . charge my account. Refresh my heart in Christ. . . . Prepare a guest room for me. . . .
V. Conclusion		
A. Peace Wish	[absent]	[absent here but present elsewhere]
B. Greetings	Many salutations to your wife and to Serenus and to all who love you, each by name.	Epaphras, my fellow prisoner in Christ Jesus, sends greetings to you, and so do Mark, Aristarchus, Demas, and Luke, my fellow workers.
C. Kiss	[absent]	[absent but present elsewhere]
D. Close	Goodbye.	The grace of the Lord Jesus Christ be with your Spirit.

Although we can draw no firm conclusions from this brief comparison, the parallels are obvious. Obviously, Paul's relationship to Christ dictated some change of emphasis. The sender is described as a "prisoner for Christ Jesus," and the close goes beyond "good-bye" to place both his addressees and Paul himself in the presence of "Jesus Christ." Other similarities and differences will become clear in our discussion below. We shall now turn to consider each part.

THE SALUTATION

The salutation is one of the most stable elements in the ancient letter. The form is rather precise. Unlike our modern letter, the salutation includes the names of both sender and recipient, and a greeting. In spite of the stereotypical letter opening, it remained pliable in the hands of Paul. In Philemon, Romans, and Galatians we see how Paul molded the salutation to serve the purpose in the letter as a whole. In Philemon Paul addressed the master of the runaway slave Onesimus, who was seeking Paul's protection.

Through Paul, who was in prison at the time, Onesimus was converted (v. 10), and Paul reminded Philemon, Onesimus's owner, that Paul's apostolic status gave him a prior claim on Onesimus. While he was in prison, Paul needed the slave's assistance. Nevertheless, Paul reported that he was returning Onesimus, requesting that the slave be treated "like a brother." The question inevitably arises: Does the treatment of a slave like a brother affect the relationship of owner to owned?

In Romans we see Paul's most original adaptation of the conventional letter opening. Writing to churches he had neither founded nor visited, Paul was eager to establish the "orthodoxy"[3] of his gospel and the legitimacy of his apostolic claim. In some quarters Paul was looked upon as a theological maverick, an imposter, and an interloper in the apostolic circle. It is quite likely that Paul's awareness of slanderous rumors about him inspired the expansion of the salutation to defend his gospel and his call (Rom. 1:1–7).

Citing church tradition, Paul underscored the fact that the message he proclaimed was no dangerous innovation but was anchored in the promises God made "through his prophets in the holy scriptures" (Rom. 1:2). Drawing

---

3. I realize that to use the term "orthodoxy" in this period is anachronistic. For the sake of convenience I use it, nevertheless, recognizing that soon after Paul's day fierce debates would define the shape and outlook of the Jesus movement and the veracity of Paul's apostolic claims and his gospel.

on traditional formulations, Paul summarized his gospel for all to judge. He wrote of Jesus' descent from David, God's designation of Jesus as "Son of God" through the resurrection, and his own appointment as apostle to the Gentiles by the risen Christ (1:3–6). We see, therefore, how already in the salutation Paul defended the authority of his apostleship and the nature of his gospel. By inserting traditional material into the salutation, he aimed to refute the slanderous rumors that he was an apostle of discord. By showing the integral place of his mission in God's plan, Paul sought the support of the Roman church for his mission to Spain.

The salutation in Galatians, likewise, shows how brilliantly Paul could bend stereotypical conventions to serve his purposes and how attending to his use of traditional forms offers clues to his purpose. In Galatians 1:1 Paul referred to himself as "an *apostle*—sent neither by human commission nor from human authorities, but through Jesus Christ and God the Father, who raised him from the dead."

With the formalities of the letter opening out of the way, Paul plunged into the body of the letter. What has been hinted at in the salutation then became explicit. Instead of the traditional thanksgiving, Paul inserted an expression of astonishment at the behavior of the Galatians. In Galatians 1:10 Paul began a vigorous defense of his apostleship that stretched through chapter 2. He lashed out at those who slandered his apostleship and discredited his gospel. By asserting that his gospel was "not of human origin" (1:11–12), but came directly from Christ, he sought to establish his independence of the Jerusalem circle and to defend the authenticity of his message as a divine revelation.

It is likely that some in the Galatian church saw in Peter, James, John, and others a direct, historical link to Jesus that Paul could not claim. Since he received his gospel from human agents, it ipso facto was less legitimate. So already in the salutation opening the letter, Paul sought to establish the integrity of his apostolic credentials and the legitimacy of his gospel. Thus, once again, we see that by noting Paul's alterations of stereotypical letter forms we gain some insight into his epistolary designs.

THE THANKSGIVING

More than any other secondary work, Paul Schubert's epochal *Form and Function of the Pauline Thanksgivings*[4] stimulated an interest in the literary design of Paul's letters. His hypothesis is still valid, namely, that the thanksgiving is

---

4. Paul Schubert, *Form and Function of the Pauline Thanksgivings* (Berlin: Alfred Töpelmann, 1939).

a formal element of most Pauline letters, that it terminates the letter opening, signals the basic intent of the letter, and may serve as an outline of the major topics to be treated in the body of the letter.[5] Coming immediately after the salutation, the thanksgiving appears in all of Paul's letters except Galatians (Gal. 1:6).

In 1 Corinthians 1:4–9, for example, Paul linked references to the charismatic speech and knowledge of the Corinthian converts to an allusion to the future "day of our Lord Jesus Christ." A study of 1 Corinthians will show that Paul thus signaled to the reader his basic concern. Scholars have long noted that the Corinthian preoccupation with "wisdom" (1:18–4:21) and charismatic speech (chaps. 12–14) sprang from a religious enthusiasm that claimed salvation in this world. Paul's reference in the thanksgiving to the future "day of our Lord Jesus," therefore, may indicate his resolve to adjust the eschatological perspective of his Corinthian converts. His emphasis on a future "day of the Lord" could also qualify the religious pretentions of his converts.

The thanksgiving in 2 Corinthians 1:3–7 functions like that in 1 Corinthians 1:4–9 in the way it offers a preview of a major emphasis of the letter body.[6] Paul alluded to the abundance of his sufferings through which he mythically participated in the sufferings of Christ. He invited his addressees to share in "our sufferings," so that they might also share in "our comfort." Against those who sought to validate their claims with visions, mighty works, prodigies of the Spirit, charismatic eloquence, and exegetical superiority, Paul exalted his imprisonments, beatings, shipwrecks, and other afflictions as signifiers of divine power (2 Cor. 11:20–12:10). What his adversaries took to be the "stench of death" raised by signs of physical vulnerability and apostolic mendacity, Paul called the "aroma of Christ" (2 Cor. 2:14–17). In 2 Corinthians 6:3–10 he defined his suffering, persecution, and poverty as a lens through which the power of God could be clearly seen. Sharing in the sufferings of Christ, Paul claimed, legitimated his ministry under attack (see 7:5–12).

The thanksgiving in 2 Corinthians offers a sober reflection on a troubled relationship between Paul and his converts and serves as a window onto the broad landscape treated in this document.

---

5. Erich Fascher, "Briefliteratur, urchristliche, formgeschichtlich," in *Die Religion in Geschichte und Gegenwart*, 3rd ed. (Tübingen: J. C. B. Mohr [Paul Siebeck], 1957), 1:1412–16.

6. The situation in 2 Corinthians is complicated by the likelihood that the present document is an anthology of letter fragments. For a plausible hypothesis regarding the number of letter fragments included in 2 Corinthians and their arrangement, see Calvin Roetzel, *2 Corinthians*, Abingdon New Testament Commentaries (Nashville: Abingdon Press, 2007).

An additional word is necessary regarding the aforementioned passage. James M. Robinson showed that Paul's thanksgivings hardly follow a fixed epistolary pattern.[7] He noted how the apostle could graft liturgical material onto traditional epistolary forms. In 2 Corinthians 1:3, Paul merged a Hellenistic form with Jewish liturgical material to create an impressive hybrid: "Blessed be the God and Father of our Lord Jesus Christ." That innovation shows that Paul did not slavishly follow a precut pattern but created his own. Moreover, we should not assume that this was a conscious, manipulative exercise on Paul's part, any more than our own use and modification of letter-writing conventions are crassly self-conscious. As hinted at in the previous paragraph, this thanksgiving reflected on the recent troubled relationship with the Corinthians. If the thanksgiving of 2 Corinthians 1:3–11 is allowed to follow the angry Pauline "letter of tears" (2 Cor. 10:1–13:10), then its softer tone seems entirely apt (see discussion below).

THE BODY OF THE LETTER

After the thanksgiving, the reader enters a vast and varied conversational world. Its landscape is as broad as Paul's theological understanding and as diverse as the needs of the churches. But in spite of the range and variety of the body of the letters, there is a pattern that reoccurs throughout. A request or disclosure formula (e.g., "I beseech you . . ." or "I would not have you ignorant . . .") often signals crossing from the thanksgiving into the body. Similarly, the letter ending is usually marked by an announcement of Paul's travel plans or a contemplated visit by the apostle.[8]

Galatians alone lacks any reference to Paul's travel plans. Robert Funk's explanation of this omission is attractive. He saw in Galatians 4:12–20 a substitute for the usual reference to an upcoming apostolic visit. In that passage Paul reflected on his previous visit and wished that he could return again (but of course he could not). In the view of Funk, "This is a travelogue in a situation where travel . . . is out of the question, i.e., in a situation where Paul cannot add the promise of an oral word to

7. James M. Robinson, "The Historicality of Biblical Language," in *The Old Testament and Christian Faith*, ed. Bernard W. Anderson (New York: Harper & Row, 1966), 270. He thinks Galatians and Romans were exceptions to this rule for good and sufficient reasons.

8. Robert W. Funk, *Language, Hermeneutic, and Word of God* (New York: Harper & Row, 1966).

the written word, he recalls the previous oral word and wishes he might renew it."[9]

The function of the travelogue, he claimed, was to reinforce the written word with the promise of an apostolic visit. Others have noted an autobiographical section, or a report by Paul on his activity, near the beginning of the body in most letters. In Galatians he spoke of his relationship to the Jerusalem church (Gal. 1:10–2:21). In 2 Corinthians he reported on the hardships he had suffered (2 Cor. 1:8–2:13). In Philippians he spoke of his imprisonment (Phil. 1:12–26), and in 1 Corinthians he recalled his ministry among his addressees (1 Cor. 1:10–17). In each case this autobiographical note was fully integrated into his theological argument. These reports impinged directly on the situation of his readers, for by reciting demands made on him, Paul warned his hearers that like demands might be made on them. We see, therefore, that although the topography of the body of the letter is necessarily less predictable than that of the thanksgiving, there are guideposts to lead the reader through it. Since the body embraces the full range and richness of Paul's theological outlook, we should expect it to offer difficulties, but we should be prepared also for pleasant surprises. Functionally, therefore, the body and thanksgiving of the letter complement each other.

As Funk well said: "The thanksgiving looks back . . . on the effects of grace already experienced. . . . the body . . . [looks ahead and] calls the readers again into the presence of Christ, that the word of the cross may take effect anew."[10]

PARAENESIS (ETHICAL INSTRUCTION AND EXHORTATION)

The letters contain at least three different types of ethical instruction. First, there are clusters of unrelated moral maxims, strung together like beads on a string. Often there is little to hold them together except their similarity of form or a catchword carried over from one to another. A good example of this type of material appears in Romans 12:9–13:

> Let love be genuine; hate what is evil, hold fast to what is good; love one another with mutual affection; outdo one another in showing honor. Do not lag in zeal, be ardent in Spirit, serve the Lord. Rejoice

9. Ibid., 268. Funk also believed that the location of the announcement of his travel plans at the end of the letter is explicable in terms of Paul's imminent visit to Rome and the purpose the letter serves in preparing for that visit.

10. Ibid., 249.

in hope, be patient in suffering, persevere in prayer. Contribute to the
needs of the saints; extend hospitality to strangers.

In this short paragraph thirteen different injunctions and at least twelve different topics appear. Not one of them has much to do with any other. While
we shall return to this discussion in the next chapter, it is important here to
say that Paul was probably dependent on tradition for this type of material.[11]

Second, scattered throughout Paul's letters we find lists of virtues and vices
in which Jewish and Hellenistic traditions were merged.[12] These lists, like
those of the injunctions above, contain items that have only the most casual
relationship to each other. In Galatians 5:19–23, for example, we find such a
catalog:

> Now the works of the flesh are obvious: fornication, impurity, licen-
> tiousness, idolatry, sorcery, enmities, strife, jealousy, anger, quarrels,
> dissensions, factions, envy, drunkenness, carousing, and things like
> these. . . . By contrast, the fruit of the Spirit is love, joy, peace, patience,
> kindness, generosity, faithfulness, gentleness, and self-control.

The third type of paraenetic material offers a prolonged exhortation or
homily on a particular topic.[13] Strongly reminiscent of an oral situation,
these materials are highly personal and supportive (e.g., "I became your
father," 1 Cor. 4:15). Pastoral in tone, such exhortations appear frequently
throughout Paul's letters. The bulk of 1 Corinthians (chaps. 5–15) probably
belongs to this type of material. Paul there deals one by one with problems
brought to him in an oral report by Chloe's people and by a letter from the
church.

First Thessalonians 4:13–18 and 5:1–11 well illustrate this paraenetic
style. Both sections treat topics of concern to Paul's readers: the resurrection
of the dead and the unpredictable suddenness of the end. Both close with
an exhortation ("Therefore encourage one another with these words," 4:18;
"Therefore encourage one another and build up each other," 5:11).

It is helpful to distinguish individual paraenetic units from sections of paraenetic material. Individual units (including types 1 and 2) appear haphazardly

11. Martin Dibelius, *Der Brief des Jakobus*, 11th ed. (Göttingen: Vandenhoeck &
Ruprecht, 1964), 15ff.

12. For relevant Hellenistic traditions, see Francis W. Beare, "The Epistle to
the Colossians, Introduction," in *The Interpreter's Bible*, ed. George A. Buttrick et al.
(Nashville: Abingdon Press, 1955), 11:133ff. For Jewish and Hellenistic background,
see Siegfried Wibbing, *Die Tugend und Lasterkataloge in Neuen Testament* (Berlin: Alfred
Töpelmann, 1959).

13. David G. Bradley, "The *Topos* as a form in the Pauline Paraenesis," *Journal of
Biblical Literature* 72 (1953): 238–46.

throughout all of the letters. But the paraenetic section knits together the body of the letter and stretches to the conclusion (Galatians, Romans, 1 Thessalonians, and possibly 1 Corinthians and Philippians). Although some of this instruction or exhortation has little specific relevance for any particular church, Paul often tailors general ethical traditions to fit particular needs. General admonitions to refrain from vengeful acts, to do good to outsiders, to obey the leaders, and to build up the church occur with some regularity in the epistles. But these act not as a rulebook suitable for every problem; rather, they are focal instances of how the gospel is to take effect. This material comes from multiple sources, and nowhere does Paul proclaim it as original. His weaving of it into the fabric of the letter, however, shows a master's hand at turning general moral saws to specific and concrete account.

CONCLUSION OF THE LETTER

Unlike the opening, the conclusion of the letter has received scant attention. Increasingly, however, scholars have discovered clues in it to the letter's agenda.[14] Analysis of the conclusion has identified its parts and the uses to which Paul may employ the endings.

Like the letter opening, the conclusion is a stable element in the epistolary structure where we usually find a peace wish, greetings, and a benediction (or grace). Occasionally, we see an apostolic pronouncement; generally, all of this is preceded by a summary of last-minute instructions. Bridging the gap between the instruction cluster and the conclusion is the peace wish. Once Paul crossed that threshold, he was committed himself to parting and would soon end the conversation.

The peace wish, of course, did not originate with Paul. The *shalom* (peace) greeting of the Semitic letter was familiar to him. Used both in meeting and parting, the word "peace" expressed a desire for the total well-being (bodily health as well as inner peace) of the person. Reminiscent of the coveted "blessing" of the Hebrew Scriptures, the *shalom* greeting often went beyond the simple exchange of amenities to a joint affirmation of faith. This peace wish occupied the ultimate position in the conclusion of the Semitic letter. In this regard it corresponded to the "good-bye" (*errōso*) of the Greek letter as the final wish for the well-being of the recipient (e.g., "you will do me a favor

14. Gordon Wiles, *Paul's Intercessory Prayers* (Cambridge: Cambridge University Press, 1973); see Calvin Roetzel, "1 Thessalonians 5:12–28: A Case Study," *Proceedings of the Society of Biblical Literature* 108 (1972): 2:367–83. See also Harry Y. Gamble, *The Textual History of the Letter to the Romans* (Grand Rapids: Eerdmans, 1977).

by taking care of your bodily health"). The peace wish for Paul, however, occupied a penultimate position in the conclusion.

In the letter opening Paul usually greeted his converts with a grace, putting both parties in the presence of God (e.g., "Grace to you and peace from God our Father and the Lord Jesus Christ"). In the conclusion, greetings were sandwiched between the peace wish and the grace, and thus the closing peace wish echoed the opening greeting and closed the circle: (opening) grace and peace, (closing) peace and grace. Before parting, Paul once again placed himself and his hearers in the presence of God, and the note of the peace wish extended God's presence beyond this meeting point of the present letter and the future divine saving presence ("live in peace; and the God of love and peace *will be with you*," 2 Cor. 13:11 AE).

After the concluding peace wish, Paul's mind opened out onto the possibilities ahead. The peace wish was more than a priestly benediction. It gathered unto itself the major concerns of the letter. In 1 Thessalonians, for example, Paul addressed a demoralized and distressed church. Some members had died before the expected return (*parousia*) of Christ; others fixed on the imminent end had fallen into sloth (1 Thess. 4:9–11).

So the peace wish of 1 Thessalonians reiterated Paul's major concerns. By declaring that God will preserve the believer's "spirit and soul and body" blameless at the end, he affirmed a future that some doubted and others mistakenly already claimed in the present. Thus once again Paul bent a stereotypical form to his own immediate theological ends.

Occasionally a prayer request (e.g., "Beloved, pray for us," 1 Thess. 5:25) stands adjacent to the peace wish. Although it has no exact parallel in the papyrus letters, it may have its counterpart in the assurance of remembrance in the letter opening and in the closing request to keep the writer in mind. The Hellenistic letter often opened with the assurance "I pray for your health" and concluded by asking, in turn, for the recipient's prayerful thoughts. One writer, for example, who complained that he was having difficulty navigating the river past the Antaeopolite nome, requested prayers on his behalf: "Remember the night-festival of Isis at the Serapeum."[15] Likewise, at the beginning of 1 Thessalonians, Paul included his addressees in his prayers (1:2), and before closing, he asked them to include him in theirs (5:25; see also Rom. 1:9 and 15:30). By such usage, Paul modeled the vital reciprocity of life in the family of God. In the opening announcement of his prayer for them and in the closing request for their prayer, he demonstrated a corporate rhythm of giving and receiving in a shared world.

15. *The Osyrhynchus Papyri*, ed. Bernard Grenfell and Arthur Hurd (London: Oxford University Press, 1910), 3:261–62.

Following the peace wish and prayer request, the impending separation between Paul and his readers becomes more prominent.[16] The closing greeting from Paul and his coworkers and the command to greet one another signaled the imminent end of the epistolary meeting. Even where it was not explicitly stated, it was to be assumed that this greeting would be conveyed by the kiss. Some view this kiss as a prelude to the celebration of the Eucharist. Although Paul's letters were read to the gathered church, and might introduce a celebration of the holy meal, there is little internal evidence to support the view that the kiss introduced the Eucharist. Rather than liturgical gesture,[17] the kiss functioned as a greeting that Paul harnessed to serve his epistolary interests. Through the command "greet one another with a holy kiss," Paul reaffirmed the relationship created by Christ between himself and his spiritual family, and also between the members of the congregation (1 Thess. 5:26).[18]

The benediction, "the grace of our Lord Jesus Christ be with you," is the most stable of the concluding elements. Appearing in every complete letter, this closing formula varies little. Here again Paul bent an epistolary convention to his Christ perspective (e.g., "The grace of the Lord Jesus be with you," 1 Cor. 16:23). Occasionally, however, a solemn warning or sober adjuration preceded the benediction. The tone of 1 Corinthians 16:22 is especially somber: "Let anyone be accursed [anathema] who has no love for the Lord." In the other letters similar adjurations appear in the same position (1 Thess. 5:27 and Gal. 6:17). It is improbable that the Corinthian warning is a eucharistic formula that aims to exclude unworthy or unbaptized persons from participation in the Lord's Supper. More likely, the Corinthian command is a decisive reminder of the central exhortation of the letter. The warning included those who curse Jesus (1 Cor. 12:3), those who hurt a brother or sister through arrogant use of their charisma, and those who profaned the body of Christ. In this pronouncement Paul addressed the total epistolary situation in which the loveless behavior of some believers threatened to destroy the church.

Galatians 6:17 contains another apostolic warning: "Let no one trouble me, for I carry on my body the marks of Jesus" (AT). It is possible that Paul intended to draw an unfavorable comparison between the "good showing in the flesh" (i.e., circumcision) of his addressees and the "marks" of Jesus (scars) that have been inflicted on his (Paul's) body by beatings, shipwrecks, and other afflictions. Paul apparently understood his own suffering as a replication of

---

16. Heikki Koskenniemi, *Studien zur Idee und Phraseologie des griechischen Briefes bis 400 nach Christus* (Helsinki: Akateeminen Kirjakauppa, 1956), 169–80.

17. See Calvin Roetzel, *Judgment in the Community* (Leiden: Brill, 1972), 145, 161.

18. Victor Paul Furnish, *Theology and Ethics in Paul* (Nashville: Abingdon Press, 1968), 55. See 3rd ed., 2009.

that of Jesus; consequently, to trouble the apostle, the Lord's representative, was to injure the Lord himself.

These adjurations may grate against modern sensibilities. They sound mean and vindictive. Yet they are understandable, in terms of Paul's sense of his mission. Thus Paul set himself in the tradition of the prophets of old commissioned to speak the word of YHWH for judgment and healing. Sometimes, of course, the line between the apostle's words and divine utterances was blurred. But believing himself appointed as an apostle of the risen Christ, Paul represented Christ to his hearers for judgment and healing; thus, in his view, the words he spoke carried the authority of the one who sent him.

Evidently Paul viewed the letter as an instrument of his apostleship. Thus it assumed an official quality beyond the usual correspondence between friends. The letter that served as an extension of Paul's apostolic presence placed the community in the Lord's presence with everything such a status promised and demanded. So although Paul's letters are highly personal and at times deeply moving, we fail to appreciate their scope and power if we ignore their apostolic character and communal significance.

Those qualities set Paul's letters apart from the papyrus model. Paul's letters are suffused with a strong theological emphasis quite unlike that of the papyrus letters. Moreover, the papyrus letters concern themselves primarily with daily concerns, whereas the Pauline letters are informed by a strong ideological tendency. These differences led Klaus Berger, a noted German New Testament scholar, to assert that the letters of Cynic philosophers resemble the Pauline letters.[19] In the way they exhorted students to avoid any pleasure that fostered injustice, in the way they promoted asceticism or provided a philosophical justification for begging, Berger saw a family resemblance to the Pauline letter.[20]

The Cynic letters to which Berger appeals, however, have little in common with Paul's letters. Almost all of them are pseudonymous, and some of them were written over a century after the death of the author to whom they are attributed. The letters themselves are more like diatribes or treatises on a given topic than an intimate conversation between two separated parties. Where the formulaic letter closing in Paul's letters is developed to reflect Paul's religious kinship with his addressees, the closing of the Cynic letters is often missing altogether or contains only a few words. It is more likely that

19. Klaus Berger, "Hellenistische Gattungen im neuen Testament," in *Aufstieg und Niedergang der römischen Welt*, ed. Hildegard Temporini and Wolfgang Haase (Berlin: Walter de Gruyter, 1984), part 2, vol. 25/2: 1326–63.

20. For the data informing this article, Berger relies heavily on Abraham J. Malherbe, *The Cynic Epistles: A Study Edition* (Missoula, MT: Scholars Press, 1977), 38–39, 64–65, 178–79, 76–77, etc.

Paul's style is influenced not only by the form of the stereotypical papyrus letter but also by rhetorical strategies of persuasion, consolation, comfort, admonition, and argumentation that were popular in the Hellenistic and Jewish worlds.[21]

While fewer than 125 Hebrew and Aramaic letters have survived from this period, the Semitic letter tradition also contributed something to Paul's style. The peace wish, for example (e.g., "Grace to you and peace"), which appears in all of Paul's letters (1 Thess. 1:1; Gal. 1:3; 1 Cor. 1:3; 2 Cor. 1:2; Phil. 1:2; Phlm. 3) had deep roots in a venerable Hebraic tradition. As early as the sixth century BCE, for example, a letter etched on a piece of broken pottery at Lachish in Israel opens with a peace wish: "Thy servant Hoshiah hath sent to inform my lord Yaosh: May YHWH cause my lord to hear tidings of peace [*shalom*]."[22]

We see, therefore, how Paul was influenced by a rich and varied letter-writing tradition. Through the skillful use of his pen and by bending these traditions to serve his ends, Paul so skillfully and creatively used the epistolary tradition as to have had an enormous impact on the emerging identity of the early church. But Paul's letter writing skill was aided by the growing importance of the letter in the Hellenistic age.

American immigrants shared their letters from "home" with the whole community. Long before I ever traveled to Germany or visited the home village of my German grandparents, I had heard of Emma's new baby and was privileged to eavesdrop on conversations about information in the latest letters from the old country. So also in the first century, receiving a letter was rare and precious, and a community event. All people—rich and poor, underclass and privileged, patrons and slaves, men and women—experienced the reception of a letter as an exciting event that most often was shared with family, friends, and even the entire town. Letters were precious because they put persons in the presence of the absent ones, offered news, and brought encouragement, consolation, and instruction. Thus one can easily understand why they were treasured and kept. So even though the theological depth and practical guidance of Paul's letters played a major role in their collection, preservation, and inclusion in the New Testament canon, the importance of the letters qua letters also made a contribution.

To summarize, we have noted the importance of reading Paul's letters as letters, and we have seen how Paul constrained to his own use the epistolary

---

21. Stanley K. Stowers, *Letter Writing in Greco-Roman Antiquity* (Philadelphia: Westminster Press, 1986).

22. Ostracon III, in *Ancient Near Eastern Texts Relating to the Old Testament*, 2nd ed., ed. James B. Pritchard (Princeton, NJ: Princeton University Press, 1955), 322.

conventions of his time. We have observed how Paul's message informed and even transformed his medium. Although the letter was for Paul the most effective means of conversation between separated persons, it was more. It was an extension of his apostleship. A modern reader aware of the subtle interplay between form (medium), content (message), and agent (apostle writer) may more fully appreciate the subtlety of Paul's gospel and the influence these letters have had on their readers over the centuries.

Paul founded cells of converts across Asia Minor and into Europe. In his absence they struggled to survive, to understand and apply his gospel, to keep the Christ experience alive, to experiment with the freedom gained, to meet life's daily challenges, to face recurring doubts, to test the truth of his apostolic claim, and to assess his fundamental honesty. Paul's letters bridged the temporal distance between him and his converts, placed him in their presence and them in his (Gal. 4:13–14; 1 Thess. 2:1–11; 3:3–4), and recalled their shared experience (Rom. 1:8–9; 1 Cor. 5:1–5; Phil. 1:3–8; 1 Thess. 1:2; 1 Cor. 1:4–6).

The letters, however, did more than bridge the distance between separated parties; they also offered a device to exhort, advise (1 Thess. 5:23; 1 Cor. 1:8; Phil. 2:15), to comfort and console (2 Cor. 1:3–7), and to remind converts of what they tended to forget (1 Thess. 2:1–2, 9; 4:1–2, 13; 5:1–2). The letters also offered a vehicle for responding to criticisms so damning that if sustained, they might fatally compromise Paul's mission (Gal. 1–2; 2 Cor. 10:1–13:10; and possibly Phil. 3). Paul prevailed, at least in part, not only because of his theological brilliance, but also because of his skillful manipulation of epistolary traditions to his use.[23]

23. Paul sometimes dictated his letters to a secretary (amanuensis), appending a conclusion in his own hand (e.g., Gal. 6:11–18). Likewise 1 Cor. 16:21–24 displays an autograph. Although the secretary self-identifies in Rom. 16:22, whether chapter 16 was a part of the original letter is disputed. On the strength of these two or three references, it is arbitrary to conclude that Paul dictated all of his letters.

4

Traditions behind the Letters

Why do we appeal to tradition? Why do we quote famous people, poets, novelists, orators, and scholars? Why do we appeal to texts, historical precedent, and even legend and myth? It is not just to enliven our speech, though it does do that. It is not just to overcome the impoverished nature of our vocabulary, though it does do that. It is not just to amuse, though it does that also. Rather, it is because the tradition opens up in us a level of insight or understanding that we did not know existed. Through the shared experience of the ages, we are delivered from a trivialized view of the human and nonhuman world and are able to appreciate more fully the heights and depths of the human spirit.

For Paul those heights and depths were known through the historic interaction between God and Israel into which he read the death, resurrection, and expected return of Christ. Through our study of his use and interpretation of those materials, we stand to gain a better appreciation of Paul the man and of his very real letters dealing with life's greatest religious and human moments.

From the outset our investigation faces the difficulty of locating and deciphering the traditions behind the letters. Early in Galatians, for example, Paul declared that his message was "not of human origin" but came "through a revelation of Jesus Christ" (Gal. 1:11). Elsewhere, however, Paul summoned church tradition and Scripture, the primitive gospel, liturgical formulas, Christ hymns, prayers, confessions, and traditional ethical admonitions to enliven and strengthen his conversation with his converts. Real people composed and transmitted these traditions; so how could the apostle claim that his gospel did not have a human origin?

The statement above from Galatians about independence does not reveal an inconsistency so much as it reveals the seriousness of the challenge there to his apostolic adequacy. Galatian antagonists had charged that Paul's Gentile Gospel was inferior to that of the core disciples—Peter, James, and John—and needed correction. That attempt to impugn Paul's apostleship automatically devalued his gospel. By his own admission he had never known the earthly Jesus. His gospel to the Gentiles differed dramatically from that preached by the Jerusalem "mother church," aroused suspicion in some quarters, and was deemed to be an outrageous novelty to critics. He claimed that a vision authorized him to be an apostle, but all kinds of folks, good and ill, claimed visions; suspicion of such visionaries abounded. Galatian critics, possibly from Jerusalem, who viewed Paul's proclamation as woefully deficient and in need of correction, had intruded. They sought to supplement it with a religious calendar including the observance of "days, and months, and seasons, and years" (4:10), and they advocated circumcision as a prerequisite for admission to God's elect.

Their worship of "elemental spirits," when added to the practices noted above, for Paul was equal to slavery (4:9) and provoked him to scorn this Galatian amalgam as "no gospel at all." His fury erupted into a dual curse on his rivals, and without denying the importance of traditional formulas, he claimed Christ as *the* primal authority for his preaching (1:11).

Once the harshness of 1:11–12 is recognized, Paul's need to affirm the origin of his call in Christ became a claim that trumped all others. He could and indeed did often ascribe to Jesus what in reality came from the church and did so with no sense of inconsistency (e.g., 1 Cor. 11:23–25). Since he viewed the church as the Lord's community, to his mind what came from the church was from the Lord. Nevertheless, the identification of traditional elements is valuable for our understanding of the letters. These traditional materials reveal important theological emphases, views of Scripture, and also Paul's own religious background. Understanding his use of that material, however, is as important as recognizing the selections he makes.

In every letter Paul adapts traditional materials to address problems as diverse as dealing with sex, taxes, divorce, legal disputes, money, power, basic human respect, and even those dealing with the marks of a *true* apostle, the reconciliation of the world, the grand design of God's rule, and the theological basis of hope.

Tradition for Paul was no "thing in itself" whose meaning was transparent. The past required interpretation and application. For Paul, traditional materials were hardly inert deposits or fossils from an archaic past; rather, they were dynamic realities coming out of a living past that addressed the present and anticipated the future.

In the discussion below we note selected traditional materials that shaped Paul's thinking in important ways.

THE KERYGMA

It may surprise some that Paul did not begin his mission as an apostle of Christ with a prefabricated theological system that he simply plopped down on every new context. Paul's theology was an emergent one, hammered out in the crucible of conflict and refined by controversy. There is evidence that his mind sometimes changed in the heat of these exchanges (e.g., note the more favorable view of law in Romans than in Galatians). That openness to change, however, hardly meant that there was nothing solid at the heart of his gospel.

C. H. Dodd, the late, great, and venerable scholar from Cambridge, once taught us that the apostle shared a basic gospel structure with the early church. Although the emphasis of Paul's preaching and his interpretation of the kerygma of the early church differed from that of his predecessors in certain areas, Dodd argued that there was mutual agreement in the emphases noted below:

a. The arrival of the messianic age as foretold by the prophets.
b. The inauguration of this new age in the ministry, death, and resurrection of Jesus.
c. The exaltation of Jesus.
d. The presence of the Holy Spirit signifying Christ's "power and glory," and announcing the end times.
e. The imminent return of Jesus as the consummation of the messianic age.
f. The call to repentance coupled with an offer of forgiveness.[1]

Although these elements appear nowhere altogether in the same place, most of them surface somewhere in Paul's letters. The following list shows where some of those elements are found:

Romans 1:2, prophecy fulfilled
Romans 1:3, 4 and Galatians 1:4, messianic age inaugurated
Romans 8:34 and Philippians 2:9, death and exaltation of Christ
Romans 8:26–30, the Spirit's presence
1 Thessalonians 1:10, 4:13–18, Christ's return
Romans 10:9, call to repentance and to welcome returning Christ

First Corinthians 15:3–7 is a classic example of Paul's incorporation of that primitive tradition into his instruction for converts. Some seem to be convinced that they already shared in the resurrected life; true to a Greek hope to

---

1. C. H. Dodd, *The Apostolic Preaching and Its Developments* (London: Hodder & Stoughton, 1936), 21–23.

be free of the body, they questioned Paul's view of the body. In response Paul offered the following:

> For I delivered to you . . . what I also received,
> that *Christ died for our sins* in accordance with the scriptures,
> that *he was buried,*
> that *he was raised* on the third day in accordance with the scriptures, and
> that *he appeared to Cephas, then to the twelve.* (AE)

EUCHARISTIC AND BAPTISMAL FORMULAS

In his instructional materials Paul often alludes to traditions that his address-ees were expected to know. The 1 Corinthians 6:11 reference to washing points to baptism. A baptismal tradition also appears in Romans 6:4–5, where Paul says,

> Therefore we have been buried [past tense]
> with him by baptism into death. . . .
> and if we have been united with him in a death like his,
> we will certainly be united [future tense] with him
> in a resurrection like his.

Similarly, in 1 Corinthians 11:23–25 Paul directly quotes the eucharistic liturgy:

> I received from the Lord what I also handed on to you, that the Lord Jesus on the night when he was betrayed took a loaf of bread, and when he had given thanks, he broke it and said, "This is my body that is for you. Do this in remembrance of me." In the same way he took the cup also, after supper, saying, "This cup is the new covenant in my blood. Do this, as often as you drink it, in remembrance of me."

THE LANGUAGE OF PRAYER

Paul frequently alludes to prayer and in some places bursts into a sponta-neous doxology (e.g. Rom. 7:25) offered in response to the rhetorical ques-tion "Who will deliver us from this body of death?" The answer burst forth: "Thanks be to God through Jesus Christ our Lord." Some of his prayers are simply a full heart's outpouring, but others have a traditional ring (Gal. 1:5; Phil. 4:20). Often it is difficult to distinguish between prayers that Paul created and those he cited. It is possible, however, to recognize frag-ments of traditional prayers in the letters. Words such as *amen* (Gal. 6:18;

1 Cor. 14:16; and 2 Cor. 1:20), *maranatha* (Aramaic for "Our Lord, come"; see 1 Cor. 16:22), and *abba* ("Father"; see Gal. 4:6; Rom. 8:15) all belong to a prayer tradition that predated Paul.

HYMNS

For generations before the time of Jesus, hymns of praise had been rising to God from temple and synagogue. It is natural, therefore, that the early church, rooted in a Jewish religious culture, would be a singing church. While the early hymns of the congregations were from the Psalms, the church soon created new songs appropriate to its Christ status. Traces of this early hymnody appear in Paul's letters as well as the rest of the New Testament (e.g., Col. 1:15–20; 1 Tim. 3:16; Eph. 5:14). The rhythm, parallelism, clearly defined strophes, poetic expression, and the absence of Pauline vocabulary or ideas establishes Philippians 2:6–11 as a pre-Pauline Christ hymn. Even in English translation (RSV) its hymnic character is obvious:

Pauline Introduction
Have this mind among yourselves,
Which you have in Christ Jesus,

Hymn

I
Who, though he was in the form of God,
Did not count equality with God
A thing to be grasped,

II
But emptied himself,
Taking the form of a servant,
Being born in the likeness of men.

III
And being found in human form
he humbled himself
and became obedient unto death [even death on a cross].[2]

IV
Therefore God has highly exalted him
and bestowed on him the name
which is above every name.[3]

2. "Even death on a cross" was most likely inserted here by Paul.
3. My translation follows Ernst Lohmeyer's arrangement in his *Der Brief an die Philipper*, 19th ed. (Göttingen: Vandenhoeck & Ruprecht, 1954), 96–97.

WORDS OF THE LORD

In 2 Corinthians 5:16 Paul wrote, "though we once knew Christ from a human point of view, we know him no longer in that way."[4] Some scholars see this statement as evidence that Paul was personally acquainted with Jesus. If Paul did know Jesus during his ministry, however, it is astonishing that he would barely mention the words and deeds of Jesus in the entire letter corpus. For example, if we had to depend on Paul for information about Jesus' life, we would know only the obvious that he was "born of woman" (Gal. 4:4), that he was in David's line (Rom. 1:3), and that he died on a cross (Phil. 2:8; 1 Cor. 1:23). We would not know his mother's name, that he had sisters, that he taught in parables, or that his ministry was centered in Galilee. If Paul were silent about the words and deeds because he assumed they were known to his readers, then it is strange that he quoted Jewish Scriptures even when he presupposed that they were familiar to his readers. Moreover, even though Paul often summarized his own preaching, Jesus' ministry received little emphasis (1 Cor. 2:1–2).[5] Although Paul expressed little interest in Jesus' ministry or the content of his preaching, he did stress three items: the cross, the resurrection, and Jesus' return. Those epic salvific moments were anchored in history, Paul argued, but they transcended history. As in the Gospels, the words of Jesus that Paul did quote or to which he alluded assumed a transcendent character. Even though the letters cited Jesus infrequently, in Paul's ethical teaching, Jesus sayings, while few in number, were weighty.[6] Let us survey selected sayings of Jesus.

a. Quotations from Jesus (italics added)

(1) 1 Cor. 7:10–11	To the married I give this command—not I but the Lord—that the *wife should not separate from her husband . . . and that the husband should not divorce his wife*. (See Matt. 5:32; 19:9; Mark 10:11–12; Luke 16:18.)
(2) 1 Cor. 9:14	The Lord commanded that *those who proclaim the gospel should get their living by the gospel*. (See Luke 10:7, the laborer deserves his wages.)

4. The Greek may suggest an unreal past condition, "even if I had known him (which of course I didn't) . . ." Since we cannot be sure that such was Paul's intention, the following discussion is necessary.

5. Victor Paul Furnish, *Theology and Ethics in Paul* (Nashville: Abingdon Press, 1968; rev. ed. 2009), 55.

6. Joseph A. Fitzmyer, *Pauline Theology—A Brief Sketch* (Englewood Cliffs, NJ: Prentice-Hall, 1967), 13.

(3) 1 Cor. 11:23–24	The Lord Jesus . . . said, *"This is my body that is for you. Do this in remembrance of me."* In the same way he took the cup also, after supper, saying, "This cup is the new covenant in my blood. Do *this, as often as you drink it, in remembrance of me."* (See Matt. 26:26–28; Mark 14:22–24; Luke 22:19–20.)
(4) 1 Thess. 4:16	The Lord himself, with a cry of command,[7] with the archangel's call and with the sound of God's trumpet, will descend from heaven, and the dead in Christ will rise first.
(5) 1 Cor. 14:37	which alludes to but does not quote a saying.

b. Echoes of Sayings

(1) 1 Cor. 4:12	When reviled, we bless, when persecuted, we endure.
Rom. 12:14	Bless those who persecute you; bless and do not curse them.
Luke 6:28	Bless those who curse you; pray for those who abuse you.
(2) 1 Thess. 5:15	See that none of you repays evil for evil.
Rom. 12:17	Do not repay anyone evil for evil.
Matt. 5:39	Do not resist an evildoer.
(3) Rom. 13:7	Pay to all what is due them—taxes to whom taxes are due.
Matt. 22:15–22	Then the Pharisees [asked.] ". . . Is it lawful to pay taxes to the emperor, or not?" . . . Jesus aware of their malice, said, ". . . Show me the coin used for the tax. . . . Give . . . to the emperor the things that are the emperor's, and to God the things that are God's."
(4) Rom. 14:13	Let us therefore no longer pass judgment on one another, but resolve instead never to put a stumbling block or hindrance in the way of another.
Matt. 7:1	Do not judge, so that you may not be judged.
(5) Rom. 14:14	Nothing is unclean in itself.
Mark 7:18–19	"Do you not see that whatever goes into a person from outside cannot defile, since it enters, not the heart but the stomach, and goes into the sewer?" (Thus he declared all foods clean.)
(6) 1 Thess. 5:2	The day of the Lord will come like a thief in the night.
Luke 12:39–40	If the owner of the house had known at what hour the thief was coming, he would not have let his house be broken into. . . . You also must be ready, for the Son of Man is coming at an unexpected hour. (See Matt. 24:42–43.)

---

7. Lloyd Gaston, *No Stone on Another* (Leiden: E. J. Brill, 1970), 407–8, made a good case for the authenticity of this saying.

(7) 1 Thess. 5:13	Be at peace among yourselves
Mark 9:50	Be at peace with one another.
(8) 1 Cor. 13:2	If I have faith, so as to remove mountains . . .
Matt. 17:20	If you have faith the size of a mustard seed, you will say to this mountain, "Move . . ." and it will move.

PARAENETIC TRADITION

Over a generation ago, Martin Dibelius noticed the traditional nature of Paul's ethical instructions (paraenesis).[8] Exhortation, characterized by a terse, gnomic style, these materials usually fall near the end of Paul's letters (e.g., Gal. 5:13–6: 10; 1 Thess. 4:1–5:22; 2 Cor. 13:11) and possess a certain uniformity in content and vocabulary.

Admonitions to do good and to avoid evil, warnings against immorality, exhortations to nonviolence, and encouragement to be subject to governing authorities, edification of the church, and kindness to outsiders all appear in more than one of Paul's letters. Since these concerns are shared in many early Christian writings (1 Peter, Ignatius, Hebrews, *1 Clement, Barnabas, Hermas,* the *Didache,* and the Pastoral Epistles), it appears that the main contours of Paul's paraenetic materials did not originate with him but were the common property of the early Jesus movement.

Almost unanimously scholars agree that Paul appropriated ethical injunctions but add that he deployed them in a way appropriate to each addressee. Until recently most scholars followed Dibelius, who held that paraenesis targeted no particular situation. Arguably, to attribute all of the sins enumerated in the vice lists to particular churches would be mistaken.[9] Recently, however, support for Dibelius's view has weakened.[10] If Paul gave immediate application to other traditional materials[11] like the thanksgiving and conclusion, would he not also mold the paraenetic tradition to each epistolary situation? Furnish has convincingly shown[12] how Paul gave specificity even to general lists of virtues

8. Martin Dibelius, A *Fresh Approach to the New Testament and Early Christian Literature* (New York: Charles Scribner's Sons, 1936), 143.

9. Dibelius correctly noted this in *A Fresh Approach,* 143ff. W. D. Davies, *Paul and Rabbinic Judaism* (London: SPCK, 1955), 136 and Hunter, *Paul and His Predecessors* (London: SCM Press, 1961), 52–55 shared this view.

10. Robert W. Funk, *Language, Hermeneutic, and Word of God* (New York: Harper & Row, 1966), 270, and Furnish, *Theology and Ethics in Paul*, rev. ed., decisively qualify Dibelius's view.

11. Funk, *Language,* 33–34.

12. Furnish, *Theology and Ethics in Paul,* 84–85.

and vices. The vice list, for example, in 2 Corinthians 12:20–21 deals with divisive behavior (bickering, pettiness, arrogance, etc.), antisocial acts like anger, selfishness, slander, gossip, and sexual immorality—all of which characterize Corinthian behavior mentioned elsewhere.[13] Therefore, we go with Furnish that even the general lists have specific applicability when used by Paul.

In 1 Thessalonians 5:16–18 also, Paul adopted a general paraenetic tradition to a specific situation, and did so to exhort the discouraged to persevere.

Noticing the traditional nature of Paul's ethical instructions, Dibelius suggested that "[we] know now that the apostle drew on pre-Pauline or even pre-Christian traditions for his moral exhortations to do good. He encouraged and admonished:

> *pantote* (always) rejoice,
> *adialeiptos* (without ceasing) pray,
> *en panti* (in everything) give thanks." [14]

In his parallel construction, the adverbs and prepositional phrase stood in the emphatic position, and the repetition of key emphases—"always," "without ceasing"—hammered home the main point: the need for perseverance and persistence in the life of faith.

In 1 Thessalonians 4:13 we learn that death had invaded this inspired community; blinded by disappointment and discouragement, some wanted to give up. Misguided enthusiasts quit work to await the coming (*parousia*) of the Lord, and they soon became a burden on others. Both the freeloaders and the disillusioned, the brazen and the timid, received the same admonition to persevere in the life of faith. For their comfort or discomfort, Paul reminded them that Christ will return to judge the world and to rescue his own, whether living or dead. In the meantime, he admonished them to hold fast to the life of faith and retain hope, for "this is the will of God" (5:18). Over and over again Paul urged the faltering to do "more and more" good (4:1, 10; 5:11).

We see how Paul structured traditional paraenetic materials, adding key words or phrases, to underscore the fundamental point of the letter: the need for steadfast endurance. We see here, therefore, that even traditional materials, as general as they may seem to us, had specific and immediate relevance for the Thessalonian church. Although Dibelius correctly maintained that the paraenetic sections were hardly the property of Paul to the same degree as were the sections of sustained theological argument, he was only half right. To call the paraenetic materials a "bag of answers for oft-recurring problems and

13. David G. Bradley, "The Topos as a Form in the Pauline Paraenesis," *Journal of Biblical Literature*, 72 (1953): 246.

14. See Roetzel's work cited note 14, previous chapter.

questions common to the members of different early Christian communities" and the essence of a bourgeois[15] mentality was clearly in error.

Types of Paraenetic Tradition

Wisdom Sayings

Wisdom materials, rooted in everyday experience, need not make explicit theological claims but may move easily across ethnic and class boundaries. They may spring as easily from the lips of the peasant woman as from the educated scribe. Note, for example, Paul's appeal to such materials to instruct, admonish, and correct the addressees.

1. "You reap whatever you sow" (Gal. 6:7).
2. "The one who sows sparingly will also reap sparingly, and the one who sows bountifully will also reap bountifully" (2 Cor. 9:6).
3. "Bad company ruins good morals" (1 Cor. 15:33).
4. "A little yeast leavens the whole [lump] batch of dough" (Gal. 5:9).

Vice and Virtue Lists

As a part of the cultural vernacular these lists stood ready when the need arose for correction or exhortation.

1. They were filled with every kind of "wickedness, evil, covetousness, [and] malice. Full of envy, murder, strife, deceit, craftiness, they are gossips, slanderers, God-haters, insolent, haughty, boastful, inventors of evil, rebellious toward parents, foolish, faithless, heartless, ruthless" (Rom. 1:29–31; see also Gal. 5:19–21; 1 Cor. 5:10–11; 6:9–10; 2 Cor. 12:20).
2. "The fruit of the Spirit is love, joy, peace, patience, kindness, generosity, faithfulness, gentleness, and self-control" (Gal. 5:22–23; see also Phil. 4:8, which includes prominent Greek philosophical terms like *prosphilēs*, "lovely"; *euphēmos*, "gracious"; *arētē*, "excellence"; and *epainos*, "praiseworthy").

Imperative Cluster

"Let love be genuine; hate what is evil, hold fast to what is good; love one another with mutual affection; outdo one another in showing honor. Do not lag in zeal, be ardent in spirit, serve the Lord. Rejoice in hope, be patient in suffering, persevere in prayer. Contribute to the needs of the saints, extend hospitality to the stranger" (Rom. 12:9–13).

---

15. See Dibelius's work cited above, note 8.

Developed Exhortation or Topical Moral Essay

(See the sustained admonition concerning the mutual responsibility of the strong and weak in Rom. 14:1–15:13; also note 1 Thess. 5:1–11.)[16]

The discussion above underscores how Paul drew on early Christ tradition as well as Jewish and even "pagan" sources. Paul freely used the epistolary conventions of his time and frequently tapped a vast reservoir of Christian and non-Christian paraenesis. The alert reader will spot these and other traditional materials in reading the letters. Sometimes Paul identified them with phrases like "I delivered what I also received, that . . ." or "it is written that . . ." or "this we declare by the word of the Lord, that . . ." Elsewhere only a break in the context, an interruption in the stream of thought (e.g., Phil. 2:6–11), or an unusual construction of words or sentences signals his use of sources. In other cases unusual vocabulary or theological statements that sound uncharacteristic of Paul may arouse suspicion that traditional elements are present. But we must notice not merely that certain materials were appropriated, but also to what specific end. Fully as important as what was used is how it was appropriated.

How, the reader should ask, did Paul use traditional elements to address the problems of his readers? How did he bend the traditional elements to serve his theological arguments and to engage his readers in conversation? Where and why did his theological outlook require alteration in the application of the tradition, and what do these alterations reveal about the intent of the issues under discussion or debate between Paul and his conversation partners? Although these questions are sometimes unanswerable, they are worth asking nevertheless, for through them may come a heightened awareness of the horizons of Paul's thought and the issues under discussion. Also, questions about Paul's use of tradition may reveal new strategies of Paul's theologizing.

16. Of course those who argue for the authenticity of Colossians and Ephesians would add another category—rules for the domestic life (*Haustafeln*). For example, see Col. 3:18–22: "Wives be subject to your husbands, as is fitting in the Lord. Husbands love your wives. . . . Children obey your parents. . . . Slaves obey your masters in everything . . ." (cf. Eph. 5:21–6:9). Such instruction is unparalleled in the undisputed Pauline letters.

5

The Letters as Conversations

Dealing as they do with such mundane matters as sex, taxes, diet, lawsuits, circumcision, ecstatic speech, and intramural quarrels, Paul's letters bear the unmistakable imprint of this world. Among other things, the concreteness of the letters shows that Paul took his readers seriously and how painstakingly he strove to interpret his gospel for their everyday life. Once we realize how the ferment in the churches prescribed the scope if not the content of Paul's writings, it may become obvious how Paul's theologizing addressed real life situations in the churches.[1]

Study of the epistles isolated from their contexts resembles reading answers at the end of an algebra book without the corresponding problems. Any one of the excellent summaries of Paul's theology would give the reader a grasp of' the range and diversity of Paul's thought. This study will focus instead on the interaction between the apostle and his churches, in the hope that the reader will gain a deeper appreciation of the vigor and ingenuity of Paul's emergent theology. While the conversations dealt with life-and-death theological issues, they always took place in a context that informed them.

---

1. Joseph A. Fitzmyer, *Paul and His Theology: A Brief Sketch*, 2nd ed. (Englewood Cliffs, NJ: Prentice-Hall, 1988), is excellent. Rudolf Bultmann, *Theology of the New Testament*, trans. Kendrick Grobel (New York: Charles Scribner's Sons, 1951) is now almost a classic. Victor Paul Furnish, *Theology and Ethics in Paul*, 3rd ed. (Nashville: Abingdon Press, 2009), offers a brilliant treatment of the major currents in Pauline interpretation. The Pauline Theology Group of the Society of Biblical Literature produced four volumes of collected essays by the outstanding scholars in the field. See *Pauline Theology*, vols. 2–4, ed. E. Elizabeth Johnson and David M. Hay (Minneapolis: Fortress Press, 1993, 1995, 1997).

Sunrise over the Aegean Sea (Courtesy of
Warren Kendall; used by permission)

The voices of Paul's converts and antagonists, however, we must strain
to overhear. Essential to reconstructing conversations, modern or ancient,
is some sense of their order. However, since none of the Pauline letters were
dated, any reconstruction is difficult and oft disputed. The outline below aims
to provide a rough guide to the chronology of Paul's ministry. Even if parts
of the chronology are debatable, their proposed order aims to help the reader
gain a sense of the larger narrative of the relationship of Paul's preaching to
the defense of his Gentile mission, the order in which his letters were written,
and the real life issues they addressed.

Miletus Roman Road
(Courtesy of Warren Kendall;
used by permission)

Via Egnatia (Courtesy of Warren Kendall;
used by permission)

While the construction is at points hypothetical, most scholars agree that Paul's apostolic mission began in the thirties and ended with his death in the early sixties. Almost all scholars agree that the evidence of the letters is more reliable than that of Acts. While some scholars arrange the letters in a different order, almost all agree that the seven letters were written in the fifties. Given the distance from us of that far horizon and the complexity of the record, it is amazing that we have as much agreement as we do.[2]

Charting the letters' chronology depends on their tie to an absolute fixed peg casually mentioned in Acts 18:12–17. There Luke referred to Paul being brought before the Roman proconsul Gallio, chief Roman administrator of Achaia. One can still see the elevated stone platform (bema) on which the proconsul stood to pass judgments and issue official orders. Acts reports that during his Corinthian ministry, Paul was apprehended and brought before Gallio to answer charges made. Fortunately, we are able to place Gallio's tenure in Corinth and locate this event most probably in the late summer or fall of 52 CE. when that Roman official voluntarily or involuntarily returned to Rome. From that date we date Paul's Corinthian experience and the letter before it (1 Thessalonians) and those after. Using that chronological peg, let us compose a probable chronological narrative of Paul's life and ministry.

---

2. Please note that with the use of only one absolute chronological peg, the dates under question for Paul's letter composition span only a decade.

Chronological Outline of Paul's Apostolic Ministry[3]

Jesus' crucifixion	ca. 30	
Paul's call to be an apostle	ca. 34	Gal. 1:15, 16
Ministry in Arabia	34–37	Gal. 1:17
Escape from Damascus	37–38	2 Cor. 11:32–33
First Jerusalem visit (two weeks)	37 or 38	Gal. 1:18
Mission to Syria/Cilicia	38–47	Gal. 1:21
Second Jerusalem visit: Gentile mission endorsed	ca. 47	Gal. 2:1–10
Claudius's edict expelling Jews from Rome	49	Acts 18:2
Mission in Greece and Macedonia	48–52	Acts 15–18
Corinth and Achaia	50–52	Acts 18:1–3

Chronological Outline of Paul's Writings[4]

1 Thessalonians	ca. 50	
Arraignment before Gallio in Corinth	52	Acts 18:12–17
Ephesian and Macedonian sojourn	52–57	
Lost letter to Corinth (from Ephesus)	52	1 Cor. 5:9
1 Corinthians	53	
Galatians	ca. 55	
2 Corinthians (multiple letters)	54–57	
Philippians (from Ephesian prison)	ca. 56	
Philemon (from Ephesian prison)	ca. 56	
Winter in Corinth (dictates *Romans*)	57	
Leads offering delegation to Jerusalem	spring 58	Rom. 15:25–33
Arrest in Jerusalem and transfer to Rome for trial	ca. 58–59	Acts 25:4–28:16
Execution	ca. 60–64	*Acts of Paul & Thecla* 11:1–7

---

3. A useful treatment of key issues in the life and legacy of Paul can be found in *The Cambridge Companion to St Paul*, edited by James D. G. Dunn (Cambridge: Cambridge University Press, 2004) in paper.

4. See Calvin Roetzel, "Chronology of Paul's Life and Letters," in article on "Paul," in *The New Interpreter's Dictionary of the Bible* (Nashville: Abingdon Press, 2009), 4:411. Older works available include Robert Jewett, *A Chronology of Paul's Life* (Philadelphia: Fortress Press, 1979) and Gerd Lüdemann, *Paulus, Der Heidenapostel*, vol. 1, *Studien zur Chronologie* (Göttingen: Vandenhoeck & Ruprecht, 1980). For the relevance of this discussion for our understanding of Paul's theology, see John C. Hurd Jr., "Pauline Chronology and Pauline Theology," in *Christian History and Interpretation*, ed. William R. Farmer (Cambridge: Cambridge University Press, 1967), 225–48.

Bema (Courtesy of Calvin J. Roetzel; used by permission)

THE THESSALONIAN CORRESPONDENCE (CA. 50 CE)[5]

Ministry in Macedonia

After his release from prison in Philippi (1 Thess. 2:2), Paul's mission took him to Thessalonica with coworkers Timothy and Silvanus. While plying a trade to earn bread, Paul preached, he said, "in power and in the Holy Spirit and with full conviction" (1:5). Gentile converts turned to God from their "idols" to embrace the apostle's gospel (1:5–6, 9–10; 2:2–9; 3:2). Exactly how and where he preached we simply do not know, but at its core stood an emphasis on the death of Jesus, his resurrection by God (1:10; 4:14), and the promise of his imminent return to consummate the arrival of the new age (2:19; 3:13; 4:15; 5:23).

5. See note 4 above.

Arch of Galerius in Thessalonica (Courtesy of Warren Kendall; used by permission)

The Report of Timothy

To avoid the charge that they were religious hucksters peddling a message for gain, Paul and his companions worked "night and day" for support while they shared God's good news. Occasionally, money from the church in Philippi (Phil. 4:16) supplemented their meager earnings. At first, Paul's example gave his gospel an authentic ring and enjoyed good success in Thessalonica. But eventually he met resistance and left the city; whether the departure was voluntary or forced, we do not know (1 Thess. 1:9–10; 2:15). During his trek south worries about the troubled church left behind haunted him.

Concerned about the usual problems facing converts in a fledgling church, Paul felt an almost irresistible urge to return to Thessalonica, but he was "hindered," he said (2:17–18). Tortured with worry, he dispatched Timothy to remind the believing cell of his teachings (3:1–3), to encourage those struggling, and to return with his report. Weeks later, Timothy rejoined Paul hundreds of miles to the south in Corinth and reported on problems in the Thessalonian church and the lingering doubts about the apostle festering there. Timothy may have carried a letter from the Thessalonians to supplement his oral report, but if so, only the faintest traces are visible.[6]

In spite of his best efforts, Paul had not escaped the charge that his preaching was for personal gain. His sudden departure would have fed suspicions that Paul—like other wandering preachers, teachers, and philosophers—had breezed into town, covered his greed with false rhetoric, lined his pockets with money from gullible believers, and then skipped town when he came under fire. Certain Jews, convinced that his gospel accepted pagan Gentiles into God's elect without requiring circumcision and law observance, may also have accused Paul of "error" and "uncleanness" (2:3 RSV; "deceit" and "impure motives" NRSV): error because his gospel did not come from God and uncleanness because he taught disregard for the laws of Torah. But that supposition is only a guess, for there is not one Scripture citation in 1 Thessalonians that is unusual if Paul were responding to Jewish critics.

Timothy's return, however, brought good news as well as bad. On the plus side, he reported that Paul still enjoyed support in spite of the brutal persecution of his converts there. Coercion and intimidation abounded for association with Christ, for participation in this "sect" (1:4–6; 2:1–2; 3:3–4), and for neglect of traditional religious rites. That pressure, when coupled with the brute face of the premature death of believers expecting to live to see Christ's return, had sparked a crisis of belief in the community. Some worried that Paul's promise of the imminent return of Christ was false (4:17); others had lost hope; and still others whose loved ones had died despaired of ever again being with them (1:3; 2:19; 4:13; 5:8). Timothy also reported that the urgency of Paul's commands to live a life in readiness for Christ's return had escaped those ignorant of Jewish laws and customs. He reported tensions between

---

6. If the Thessalonian converts did indeed send a letter, it may have solicited guidance on three items: (1) Paul exhorted the converts to love one another, but what form should love take toward the eschatological enthusiasts who in expectation of the imminent end of the world had quit work and were sponging off of diligent workers? (2) Some believers had died. Did their death imply that God deemed them unworthy of the kingdom? (3) Converts had tried to live in readiness for an end that Paul predicted was at hand. Did its delay mean that Paul's prediction was false? When would it come? In 1 Corinthians the phrase, *peri de*, "now concerning," was a marker of topics on which the Corinthians had written for guidance. A similar phrase appears in 1 Thess. 4:9 and 4:13, and a variation of the phrase appears in 5:1. Did that prove that the Thessalonians wrote a letter to Paul? Obviously, more letters were exchanged than have survived, and presumably some were from these little house churches. Can we find subtle traces of them in Paul's letters?

those so caught up in the earnest expectation of the end of the age that they quit work and burdened others.[7]

Naturally, resentment flared when hard-pressed believers had to care for those idlers (5:14). Except for these concerns, Timothy's report was positive. A great reservoir of goodwill and affection remained for Paul (3:6). Despite the loss of hope, faith and love remained. But the problems Timothy reported were real enough to prompt Paul's response sketched below.

Paul's Letter to the Thessalonians

Instead of the harsh polemic of other letters, this epistle blossoms with assurance and comfort, gentle admonition and conciliation, encouragement and affection. Reflecting Paul's sensitivity to the pagan past of his addressees and to their persecution and discouragement, Paul appropriated inclusive election and familial language to locate them in a surrogate family of believers. The thanksgiving assured them that they were "beloved of God" and chosen (1:4). He made persecution and election correlates of life in Christ (1:6; 2:12–16; 3:3); and for those rejected by family, friends, and associates, he surrounded them with a circle of care. While his warm and inclusive language could hardly erase the loneliness, confusion, and even desperation of being outcast, it constructed a surrogate household to nurture, encourage, remind, support, and console (5:14). Headed by the great patriarch, "God the Father" (1:1), his "beloved" (1:3–4), this new family supported "brothers and sisters" (*adelphoi*, used eight times for emphasis). Paul emphasized his love and care for them. He recalled being "gentle" among them like a wet nurse caring for her children (2:7) and of being a father nudging his little ones along (2:11–12). This special relationship through Christ (1:1), it noted, set them apart from those behaving with "lustful passion, like the Gentiles [as if they were no longer Gentiles] who do not know God" (4:5). And it reassured ruptured families that they could look forward to the imminent return of Christ, when they would join with those torn from their embrace by death.

Paul also admonished the idle to work with their hands; he encouraged the disheartened offering them a new cause for hope. He reassured them that the departed dead believers would precede the living into God's future kingdom. He admonished the fainthearted to persevere "more and more," he urged teachers to use care in teaching, and he gently admonished all to persist in faith and love with hope. Note that in Paul's great triad of faith, hope, and

---

7. The Greek word *ataktoi* refers not just to the "idle" (1 Thess. 5:13), as is often assumed, but also to the creators of disorder (see 1 Cor. 14:40 also).

love was adjusted to place desperately needed hope in the ultimate position of emphasis.

Outline of Paul's Letter to the Thessalonians

1. Address and Salutation	1:1
2. Thanksgiving	1:2–10; 2:13; 3:9–10
3. Personal Defense	
a. Recollection of the mission	2:1–16
(1) Paul's pastoral work	2:1–12
(2) Believers' response	2:13–16
b. The mission of Timothy	2:17–3:13
(1) Paul's desired visit	2:17–20
(2) Timothy sent	3:1–5
(3) Timothy's return and report	3:6–10
(4) Prayer	3:11–13
4. Ethical Exhortation and Instruction	
a. The ethical demands of the gospel	4:1–12
(1) Previous instructions	4:1–2
(2) Excludes sexual impurity	4:3–8
(3) Mutual love	4:9–10
(4) Idleness	4:10–12
b. Concerning the dead in Christ	4:13–18
c. Concerning Christ's return	5:1–11
d. Final instructions	5:12–22
5. Closing (Peace Wish, Kiss, Apostolic Command, and Benediction)	5:23–28

THE CORINTHIAN CORRESPONDENCE (CA. 53–57)[8]

Paul came to Corinth, he said, in "fear and in much trembling" (1 Cor. 2:3). Perhaps he was afraid that he would receive the same harsh treatment that had cut short his ministry in Thessalonica. But what he feared might be a ministry of just a few weeks, Luke suggests (Acts 18:11), stretched into a year and a half, and the gospel that first took root in the city enjoyed success in the surrounding countryside as well (2 Cor. 1:1). During his stay in Corinth, Paul received assistance from Aquila and Prisca, Jewish Christian refugees from

---

8. A useful summary of recent secondary literature and of issues is available in Gordon D. Fee, *The First Epistle to the Corinthians* (Grand Rapids: Eerdmans, 1987), but a more recent accessible commentary is Richard A. Horsley, *1 Corinthians*, Abingdon New Testament Commentaries (Nashville: Abingdon Press, 2011). See also Margaret M. Mitchell, *Paul and the Rhetoric of Reconciliation: An Exegetical Investigation of the Language and Composition of 1 Corinthians* (Louisville, KY: Westminster/John Knox, 1991) for excellent bibliographical sources and an insightful interpretation.

Corinth Fortress and Temple of Aphrodite
(Courtesy of Warren Kendall; used by permission)

Rome who "risked their necks" for him and earned the gratitude of all of the Gentile churches (Rom. 16:3–4; see also Acts 18:1–4).

While in Corinth Paul evidently spoke in tongues (1 Cor. 14:18) and demonstrated other charismatic gifts ("signs and wonders and mighty works," 2 Cor. 12:12). In the face of the "impending distress," that is, "woes" of the end time, Paul chose to remain celibate (1 Cor. 7:7, 26). Evidently his celibacy profoundly affected some in the congregation, prompting Paul later to devote an extensive discussion to both marriage and ecstatic speech.

Acts reports that after leaving Corinth, perhaps ordered to do so by the Roman official Gaius, Paul settled in Ephesus for three years (ca. 52–55). Among others, Timothy, Titus, Aquila, and Prisca worked with him there. Apollos also, an Alexandrian Jew who trailed Paul to Corinth, enjoyed good success there for a time and followed him to Ephesus. According to Acts 8:24–28, Apollos's eloquence, agile and imaginative exegesis, enthusiasm, debating skill, and resourceful, charismatic personality endeared him to the Corinthians. One need hardly assume that Apollos caused the problems in Corinth, but his presence there may have aggravated the enthusiastic tendencies disturbing the church.

While at Ephesus, Paul wrote a letter, now missing, that addressed problems in the Corinthian church (1 Cor. 5:9).[9] Our 1 Corinthians, written later, curtly noted that Apollos was then unwilling to return to Corinth but would return "when he has the opportunity" (1 Cor. 16:12). From this scant information it is a bit too bold to assume that Paul suspected that Apollos once encouraged the excesses in Corinth and now was unenthusiastic about his return. But from 1 Corinthians we learn of a religious enthusiasm of the cell of converts there who understood that life in Christ bestowed gifts of the Spirit that became a marker of authentic life in Christ. Ecstatic speech may have been thought to induce salvation, rather than salvation inducing speech. "The language of angels" as it was called (1 Cor. 13:1) may have become a metric for deciding who was in tune with the divine or who had "knowledge."

Some may have claimed that their recognition that idols had no real existence allowed them to attend pagan celebrations, participate in pagan cultic meals, and even eat meat offered to idols. It is possible that this "knowledge," when coupled with the creed that in Christ "there is neither male and female" (Gal. 3:28), led some to try living above mere accidental gender distinctions. "Spiritual marriages" may have allowed men and women to live a celibate life together. If such a lifestyle did in fact develop, then we can understand how the missing first letter, mentioned in 1 Corinthians 5:9, admonished believers not to associate with sexually immoral persons.

Outline of Paul's Complex and Extended Corinthian Relationship

The apostle's interaction with the Corinthian church was a troubled one, and 1 Corinthians came at an early stage of that relationship. The following summary of that interaction is offered to assist the reader (52–58 CE).

  1a. Paul's preaching in Corinth.
  1b. Hearing before Gallio.
  2. Letter A: To the Corinthians (1 Cor. 5:9) (missing).
  3. Corinthians to Paul (1 Cor. 7:1) (missing) and oral report (1 Cor. 16:17).

9. Some see 2 Cor. 6:14–7:1 as a fragment of this missing letter, since it clearly was an insertion and since it also deals with immorality, the theme of the first letter (1 Cor. 5:9). Joseph A. Fitzmyer, however, has argued convincingly that the language of 6:14–7:1 is more characteristic of Qumran texts than of Paul. See his "Qumran and the Interpolated Paragraph in 2 Corinthians 6:14–7:1," in *The Catholic Biblical Quarterly* 23 (1961): 271–280. See also work by Fee cited in note 8 above.

Temple of Apollo (Courtesy of Warren Kendall;
used by permission)

4. Letter B: 1 Corinthians response to oral and written communication. Carried by Timothy.
5. Letter C: Paul's third letter, 2 Cor. 8, carried by Titus and the "brothers." Urged completion of the offering project. Suspicions surface about Paul's conduct and fitness for ministry.
6. Letter D: 2 Cor. 2:14–7:4 (minus 6:14–7:1). Defended apostolic ministry. Disastrous ("painful") visit followed (2 Cor. 2:1; 7:9, 11f.).
7. Letter E: Paul crafted slashing defense (2 Cor. 10:1–13:10). Titus bore letter and defended Paul.
8. Letter F: Titus met Paul in Macedonia with good news. Corinthian church reconciled.
9. Letter G: Paul scribed reconciling letter (2 Cor. 1:1–2:13; 7:5–16; 13:11–13). Probably borne by Titus.
10. Letter H: Paul wrote 2 Cor. 9, a round-robin missive to Achaian churches. Urged completion of the offering. Carried by anonymous "brothers." Prepared for Paul's imminent arrival with delegation.
11. Paul traveled to Corinth, spent winter as Gaius's guest, and wrote the Roman churches defending his Gentile mission and announcing that

the offering from the Gentile churches for the "poor among the saints" in Jerusalem was ready, the delegation chosen, and the journey to present the offering about to begin. Begged for prayers for success (Rom. 15:26–32).

Oral and Written Responses from Corinth to Paul

Chloe's people ("slaves"?) and others (1 Cor. 16:17) arrived in Ephesus to report orally on the deteriorating situation in the home church (1 Cor. 1:11). Boasts of possessing exclusive truth and claims to exclusive religious "knowledge" may have stoked fiery antagonisms in Corinth. Conflicting claims to a superior "knowledge" gained from a favorite mystagogue (e.g., Peter, Paul, Apollos, or Christ) spawned a factionalism that imperiled the church. Such spiritual elitism fostered contempt for those with "lesser" gifts, led some to disdain the unimposing Paul, cultivated a divisive elitism (see 1 Cor. 1:10–4:21), and promoted a calloused indifference to the needs of others.

Paul's Response to the Oral Report

In what we know as 1 Corinthians we see Paul's reply to two communications from Corinth, one oral and one written. Interestingly, Paul responded in kind, sending 1 Corinthians (which was really his second letter) from Ephesus by sea (1 Cor. 5:9, ca. 53 CE) and dispatching Timothy by land (1 Cor. 4:17), probably with oral instructions. Paul's letter is intact, but for the sake of clarity we summarize his argument below.

1. Concerning Division (1 Cor. 1:10–4:21)

Why do you boast of your baptism in the name of people like me, Apollos, Peter, and even Christ? Is Christ divided? Were you baptized in the name of Paul? Does some special wisdom come in baptism through your union with Christ? Is that why you call yourselves wise, mature, and spiritual? Your boasting is silly and contrary to the ways of God. Divine wisdom looks like foolishness to society. Through a cross, or through a motley collection of people like yourselves, or through a frail and unimposing figure like me, God reveals wisdom not in strength and glory, but in weakness and shame! Christ crucified, not Christ glorified, was the heart of my gospel, and this Christ forms the foundation of the church. All work laid on that foundation by Apollos or anybody else will be tested on the last day. To those inflated with their own self-esteem and heedless of the welfare of the church, let me say: if they destroy the church, God will destroy them. Is it because you think you are so spiritual that you presume to judge Christ's apostles and think you are above Scripture (see 1 Cor. 4:6)? When I come, I will find out how really spiritual these people are.

2. Concerning Immorality (1 Cor. 5:1–6:11; 11:17–34)

a. Incest (1 Cor. 5:1–13)

I hear that a man is cohabiting with his "father's wife," all in the name of the Lord Jesus, and worse, you condone it! You say Christians are above such trivial differences as those of sex, and that life in the kingdom transcends sexuality. You tolerate behavior that even pagans scorn. Expel this offender, lest he poison the whole congregation. In doing so, he may be destroyed, but his spirit will be saved. When I wrote that you should not associate with immoral persons, I meant just such as this, not the outsiders.

b. Lawsuits (1 Cor. 6:1–11)

I hear that some of you are defrauding others, and that someone has taken a case to the civil courts. How ironic that you who someday will judge the heathen, or even angels, now turn to the heathen for justice. Must the injured party turn to the civil courts? You claim to be wise (sophos): are you not wise enough to render a decision on such matters? Great harm can be done to the church and the mission by such internal strife.

3. Concerning the Lord's Supper (1 Cor. 11:17–34)

Each one eats disregarding the needs of others and eating only for self-satisfaction. You claim to be celebrating your life in the kingdom, but instead you profane the Lord's body. Do you not know that Christ is in his community? Your selfish and greedy behavior not only insults your brother and sister; it offends the Lord himself, who is present for judgment. That is why some are sick and some have died.

Paul's Response to the Corinthian Letter

In 1 Corinthians 7:1 Paul shifted his attention to the concerns of a Corinthian letter ("Now concerning the matters about which you wrote . . ."). With the phrase "now concerning (peri de)," Paul introduced topics that Hurd claimed came from the Corinthian epistle.[10] By noting the appearances of peri de Hurd constructed an outline of the Corinthian letter to Paul (e.g.,

10. First suggested by John C. Hurd, Jr. *The Origin of 1 Corinthians* (New York: Seabury, 1965).

7:1, 25; 8:1; 12:1; and 16:1). In their letter, Hurd claimed the Corinthians cited Paul's example to support their practice of celibacy for married and unmarried believers, recalled Paul's proclamation of freedom in Christ as permission to consume meat offered to idols, and took the apostle's claim that in Christ there is neither male and female to mean that women could pray with uncovered head and actively participate in worship services. Moreover, their letter possibly noted suspicions about Paul's fixation on money for the Jerusalem poor, when so many destitute lined the streets of Corinth and populated the church. Finally, the letter requested that Apollos, who wowed Corinthians with his powerful witness, oratory, and charismatic presence, be allowed to return to them.

Corinthian Letter to Paul

After dealing with the concerns offered by the oral report from Chloe's people (slave messengers?) in 1 Corinthians 7:1, Paul began his treatment one by one of the major topics of the Corinthian letter to Paul. From the outline of their letter recovered from Paul's responses, I offer the following hypothetical but probable outline of the Corinthian letter to Paul.

1. Concerning Marriage

Given the urgency of the times, we believe married believers should refrain from sexual intercourse, and virgins and widows should not consider marriage, in order to keep themselves in a constant state of readiness to meet Christ and to enjoy the company of angels. Given the urgency of the times, we remember how you said, "It is well for a man not to touch a woman." In this we are following your example. Moreover, you yourself said that in Christ there is "neither male nor female," and that the Lord said that in the kingdom men and women are neither married nor given in marriage (Luke 20:35). As we await Christ's return, should not those of us who are married act as if we are not, and should not believers divorce any unbelieving partners?

2. Concerning Contact with the World

You wrote us not to associate with the immoral, but to do what we would need to in order to withdraw from the world. As you know, the world is full of immoral people. And how does this square with your exhortation to do "good to all"? And, did you not say, "For freedom Christ has set us free"? Don't we witness to Christ by exercising our freedom in Christ? Also, if we are free and if idols have no real existence, what harm can come from eating idol meat? Also, we know that physical things cannot defile the spirit—"Food is meant for the stomach and the stomach for food." Must we decline invitations to eat with our unbelieving friends and family and forgo a chance to witness to Christ, if the meat is not ritually pure? How can we witness to unbelievers if we offend them?

3. Concerning Worship

Since all are one in Christ, the distinctions between men and women are artificial; such physical accidents mean nothing in the kingdom of God. It is entirely appropriate, therefore, for women to pray with heads uncovered and to share actively in the service. And why should you have reservations now about speaking in tongues? We are merely following your example. Those who are unable to speak the heavenly language of angels are less gifted.

4. Concerning the Resurrection

Through baptism we have already passed from death to the resurrected life. If we have already died and been raised with Christ, then, as you said, today is the day of salvation. Also, the whole idea of the resurrection of the body is disgusting. Which body? Is it the old body or the young, the sick body or the healthy? How can you say we must prepare for the resurrection of the dead and the judgment of those raised up? How can those who have already died with Christ and been raised up, die again? Also, what do you mean by the "resurrection of the body"? The whole idea of the resuscitation of a rotten corpse is repugnant to us. Salvation brings release from our bodies; and did you not say that flesh and blood cannot inherit the kingdom of God? What good is salvation if we are still imprisoned in our bodies?

5. Concerning the Collection

Although we are poor ourselves, we will contribute to the project for the poor in Jerusalem. It would probably be best if we sent someone from our church to deliver the offering. You would not want anyone to think you were skimming off part of the gift for yourself, would you? But some wonder why we must send an offering for the poor in Jerusalem as a sign of solidarity with them. We have many, many poor here in Corinth. Should we not attend to our own first? Many of us are slaves and destitute. We are very limited in what we can give.

6. Concerning Apollos

Might you encourage Apollos to return to Corinth? He had a very effective ministry here. Some of our people miss his powerful witness, oratory, charismatic presence, and persuasive teaching of Scripture. The brothers and sisters are always asking for his return.

Letter B: Paul's response to the Letter from the Corinthians

1. Concerning Marriage (1 Cor. 7:1–40)

I fear you misunderstood my remark that it is better for a man not to touch a woman and vice versa. Because you think you are equal to angels, you claim to be above such worldly gender distinctions to keep yourselves in readiness for God's revelation.[11] The pure want to rid themselves of unbelieving partners. Some believe that continence within marriage is required. But abstinence from sex should be practiced only for a time of prayer. Widows and virgins are made to feel inferior if they marry. While there, I encouraged all to remain as I am, because of the special urgency of the times (the end is near), not because we have already overcome the world. Not everyone has the gift of celibacy. It is better to marry than to be consumed with passion.

2. Concerning Idol Meat (1 Cor. 8:1–11:1)

It is true that there is no God but one, and that idols have no real existence. Since idols do not exist, you ask, what harm comes from eating meat routinely offered to the gods in the marketplace? Indeed, believers may eat idol meat, but if my freedom causes a weaker believer to stumble, then it is best to abstain. Freedom must always be subordinated to love.

3. Concerning Distinctions between Men and Women (1 Cor. 11:2–16)

Some of you say that in Christ there is neither male nor female. It is true that I encouraged women to prophesy in the service and that you were baptized into Christ in whom there is "neither male and female," but you seek to obliterate all distinctions between male and female. Such are accidents of birth, you say, and after sharing in the new creation all such accidental distinctions should be ignored. You claim too much. While your claim is true for the future life, it is not yet realistic for this world. We are not yet angels. The Scriptures note a gender distinction. Woman was taken from the side of man (Adam), and now man is born of woman, but women and men are interdependent. Let men and women continue sharing in the service of worship, but let us maintain the distinction between and interdependence of male and female. Men, cut your hair, and women, cover your heads (or wear veils).

---

11. Note especially Luke 20:34–36, which suggests the same view: "And Jesus said to them, 'Those who belong to this age marry and are given in marriage; but those who are considered worthy of a place in that age and in the resurrection from the dead neither marry nor are given in marriage. Indeed they cannot die anymore, because they are like angels and are children of God, being children of the resurrection'" (AT).

4. Concerning Spiritual Gifts (1 Cor. 12:1–14:40)

You claim to follow my example in practicing ecstatic speech. You do well to exalt the spiritual gifts, but if those who speak in tongues despise those who do not, how does that build up the church? Strive for the higher gifts, like teaching and interpreting, gifts that edify. Allow all to contribute in their own way with whatever gift they have, and subordinate all of the gifts to love, the most excellent of all charismatic gifts (12:31).

5. Concerning the Resurrection (1 Cor. 15:1–58)

Remember the gospel that I preached, that Christ died, was buried, and was raised. Christ's raising was the first of the general resurrection soon to be completed. You say you have already been raised up, that death is behind you, that only the life of glory remains, and that therefore there is no future resurrection of the disgusting body for you. I hear also that the whole idea of the resurrection of the body is repulsive to you. Do you not know that God can give us a different body appropriate to the next life? Death has not been completely conquered; that will come in the future when God puts all enemies underfoot, and the last enemy to be destroyed will be King Death. Then and only then will we be able to say, "Death is swallowed up in victory."

6. Concerning the Collection (1 Cor. 16:1–4)

Have the collection ready when I come. I agree that someone from the congregation should accompany us to deliver the offering.

7. Concerning Apollos (1 Cor. 16:12)

I urged him to come, but it was not God's will that he come at this time. He will come later.

As a guide for reading the letter itself, the following outline is offered.

Paul Dispatched Timothy with Oral Instructions, and Timothy's Return

Paul placed 1 Corinthians (actually his second letter to Corinth) in the hands of his trusted coworker, Timothy, for delivery and its interpretation. When Timothy arrived or while he was in Corinth, he found the church still shaken by internal disputes and gravely suspicious of Paul. Neither his presence nor the letter healed the wounds opened by internal conflict. He also learned that certain Hellenistic Jewish Christian missionaries had arrived, bidding for the affection, loyalty, and support of the Corinthian church. They claimed to be "servants of Christ" (2 Cor. 11:23 RSV; 3:1–2) and professed to be apostles (2 Cor. 11:5, 13). They came armed with written testimonials to the success of their preaching elsewhere (2 Cor. 3:1).[12]

The Corinthian letter Timothy delivered to Paul in Ephesus is outlined below.

Outline of 1 Corinthians (Paul's Letter B)

1. Address, Salutation, and Thanksgiving	1:1–9
2. Concerning Disunity	1:10–4:21
a. Dissension in the church	1:10–17
b. God's vs. worldly wisdom	1:18–2:16
c. Paul preaches God's wisdom	2:6–16
d. Factions among the wise	3:1–23
e. The church's judgment of Paul	4:1–21
3. Problems of Immorality	5:1–6:11
a. Incest	5:1–13
b. Lawsuits between believers	6:1–11
4. Reply to Questions in the Corinthians' Letter	6:12–16:12
a. Introduction	6:12–20
b. Concerning sex	7:1–40
c. Concerning idol meat	8:1–11:1
d. Concerning gender distinctions	11:2–16
e. Selfish behavior at church meals	11:17–33
f. Concerning spiritual gifts	12:1–14:40 (minus 14:34–36)
g. Concerning the resurrection	15:1–58
h. Concerning the collection	16:1–4
5. Paul's Travel Plans	16:5–9
6. News of Timothy's Visit	16:10–11
7. Concerning Apollos	16:12
8. Conclusion	16:13–24
a. Closing paraenesis (ethical instruction)	16:13–18
b. Closing greeting, warning, and benediction	16:19–24

Paul Dispatched Titus and the Brothers with Oral Instructions

Paul ended 1 Corinthians (16:1–4) with specific instructions urging their preparation of their part of the offering Paul had proposed. Mitchell has convincingly argued that 2 Corinthians 8, with its rationale for the offering

---

12. Dieter Georgi, *Die Gegner des Paulus im 2. Korintherbrief: Studien zur religiösen Propaganda in der Spätantike* (Neukirchen-Vluyn: Neukirchener Verlag, 1964); Eng. trans. *The Opponents of Paul in Second Corinthians* (Philadelphia: Fortress Press, 1985) has profoundly influenced the scholarly understanding of the scope of Paul's opposition, esp. in 2 Corinthians.

and recommendation of the delegation sent to assist with the project, followed 1 Corinthians.[13] Three issues combined to complicate that venture.

First, there was the lingering conflict created by a divisive spirit, religious puffery, spiritual elitism, and totalistic claims to salvation revealed in 1 Corinthians. When Titus and the brothers arrived, they found the church still shaken by internal disputes and gravely suspicious of Paul. Neither their presence nor 1 Corinthians had healed the wounds opened by internal conflict.

Second, Hellenistic Jewish Christian missionaries had arrived, bidding for the affection, loyalty, and financial support of the Corinthian church. Claiming to be servants and apostles of Christ (2 Cor. 11:5, 13, 23) they proved to be formidable adversaries.[14]

Third, Paul probably dispatched highly commended Titus and the "brothers" with a letter of introduction and a specific program to complete the offering (2 Cor. 8, letter C)[15] project in Corinth. Rather than being eager to participate in this symbolic gesture, the Corinthians drew back. The doubts about the project and Paul's place in it, when combined with lingering internal problems and the invasion of itinerant missionary critics of Paul, fueled raging doubts about Paul's apostolic legitimacy, his motives, his honesty, and the truth of his gospel. Paul's own converts, his "children," turned against him or failed to come to his defense.

Paul's Painful Visit to Corinth

After writing a defense of his legitimacy (2 Cor. 2:14–7:1 [minus 6:14–7:1, added later by an unknown author], letter D) that was less than fully successful, Paul made a brief, "painful" visit to Corinth (2 Cor. 2:1) that failed miserably. Once in Corinth he was insulted publicly by a Corinthian Christian (2 Cor. 2:5–8; 7:12) and frustrated in his reconciling effort. He returned to Ephesus in humiliation and in disgrace (2 Cor. 12:21). His disastrous visit played into the hands of his critics. His hasty retreat lent substance to the

13. Margaret M. Mitchell, "Paul's Letters to Corinth: The Interpretative Intertwining of Literary and Historical Reconstruction," in *Urban Religion in Roman Corinth*, ed. Daniel N. Schowalter and Steven J. Friesen (Cambridge, MA: Harvard Theological Studies, 2005), 307–38.

14. Dieter Georgi, *The Opponents of Paul in Second Corinthians* (Philadelphia: Fortress Press, 1985) has joined others in claiming 2 Cor. 6:14–7:1 as an interpolated paragraph.

15. Please note that in 1 Cor. 5:9 Paul referred to a letter he wrote prior to scribing our 1 Corinthians. There he said, "I wrote [n.b.: past tense] you . . ." We of course do not have a copy of that letter. That reference makes 1 Corinthians Paul's second letter and 2 Corinthians 8 his third.

Lechaion Way in Corinth (Courtesy of Warren Kendall;
used by permission)

charge that he was cowardly. His position in the Corinthian church seemed more insecure than ever.

Paul's Fifth Letter to the Corinthians[16]

Humiliated, shamed, and angry, Paul limped away to Ephesus to ponder a response. Hunkered down in Ephesus after his public shaming, Paul scribed his fifth Corinthian epistle, letter E or "tearful letter" (2 Cor. 2:4; 10:1–13:10) to try to patch up a relationship gone sour. That tearful letter catalogues the attacks of his rivals on his fitness for ministry—on his honesty, steadfastness, sincerity, rhetorical sufficiency, and weak, "womanish" bodily presence. Hurt

16. The most influential commentary on 2 Corinthians to date is that of Victor Paul Furnish, *2 Corinthians*, Anchor Bible (Garden City, NY: Doubleday & Co., 1984). But note the more recent Margaret E. Thrall, *II Corinthians*, 2 vols. (Edinburgh: T. & T. Clark, 1994). More accessible to the nonspecialist is Calvin J. Roetzel, *II Corinthians*, Abingdon New Testament Commentaries (Nashville: Abingdon Press, 2007).

and angry, Paul summoned up some of the most brutal martial language he would use anywhere, turned it on his own converts (2 Cor. 10:1–6, 10), and appended a section that demonized and stigmatized his rivals and their supporters (2 Cor. 11:1–14).

Then, with a flash of insight, Paul appeared to realize the futility of playing the game of his rivals. A theological epiphany seems to have inspired some of Paul's most creative theologizing about the nature of power. While his critics mocked his bodily weakness (2 Cor. 10:10), Paul turned their word "weakness" to his defense. Using it in some form eleven times in one short treatise (2 Cor. 13:3, 4, 9; 11:30; 12:5, 9, 10; 13:4; 11:21, 29; 12:10), he took on the persona of a "fool" who entertained an ofttimes mocked powerful figures at public events. While his critics mocked, Paul claimed the scars etched on his back, not as signifiers of shame or weakness, but as mystical links to the beaten, humiliated, and crucified Christ. This radical ideology of power in weakness totally inverted and subverted the "dominant male discourse on the body" and elevated the trait of womanish weakness to become "the primary modes of identification and resistance." Then he directed the Corinthians once more to that which stood at the heart of his gospel at the beginning: "I decided to know nothing among you but Jesus Christ and him crucified" (1 Cor. 2:2).[17]

So anxious was Paul about the effect of this "severe" letter that he found it impossible to wait for its carrier Titus, who agreed to meet Paul in Troas. Instead of waiting there, Paul set out to meet Titus (2 Cor. 2:12–13) and finally linked up with him in Macedonia. Like a bright burst of sunlight after the passing of a storm, Titus's news brought joy to Paul. He reported that the Corinthians mourned their wrongs; they longed to see Paul (2 Cor. 7:6–7), and they had reprimanded the troublemaker/s and restored order. Paul's joy, optimism, and praise blossomed. Expressions of "complete confidence" in the Corinthians (2 Cor. 7:16) replaced other worries, and generosity that would have seemed impossible just weeks before pushed aside the threats and warnings of the tearful letter.

After hearing the good news, Paul sent Titus with a letter of thanksgiving to the Corinthian church (2 Cor. 1:1–2:13; 7:2–16; letter G). The chief offender had been disciplined; Paul expressed sorrow that his earlier letter was so severe and said he sought not the punishment of the offender but forgiveness and restoration instead. Conciliation and praise replaced the heat and hurt of the earlier letter. Now Paul's mind turned again to the offering

17. See Calvin Roetzel, "The Language of War (2 Cor. 10:1–6) and the Language of Weakness (2 Cor. 11:21b–13:10)," in *Violence, Scripture, and Textual Practice in Early Judaism and Christianity*, ed. Ra'anan S. Bustan, Alex P. Jassen, and Calvin J. Roetzel (Leiden/Boston: Brill, 2010), 77–98, and B. D. Shaw, "Body/Power/Identity: Passions of the Martyrs," *Journal of Early Christian Studies* 4 (1996): 305–11.

project, as he penned one last, brief circular letter (2 Cor. 9; letter H) to the churches of Achaia to be carried by the "brothers" and to encourage the completion of the offering project and to prepare for the arrival of Paul with a Macedonian delegation to collect and deliver the money first to Corinth then to Jerusalem.

Letter H to the Corinthians (2 Cor. 9)[18]

Filled with exhortation to complete this good work, Paul's mind raced on ahead to the apocalyptic moment when the Gentile pilgrimage to Jerusalem would offer the gifts and praise that the prophets reserved for the end time (e.g., Isa. 2:2–3; 60:5). Caught up in the ecstasy of that anticipated moment, Paul inserted the reader into a great cosmic narrative. He shifted the gaze of his Achaian Gentile readers to Jerusalem, where their voices would join with those of the Jewish Christians in spontaneous praise. Paul gave play to his imagination and improvised a narrative so grand it almost takes the breath away. He joined Gentile and Jew in the glorification of God, and all of the past quarrels with Peter and James of the mother church were swept aside.

Instead, the prospect of this glorious outcome inspired Paul to a spontaneous cry: "Thanks be to God for his indescribable gift!" (2 Cor. 9:15). One can almost sense the quiet that would settle over the little house-church cells in Achaia as this letter was read and as it bestowed on their offerings, whether small or great, a place in a scenario almost too great to imagine. With this offering the great reconciling work of God in Christ placed them on the threshold when Jew and Gentile believers would stand together in solidarity.

When we next hear from Paul, he is in Corinth with Gaius his host, that is, Gaius the wealthy convert whom Paul baptized on his founding visit (1 Cor. 1:14). The collection stood ready for delivery; the delegations from Macedonia and Achaia had gathered to set out in April with the return of the shipping season. The brilliance of Paul's earlier inspired moment now faded as he recalled his last angry meeting with Peter and those with James. A somber Paul wrote the Roman church soliciting their prayers for a successful delivery of the offering to the poor among the saints in Jerusalem. A rejection of that offering by the Jerusalem church would have been catastrophic and would have been tantamount to their saying, "We want nothing to do with you." The world Paul earlier created for his reader was unfinished, a world that a realized eschatology could never provide.

18. See Roetzel, *II Corinthians*.

With the letter to Rome dispatched, this letter written, and the journey to Jerusalem about to begin, Paul's voice fell silent. But the story was interrupted at an opportune moment when hope for reconciliation burned brightly. If we were forced to rely on the later Acts account to learn how the story ended, the outcome might be ugly, for scholars argue that Luke's aching silence about the offering suggests that the offering was rejected.[19]

One might ask if this discussion of the literary integrity of 2 Corinthians really matters. Why not simply read 2 Corinthians as it is? Why appeal to an unprovable hypothesis to make sense of this exchange? We do so because there is no alternative. Since no text is self-interpreting, no interpreter simply takes the text as it is. One views a text through the optic one brings to it, and all readings are hardly created equal. In making a decision about a reading, one must assess the evidence pro and con. We have tried to follow that guideline here in the full awareness the historical imagination can assist our approach to the world of the text.

We must necessarily engage in such acts of historical imagination to capture the dynamic and theological creativity that is revealed in the shrill and soothing exchanges between Paul and his churches. Such an act of conjuring the narrative of a text defies all facile solutions; nevertheless, it is necessary if one is to capture the dynamism of Paul's theology and the way it was refined in history's crucible. The hope and aim of the scholar is that her construction will reasonably explain the issues and problems the text presents and that the conjured narrative will reveal the tensions and vitality of the interaction between Paul and this small cell of believers. While the construction of letter fragments below may look complicated, it is helpful to note that these exchanges took place over several years under a variety of circumstances.

Outline of 2 Corinthian Letter Fragments

Offering Rationale and Promotion (2 Cor. 8, Letter C)

1. Address, Salutation, Thanksgiving (missing)
2. Body of Letter
   a. Generosity appeal   8:1–15
      (1) Macedonian example   8:1–7
      (2) Apostolic appeal   8:8–9
      (3) Advice for completion   8:10–12
      (4) Gifting between equals   8:13–15
   b. Commendation of Titus and the "brothers"   8:16–24

---

19. See J. Roloff, *Die Apostelgeschichte*, Das Neue Testament Deutsch 5 (Göttingen: Vandenhoeck, 1981), 312, who argued compellingly that the silence of Acts about the offering, when the author surely knew it was being delivered, suggests that the offering was rejected.

First Defense of Paul's Ministry (2 Cor. 2:14–7:4, Letter D)

1. Address, Salutation, Thanksgiving	(missing)
2. Defense of Ministry	2:14–6:10
a. Introduction	2:14–3:6
(1) Triumphal procession with God	2:14–17
(2) Ministry adequacy defended	3:1–6
b. Ministry of new covenant	3:7–4:6
(1) Glory compared with glory	3:7–11
(2) Unveiled	3:12–18
(3) Concluding unit	4:1–6
c. Gospel: treasure in clay pots	4:7–15
d. Ministry validated in affliction	4:16–5:10
e. Ministry of reconciliation	5:11–6:1
3. Final appeal	6:11–13; 7:2–4
a. Appeal for an open-armed welcome	6:11–13
b. A non-Pauline insertion	6:14–7:1
c. Concluding appeal	7:2–4

Letter E: 2 Cor. 10:1–13:10

1. Opening	(missing)
2. Defense and response to antagonists	10:1–13:10
a. Martial language	10:1–11
b. Good and bad boasting	10:12–18
c. Persona of fool assumed	11:1–12:13
(1) Demonization of super-apostles	11:1–15
(2) Boasting contest	11:16–23
(a) Introduction to fool's speech	11:16–21a
(b) Power in weakness	11:21b–12:10
(3) Postscript to fool's speech	12:11–13
d. Final appeal and warning	12:14–13:10
(1) Apostolic visit and final defense	12:14–18
(2) Hopes and fears of the visit	12:19–21
(3) Closing threats and exhortations	13:1–10

Reconciling Letter (2 Cor. 1:1–2:13; 7:5–16; 13:11–13, Letter G)

1. The Salutation	1:1–2
2. The Blessing/Thanksgiving	1:3–11
3. Letter Body	1:12–2:13; 7:5–16
a. Introduction	1:12–14
b. Painful visit recall	1:15–2:4
c. Discipline of the offender	2:5–11
d. Anguished wait for Titus	2:12–13
e. Paul and Titus rendezvous	7:5–16
f. Titus brings news of reconciliation	7:5–7
g. Good grief "letter of tears" effected	7:8–13a
h. Consolation and confidence	7:13b–16
4. Concluding Injunctions and Grace	13:11–13

Round-Robin Offering Letter to Achaian Churches (2 Cor. 9:1–15, Letter H)

1. Letter Opening	(missing)
2. Final Offering Letter	9:1–5
3. Divine Source of Sowing and Reaping	9:6–10
4. Focus on Jerusalem and Eschatological Pilgrimage	9:11–15

While most Paul scholars recognize that our 2 Corinthians contains parts of different letters written over several years, they honestly disagree about the precise partition of the letter parts. Moreover, there is little agreement about the identity and message of the rival "superlative apostles" hounding Paul's steps. Nevertheless, most agree that 2 Corinthians opens the drapes, allowing us to view a vast landscape of contending parties; in that struggle some of Paul's most profound theologizing took place. There we find a totally revolutionary statement about the nature of power (10:1–12:10), the reconciliation of the world (5:11–21), the offering as a religious signifier of the solidarity of Jew and Gentile in the imminent arrival of the rule of God (chaps. 8 and 9), and the promise of God's strength in weakness (12:1–10). Some more recently have informally opined that 2 Corinthians was one of Paul's greatest theological achievements, if not his greatest. There is also the fascinating possibility that Paul's letters influenced, if they did not shape, Mark's later theology of the cross.

GALATIANS (52–56 CE)[20]

Paul founded the Galatian churches from a sickbed. When illness overtook him on his way through Galatia, the local people took him in and nursed him back to health (Gal. 4:13–16). During his recuperation, and after, Paul spoke

---

20. The best available discussion in English of the history of interpretation of Galatians and the major issues facing the interpreter is offered by Hans Dieter Betz, *Galatians: A Commentary on Paul's Letter to the Churches in Galatia*, Hermeneia (Philadelphia: Fortress Press, 1979). Scholars disagree on the location of these churches. According to the southern Galatian theory, they were in the region through which Paul traveled on his "first missionary journey" (Acts 13–14). This theory has the advantage of harmonizing Paul's letters with the Acts account. Those holding the northern Galatian theory point to discrepances between the Acts account and Paul's letters and further argue that Paul uses the ethnic name "Galatians" (3:1) to refer to his readers, which would better fit the inhabitants of the north, where the Galatians had settled, than residents in the southern part of the Roman province.

Those opting for the southern theory tend to date Galatians among the earliest of Paul's letters, since it is assumed that he founded the church on the "first missionary journey." Those supporting the northern hypothesis tend to date Galatians somewhat later, since it is assumed that it was on a later visit that Paul ventured to the heart of the old Celtic kingdom of Keltai near the modern Ankara, Turkey. This later theory is also of some significance if one is interested in tracing the emergence of Paul's theology

to the Galatian Gentiles (Keltai [from Celts]) of their adoption as children of God. No longer, he said, need they be slaves of this world's hostile, demonic powers (4:8–9). Through the crucified one and the gift of the Spirit, they could be liberated from the clutches of demonic powers. After hearing this "good news" and witnessing the mighty deeds of Paul (3:5), the Galatians received his gospel with enthusiasm and revered the apostle himself. Their patient had become an "angel of God," or savior. They thought him even Jesus Christ (4:14). Their devotion was so extreme that they would, if possible, have given him their very eyes (4:15).

Opposition Developed

All was well when Paul departed, but later he learned that the Galatians had adopted another version of his gospel. His apostleship was under attack, and the church was in turmoil. Whether outsiders or insiders inspired the opposition is uncertain. In any case, the nature of that opposition is clear to modern scholars. Once Paul left Galatia, his converts learned from Jewish Scriptures that the promises of God belonged to the children of Abraham and that one became a son of Abraham through circumcision, and a daughter by law observance. Abraham, the father of many Gentiles (Gen. 17:5), had received circumcision when ninety-nine years old, after receiving God's promise. Likewise, the Galatians might have reasoned that it was necessary for them, the spiritual descendants of Abraham, to receive circumcision.

Such a conclusion would have been natural in light of Genesis 17:10, which reads (with God as assumed speaker), "This is my covenant, which you shall keep, between me and you and your offspring after you: Every male among you shall be circumcised." Later, in Genesis 17:14, a divine proscription was placed on those disobeying the command: "Any uncircumcised male who is not circumcised . . . shall be cut off from his people." Word of the observance of circumcision by the Jewish Christians in Jerusalem may have strengthened the conviction of the Galatians that their males also should be circumcised. For whatever reason, by the time Paul wrote Galatians, the church was requiring all baptized males (Gentile or no) to be circumcised (Gal. 5:2, 11; 6:12–13). Their zeal for God and the Scriptures led them, and perhaps women as well, to keep other parts of the law (3:2; 4:21; 5:4, 18).

The Galatians thus attempted to revise Paul's gospel by adding circumcision to it as a requirement. They also incorporated much from the local

---

made evident in a comparison of the later Romans with Galatians. The dating of Galatians has been notoriously difficult for these reasons, and this uncertainty informs the broadest possible dating range informing the date assigned above.

religion. They continued worshiping certain "elemental spirits" (4:9) and observing "days, and months, and seasons, and years" (4:10). Of a piece with the modification of Paul's gospel were the questions raised about the apostle Paul, for it was impossible to separate the veracity of the message from the integrity of the messenger. The Galatians began to wonder if Paul were an interloper in the apostolic circle. Jesus' original followers, even Jesus' brother James, were leaders in the Jerusalem church. Their links with the Lord were biological, historical, and personal, and the authority for their leadership was unquestioned. Paul, however, was a newcomer, for it was only after Jesus' death that Paul learned of Jesus and his followers, and then only as their adversary.

How could Paul claim to be the Lord's apostle when he had not known the historical Jesus? Many of Paul's traditions stemmed from followers of Jesus, not from Jesus himself. Thus Paul's gospel was secondhand and therefore deficient. However good his intentions or impressive his preaching, Paul's gospel required emendation, that is, a supplement wider in scope, stricter in discipline, more firmly scriptural and apostolic than some claimed vision. Their appeal to Scripture was possibly developed in opposition to certain enthusiastic or libertine tendencies in Gentile churches like Corinth, and perhaps there was a danger seen in Paul's preaching of salvation by grace alone. Note, for example, Paul's warning against excesses of the Spirit that drew few distinctions between moral and immoral behavior (5:13). True to his Diaspora lineage, Paul seemed more worried about immorality than about breaching the law.

Who Were Paul's Opponents? Three Views

One scholarly judgment is that Jewish Christians from Jerusalem (of Peter or James) trailed Paul from place to place as a truth squad out to correct his dangerous innovation. This theory is that the Jewish Christian church in Jerusalem kept the law and sought to impose it on Paul's congregations, which, by claiming salvation by grace apart from law, had grown morally lax.

This view, however, suffers from the lack of any Galatian reference to such opposition. Although Paul was eager to show his independence of the so-called "pillars" in Jerusalem, he nonetheless referred positively to their endorsement of his Gentile gospel (2:9–10). Moreover, if the pillars once endorsed Paul's gospel, it is possible but unlikely that they would then actively oppose it. Moreover, the Galatian charge that Paul was dependent on the Jerusalem church for his gospel makes no sense if the Jerusalem leaders opposed him. And if Paul's opponents were Jewish Christians from Jerusalem, it is puzzling that he should have to remind *them* that one who submitted to circumcision is obligated to keep the whole law. Any Jewish Christ follower from Jerusalem would have known that that was an ancient Pharisaic principle, and it is not likely they would have neglected it. Finally, the reversion of the Galatians to the service of "elemental spirits" (4:9) and their tendency to turn Christian freedom into libertinism (5:13) could hardly have been the result of a campaign by Jewish Christians to bring all of Paul's converts into obedience to the law.

Another group, followers of Johannes Munck, a distinguished Danish scholar, hold that Paul's opponents were members of the Galatian congregation.[21] According to Munck, Paul referred to the troublemakers as "those who are being circumcised" (6:13 AT), which would be singularly inappropriate if Paul meant to refer to Jerusalem Jews, who, of course, had been circumcised long ago. On Munck's side also is the absence of a single reference to the opponents as "outsiders" (unlike 2 Cor. 10–13; 3:1). In support of Munck's view, Lloyd Gaston has shown that there were Gentile Judaizers in Asia Minor, although from a somewhat later period.[22] According to Ignatius in his *Letter to the Philippians*, "If anyone interprets Judaism to you do not listen to him; for it is better to hear Christianity from the circumcised [such as Paul] than Judaism from the uncircumcised [e.g., Gentile Judaizers]."[23]

It would have been natural for Gentile converts to conclude from reading Jewish Scripture that circumcision was required of all believers (see Gen. 17:11, 14). Inevitably, this practice would cause some to wonder why Paul had not required circumcision. Paul's silence on this issue would have been especially perplexing in light of the practice of circumcision in the church in Jerusalem. Had Paul deliberately misrepresented the gospel he received from Jerusalem by omitting the circumcision requirement? The issue is complicated by the fact that Paul, unlike Peter and James, had not known the earthly Jesus, which might have inspired the quite logical question: was not the gospel of the "pillars" more authentic than that of Paul?

Although Munck raised important questions about the identity of Paul's opponents, many scholars feel his thesis does not account for the references to behavior having nothing to do with Jewish praxis. It is especially difficult to reconcile Munck's thesis with the references to the worship of elemental spirits in Galatia, to their observance of days, months, seasons, and years, and to their libertinism.

21. Johannes Munck, *Paul and the Salvation of Mankind*, trans. Frank Clarke (Richmond: John Knox Press, 1959), 87–134.

22. Lloyd Gaston, "Paul and the Law in Galatians 2 and 3," in *Paul and the Torah* (Vancouver: University of British Columbia Press, 1987), 64–79.

23. Ignatius, *Epistle to the Philippians*, trans. Kirsopp Lake, Loeb Classical Library (Cambridge, MA: Harvard University Press, 1949), 1:245.

As another possibility, Walter Schmithals, a noted German scholar, has argued that Paul's Galatian converts were syncretists who combined features of Jewish praxis (e.g., circumcision) with items drawn from folk religion and thus tried to blend Paul's gospel with elements of their own religious and social context. Such a thesis allows for the amateurism of the Galatian observance of circumcision. For example, their unawareness of the principle that this cultic act obligated those circumcised to keep the entire law is surprising. But it does seem strange, if syncretism were the threat, that Paul should give it so little space and so much space to the Judaizing menace. Moreover, we know that Judaism was no monolithic unity in the period and that syncretistic tendencies were quite evident in certain Jewish circles.

Paul's Response

The attempts to undermine Paul's authority and supplement his gospel evoked his fiery rejoinder. In place of the usual warm, friendly thanksgiving, Paul opened this letter with an expression of astonishment: "I am astonished that you are so quickly deserting the one who called you in the grace of Christ" (1:6). He then called down a twofold curse from heaven on his rivals who were preaching "another" gospel (1:7–9). Later he excoriated those who delighted in circumcising others and suggested with bitter sarcasm that they mutilate themselves (5:12). Using an ugly pun, he fulminated that those who receive circumcision are cut off from Christ (5:4). Finally, he audaciously warned those attacking *him* that they really were opposing *Christ* (6:17).

The defense of his apostleship with the defense of his gospel was natural, for in the mind of Paul and his readers the two were inseparable. When the Galatians thus located Paul's gospel in a human source, that is, the "pillars" of the Jerusalem church, Paul insisted that the call from Christ that initiated his apostleship was independent of the Jerusalem church. For three years after his call he did not visit Jerusalem, and when he did return, it was only for a fortnight, and then not again for fourteen years. Even during his brief time in Jerusalem he maintained his independence, so he claimed, and then gained acceptance for his gospel. Later, on one occasion he publicly rebuked Peter in Antioch for his duplicity on the issue of eating with Gentiles. Moreover, Paul appealed more often to his status as an Israelite than as a Jew and thus showed a preference for a broader term than that of the Jerusalem church.[24] By arguing that Christ, not the Jerusalem leaders, commissioned him directly,

---

24. See Calvin Roetzel, "*Ioudaioi* and Paul," in *The New Testament an Early Christian Literature in Greco-Roman Context: Studies in Honor of David E. Aune*, ed. John Fotopoulos (Leiden: E. J. Brill, 2006), 3–16.

Paul tried to neutralize the charge that his gospel was a human creation (1:18–2:21).

Paul disputed the scriptural basis of his opponents' opposition. His discussion centered on Abraham, a figure important to both him and his critics. As a son of Abraham according to the flesh (Rom. 4:1; 11:1; 2 Cor. 11:21b–24), Paul knew that Abraham was an uncircumcised Gentile (Heb. *goi*) when he first trusted God's promise (Rom. 4). Abraham, Paul claimed, was thus the patron of all proselytes or Gentiles. Since God's promise was that through Abraham all the world's peoples (i.e., Gentiles) would be blessed, it is likely that the Galatians shared Paul's interest in the Abraham narrative, for in it they would have found grounds for requiring circumcision and could point to the commandment to Abraham that all of his male descendants were to undergo circumcision (Gen. 17:9–11). Any uncircumcised male would "be cut off from his people" (Gen. 17:14). Against this interpretation of the Abraham narrative, Paul appealed to Genesis 15:6, where Abraham "*believed* the Lord; and the Lord reckoned [counted] it [his trust] to him as *righteousness*" (AE). Therefore, Paul concluded, since Abraham was counted righteous on account of his faith before he was circumcised, it is faith, not circumcision, that links the children of promise with Abraham.

Paul then offered an exegesis of the Abraham narrative that some might think grotesque (Gal. 3:16): He wrote, "Now the promises were made to Abraham and to his offspring. It does not say, 'And to offsprings,' as of many; but it says, 'And to your offspring [sing.],'" which Paul read as a reference to Christ. Thus Paul implied that it was through faith in Christ, not law observance, that Gentiles became true children of Abraham. Given the benefit of modern exegetical methods, we know, of course, that Paul was unfaithful here to the intent of the Genesis material. But Paul's tendency to read himself and his community into those texts was common (see Qumran exegesis especially).

In light of Paul's positive statements about the law elsewhere, his almost totally negative characterization of it in Galatians is problematic. His statements here, however, must be read as exaggerations for effect—a polemical attempt to confute his critics. He vigorously opposed their effort to supplement his gospel with law observance for two reasons. First, it revealed distrust in the adequacy of his gospel and the God who gave it. In Jerusalem Paul had defended his right to offer full salvation to Gentiles qua Gentiles to belong to God's elect; in this letter, he met the attempt of some Galatians to assign to second-class status that qualified Paul's offer of full participation, Gentiles who entered the church through faith instead of the law.

The second reason for Paul's opposition was that the Galatian experiment with the law was amateurish. One senses Paul's disdain, if not contempt, for those who thought they could selectively observe portions of the law. Paul reminded the Galatians of a basic Pharisaic principle that evidently they had overlooked: "Every man who lets himself be circumcised . . . is obliged to obey the *entire* law" (5:3 AE). Paul said this, however, not to urge those who were keeping a part of the law to work harder to observe all 613 commandments in the Pentateuch, but to encourage his listeners to claim full membership in God's covenant people by grace, and not as righteous proselytes via Judaism.[25] Since the Galatians came to enjoy life in the Spirit through "hearing with faith," free from "works of the law," Paul would have them continue in the way of responsible freedom (Gal. 5).

Outline of Galatians

1. Address and Salutation	1:1–5
2. Expression of Astonishment[26]	1:6–9
3. Paul's Defense of his Apostleship	1:10–2:21
4. Paul's Defense of his Gospel	3:1–4:31
a. Spirit comes through gospel not law	3:1–5
b. Abraham: father of promise	3:6–29
c. Law and grace	4:1–31
5. The Gospel Applied: Freedom and Responsibility	5:1–6:10
a. Stand fast in freedom	5:1–12
b. Freedom to love	5:13–25
c. The law of Christ	5:26–6:10
6. Personal Exhortation and Conclusion	6:11–18

PHILIPPIANS (CA. 55/56 CE)

Paul probably wrote the Philippian church from a jail in Ephesus (winter of 55 or spring of 56).[27] From the time of its founding, the Philippian church had a turbulent history. Paul spoke of the shameful treatment and fierce opposition he ran into there (1 Thess. 2:2). The church was later hounded by

25. Gaston, "Paul and the Law in Galatians 2 and 3," 73–76.

26. I am indebted to the late and revered Nils A. Dahl for this insight, which he advanced in a paper given to the Paul Seminar of the Society of Biblical Literature at the 1973 meeting. The paper was entitled "Paul's Letter to the Galatians: Epistolary Genre, Content, and Structure."

27. The mention of the "imperial guard" and "those of the emperor's household" has led some to place the writing of Philippians in Rome during Paul's imprisonment there, but we now know the "imperial guard" was present in other cities, perched like frogs on the banks of the Mediterranean. Moreover, Philippians notes five communications between Paul and the church, and given the fact that it would have taken approximately eight weeks to traverse the distance between Rome and Philippi (some 730 miles by land), Ephesus seems a more likely candidate for Paul's imprisonment than Rome when Philippians was written.

outsiders (Phil. 1:29–30) and fractured by the pettiness and jealousy of insiders (3:2; 4:2–3). Some there preached the gospel out of love and respect for Paul; others preached out of partisanship (1:15–17). But throughout these difficulties, the relationship between Paul and the Philippian church remained warm, supportive, and affectionate. The Philippians supported Paul's mission financially when he was in Thessalonica (4:16) and possibly also in Corinth (2 Cor. 11:9). It gave generously to the Jerusalem collection (2 Cor. 8:1–5) and sent Epaphroditus to care for the apostle during his imprisonment (Phil. 2:25). Paul planned to return to Philippi on his way to Corinth (2 Cor. 2:13), and possibly again on his final visit to Jerusalem with the offering. And when in prison, Paul wrote movingly of his love and longing for the Philippian believers (Phil. 4:1).

When Paul wrote the letter from prison, one judicial hearing had already been held, and either Paul's condemnation (1:20; 2:17) or release (1:25; 2:24) seemed imminent. His mission continued, however, in spite of the chains. We hear that some both inside and outside the praetorian guard accepted Paul's witness (1:13). Also we hear that his testimony led to the conversion of some slaves and freedmen from Caesar's household (4:22). Through the courageous example of the apostle, timid believers became fearless (1:14). Word of Paul's imprisonment eventually leaked out to the congregation at Philippi, and considering their special reverence for him, the response was predictable, and the contacts continued. Those exchanges may be reconstructed as follows:[28]

The major objection to Ephesus as Paul's prison location is that neither he nor Acts mentions it. That silence, however, is hardly decisive, for Paul himself reports that he was imprisoned many times (2 Cor. 11:23) and suffered great affliction in Asia (2 Cor. 1:8). Moreover, Clement of Rome reports a generation later that Paul "wore chains seven times," and the later *Acts of Paul and Thecla* speaks of an Ephesian imprisonment (see Edgar Hennecke, *New Testament Apocrypha* [Philadelphia: Westminster Press, 1963–66], 2:338). Although these late traditions cannot qualify as primary evidence, they do offer important secondary support for Ephesus as Paul's imprisonment site. The decision on the provenance of the letter affects our dating of it and is relevant for the discussion of the emergence of Paul's theology. See my discussion of "Philippians, letter of," in the *Dictionary of Biblical Interpretation*, ed. John H. Hayes (Nashville: Abingdon Press, 1999), 2:280–83. In the letter Paul expresses the hope to visit Philippi a second time, which hardly seems likely from Rome. Moreover, as Romans explicitly tells us, even before Paul had reached Rome, his attention had already turned westward to Rome and beyond to Spain. In light of that preoccupation, a visit to Philippi from Rome would have required Paul to backtrack to the east before the launch of the Spanish mission. Therefore, I side with most scholars that an Ephesian provenance of the letter, even though conjectural, is the more likely possibility.

28. Philippians is so loosely structured that many have suggested that it is a patchwork of at least three letter fragments (Helmut Koester, "The Purpose of the Polemic of a Pauline Fragment [Philippians iii]," *New Testament Studies* 8 [1962]: 317n1). For

1. Having learned that Paul was a prisoner in Ephesus, the Philippians sent Epaphroditus with money for his support and with instructions for his care.
2. Paul sent a letter of thanks (now lost), and the bearer of that letter reported to the Philippians that Epaphroditus was very sick.
3. The Philippians wrote to Paul expressing:
   a. Their distress over the critical condition of Epaphroditus (2:26)
   b. A request for the return of Epaphroditus and perhaps an expression of regret that this illness prevented him from serving Paul as they intended (2:25–30)
   c. A report of a quarrel between two women in the congregation, Euodia and Syntyche (4:2–3)
   d. Concern over the efforts of local Jews to win (back?) converts that the church had gained from the God-fearers (3:2–16)
   e. Concern about immorality (3:17–20)
4. Paul sent the present letter (in whole or in part) with Epaphroditus (2:25–26)
5. A visit by Timothy to Philippi was planned, and he was to report back to Paul (2:19–23)
6. Paul planned a visit to Philippi if or when he was released (2:24)

Opposition

Have no fear of "opponents" (Phil. 1:28). Who were these opponents? What were they doing? What were they saying about Paul? Where did they come from? Although no precise description of the outlook of the opponents is possible, a rough sketch of their thought is possible. They were nagging Gentile followers to accept circumcision (3:2). They preached a partisan gospel designed to torment the imprisoned apostle (1:17). They rejected the importance of the cross (3:18) in favor of a glorious resurrected life. And they made a fetish of self-indulgence: "their god is the belly" (3:19). Owing to the absence of any sustained discussion of the law, it is unlikely that the opponents were Galatian-type Judaizers. Given their proclamation of Christ (1:17), they probably were not but might have been from the synagogue, although Jewish opposition did exist in another form in 2 Corinthians.

---

guidance here, I have followed the excellent essay by Philip Sellew, "*Laodiceans* and the Philippians Fragments Hypothesis," *Harvard Theological Review* 87 (1994): 17–28. Sellew argues that Polycarp's reference to "Paul's letters to you" in his letter to the Philippians is factually correct and that "the bishop means what he says and he knows what he is saying" (p. 24). Sellew finds additional support in the deuteropauline letter to the Laodiceans, which believes that Philippians is a collection of letter fragments and that the author has before him a copy of Philippians without 3:2–4:1. For a summary of this history, see Calvin Roetzel, "Philippians, Letter to the" in *The Dictionary of Biblical Interpretation*, 2:280–83.

The "opponents" were probably religious syncretists (see discussion on Galatians above on a Judaizing syncretism). To them Paul's gospel was just one ingredient among many in a religious stew. Circumcision was a sign and seal of the covenant. Initiation into the local mystery religion also allowed the neophyte to pass directly and completely from death to a mythic resurrected life. When added to Paul's gospel of grace and freedom in Christ, this religious stew could lead to an unusual configuration.[29]

An alternative view is that Paul addressed different types of opponents in this letter: Jews bent on winning back Gentile God-fearers, those who had slipped into immorality, and religious enthusiasts who were critical of Paul's gospel and its emphasis on the cross. Others suggest that Paul was slow to recognize the character of the opposition and is thus somewhat confused in his response. Given Paul's first confused defense of his apostolic fitness in 2 Corinthians 2:14–7:4 (minus 6:14–7:1), that is entirely possible.

Although both of these alternatives are tenable, they seem less persuasive than the first view. Given the range of Paul's opposition elsewhere, it is unlikely that he would have misjudged his opponents here. Moreover, if opposition were coming from such different groups, it is strange that the groupings are so indistinct in the letter.

Paul's Response

To those claiming to be already "saved," Paul spoke of "full" salvation as only a future possibility. In writing of sharing Christ's "sufferings" by becoming like him in his "death" in order to "attain the resurrection" in the future (3:10–11), Paul implicitly emphasized the provisional nature of present salvation and qualified the promise of his critics. A variation on the same theme appears elsewhere: "Not that I have already obtained this [resurrection] or have already reached the goal; but I press on to make it my own. . . . I press on toward the goal for the prize of the heavenly call of God" (3:12–14). Paul then called on the Philippians to imitate him and thus implicitly rejected the claimed view of those professing too much (3:15–17). His emphasis on the future not only undercut the smug and self-assured; it reassured those who stumbled and simultaneously exhorted them to "have this mind in you which was also in Christ Jesus." His recitation of the ancient Christian hymn in 2:6–11 enjoined obedience and looked forward to exaltation and triumph with Christ *in the future.*

---

29. See Walter Schmithals, "Die Irrelehrer des Philipperbriefs," *Zeitschrift für Theologie und Kirche* 54 (1957): 279ff.

Many read Paul's repudiation of his Jewish antagonists in 3:4–9 to mean that he rejected his Jewish past. Let us listen to his words: "Whatever gains I had [as a Jew], these I have come to regard as loss [dung] because of Christ" (3:7). This statement, however, is a part of Paul's polemic against the "dogs," a term loaded with contempt for those modifying his gospel and discrediting him by appealing to circumcision as the prerequisite to the new life. Paul responded in total disgust, pointing to his considerable achievements—his Pharisaic inclination, his Abrahamic connection, and even his blamelessness before the law—as "dung" (Phil. 3:8). This harsh term may suggest Paul's total rejection of his Jewish ancestry to some, but given his positive statements elsewhere (e.g., Rom. 9:1–5; 11:1; 2 Cor. 11:21b–25; 2 Cor. 3:7) and the affirmation of his Israelite heritage, Philippians 3:8 is less a repudiation made in the heat of an ugly exchange than a reevaluation of all of his experience, even his religious experience, in light of Christ.

In spite of the threats posed by internal strife and external invective, there is a genuine warmth and human tenderness in Philippians that is refreshing, especially when compared with the bitter clashes of Galatians and 2 Corinthians 10:1–13:10. Philippians shows that Paul was not always a stormy combatant or divine warrior. He was also a towering figure whose confidence in God's future led him with confidence to look past the worst that life could bring.

Outline of Philippians

1. Introduction, Salutation, and Thanksgiving	1:1–11
2. Paul's Imprisonment	1:12–26
3. Exhortation to Stand Firm against Opponents	1:27–2:18
4. Travel Plans	2:19–30
5. Letter Conclusion (Beginning)	3:1
6. Exhortation to Persevere in the Struggle against Judaizing Propaganda and Libertinism	3:2–4:1
7. Conclusion (Continuation)	4:2–23
a. Appeal for harmony	4:2–6, 8–9
b. Thanks for gifts (Possibly a fragment of a separate letter)	4:10–20
c. Closing greetings and benediction	4:7, 21–23

PHILEMON (CA. 56 CE)

Perhaps after stealing money (v. 18), Onesimus, a slave, ran away from his rich Christian master, Philemon, and Apphia. By coincidence, he found Paul in prison, converted to Christ, and assisted Paul in some way (v. 10). Paul wanted to keep Onesimus with him, and on the strength of his apostolic office he felt entitled to claim his service. Instead, he returned Onesimus to his master with this brief letter. In it Paul urged Philemon to restore Onesimus to his "household," treat him like a "beloved brother" (v. 16), and to refrain from meting out harsh punishment to which Onesimus was liable as a runaway and possible thief. That request gained weight in light of Paul's expectation of his own imminent release from prison and visit to Philemon (note his request: "Prepare a guest room for me," v. 22).

Colossians, a deuteropauline letter, in 4:9 has Onesimus traveling with Tychicus to Colossae, which might suggest that Philemon's residence was near Colossae. But that might be assuming too much, for that Colossians was by Paul is doubtful, and even if it were, to find useful evidence in it for locating Philemon's home would require that the trip of Onesimus that Colossians mentions be the same trip Paul mentioned in Philemon.

If, as many scholars hold, the Pauline authorship of Colossians is doubtful, then it is possible that the reference to Onesimus was scribed there under influence from Philemon. On this question it is best to plead ignorance and say honestly that we do not know where Philemon lived.

Outline of Philemon

1. Salutation	1–3
a. Paul as sender	1a
b. Recipients: Philemon, Apphia, Archippus, and the church	1b–2
c. Greeting	3
2. Thanksgiving	4–7
3. Body of Letter	8–22
a. Return of Onesimus	8–20
b. Apostolic visit	21–22
4. Conclusion	23–25
a. Final greeting	23–24
b. Grace and benediction	25

ROMANS (CA. WINTER OF 57–58 CE)

Letter Integrity

There once were three different manuscript versions of Romans: one ending with chapter 14, one with chapter 15, and one with chapter 16. But which one went to Rome? The scholarly consensus is that it was not the shortest version (chaps. 1–14 plus the benediction in 16:25–27), which was used, if not created, by Marcion, a second-century "heretic."[30] Given Marcion's tendency to take the

---

30. The use of the term "heretic" to apply to the early period is anachronistic, for it was only later—some would say much later—that the church gained the power to

knife to disagreeable texts and his distaste for the "Old Testament" (his term), Paul's praise of the Jewish Scriptures in 15:9–12 and 15:21 may have inspired their amputation (16:25–27). Since shorter versions of the letter surface in Latin manuscripts, however, Marcion may have simply adopted one of those.

More tenable is the view that Paul's original letter to Rome contained only chapters 1–15, plus a concluding benediction that was removed to make way for chapter 16. Some hold that chapter 16 was a later work, perhaps by Paul himself, and was probably sent to a church in the east. Because Paul spent much time there, the leading candidate for that honor is Ephesus. Even if chapter 16 were written at the same time as chapters 1–15, it was not a part of the same letter and can hardly be used to ascertain anything about the Roman situation.

The argument that the long version (chaps. 1–16) went to Rome raises a host of questions. Would Paul have known twenty-six Christians in Rome whom he could greet by name (16:3–15)? Since no other Pauline letter conclusion greets addressees by name, one wonders whether, even had Paul known twenty-six Christians in Rome, he would have greeted them. Then other letters mention many of those greeted as earlier being with Paul in the east. Prisca and Aquila were working with Paul in Ephesus when 1 Corinthians 16:19 was written (ca. 53 CE). Had they now returned to Rome (ca. 57 CE)? Paul greets Andronicus and Junia (Rom. 16:7), as "fellow" prisoners in Ephesus presumably. Had they also moved to Rome? Paul calls Epaenetus "the first convert in *Asia*" (16:5 AE), but now he also is in Rome. While such a mass movement of Paul's acquaintances to Rome may sound improbable to us, it was certainly possible.

Approximately three years before Paul wrote Romans, Nero had lifted the edict of Claudius (of 49 CE) expelling Jews from Rome (see below). In that interim between 54, when Nero lifted the edict, and Paul's dictation of Romans (57 or 58), there would have been sufficient time for Jewish Christians to return to Rome from the east, and had they done so, they might now offer a valuable bridge between Paul the apostle and the Roman churches. Such a return would explain the anomaly of Paul's final greeting.

Harry Gamble has provided textual evidence persuasive to some that chapter 16 originally belonged to the textual tradition that has Paul send this entire letter to Rome.[31] The final benediction condemning false doctrine

---

define and enforce orthodox positions. In the time of Paul, multiple versions of the gospel were disputed, and acceptance came through persuasion rather than force. As late as the fourth century Augustine was one of the first to justify physical coercion as a valuable instrument to enforce doctrinal correctness.

31. See Harry Y. Gamble, *The Textual History of the Letter to the Romans* (Grand Rapids: Eerdmans, 1977).

(16:17–19), however, points to a later situation in the east (see 2 Corinthians and Philippians), and given the multigeneration gap between Paul's dictation of the letter and the textual evidence we have, that witness is not credible. Whatever its genealogy, our challenge is to make sense of our current text.

Background of the Roman Church

We do not know who founded the Roman churches or when they were established. We know only that they had already been in existence "for many years" before Paul wrote Romans (15:23), and that there was a church in Rome in the forties when the Emperor Claudius "expelled from Rome the Jews who were constantly stirring up a tumult under the leadership of Chrestus" (Suetonius, *Claudius* 25, in *The Lives of the Twelve Caesars*). Although Suetonius's report is vague, it probably referred to heated or violent arguments in the synagogue concerning Christ. Aquila and Prisca, Paul's coworkers in Corinth (1 Cor. 16:19), conceivably were among those expelled. Meanwhile Gentile believers remained in Rome, untouched by Claudius's ban. After the death of Claudius, Nero lifted the ban in 54 CE and allowed the return of Jewish Christians. Their return may have aroused tensions in the Roman churches between Jewish and Gentile factions (cf. Rom. 14:1–15:13).

Problems within the Church

Scholars disagree about the purpose of Romans, and no thesis adequately accounts for its existence. Chapter 14 shows Paul was aware of conflict between Christians, probably Jewish and Gentile believers. One explanation suggests that a Gentile emphasis on Paul's doctrine of justification by grace, apart from works of the law, encouraged licentious tendencies (1 Cor. 5–6), and returning Jewish Christians might have taken umbrage at the moral laxity of Gentile believers and their view that the gospel forbade the observance of dietary rules (chap. 14). In spite of Gentile disdain, some Jewish believers ("weak") preferred eating no meat (14:2) to eating ritually unclean meat (14:14). Similarly, abstention from wine routinely offered to pagan gods before its sale (14:21) avoided the sin of idolatry (14:2). It was better to risk being a Jewish follower scrupulously obedient to Torah than to offend against conscience; such fervent Torah observance was preferable to encouraging immorality through emphasis on justification by grace. Enough immorality existed among Gentile followers (cf. 1 Cor. 5–7) to lend substance to the salacious rumors that Gentile rejection of the law encouraged an egregious lawlessness.

Paul had already objected to such charges with cutting rhetorical questions: "Should we continue in sin in order that grace may abound?" (6:1); "Should we sin because we are not under law but under grace?" (6:15); "Is the law sin" (7:7). The accusation that Paul encouraged the slogan "let us do 'bad things' that good may come" (3:8 AT) sparked an angry retort.

Another plausible reason for Paul's Romans was that it responded to the charge that his Gentile gospel implied that "God's promises [to Israel] had failed" (9:6). Because such a charged accusation had been flung at him before, Paul was in a position to pose rhetorical questions implying a strong negative answer: "Never, never, never! (*mē genoito!*)" (9:14 AT). Jewish Christians active in both synagogue and church were regularly ridiculed and harassed from non-Christian Israelites. Thus Jewish Christians, reviled by Gentiles for being overly scrupulous and charged by synagogue leaders with encouraging lax behavior, were in a bind. Why, these leaders might ask, do not the Gentiles first become proselyte Jews, if they wish to become heirs of God's promises? Moreover, Jewish followers claiming to be no longer "under law but under grace" may have abandoned the synagogue altogether, and were vulnerable to the charge of being called apostates (6:15). Some might ask, What kind of gospel was this that prompted believers to jettison the law as God's good gift and begin the slide into immorality? How could anyone be law observant and also accept a gospel that rejected the law? More importantly, what kind of a God is it who would make promises to Abraham and not keep them? The climax to the opening part of Romans, chapters 9–11, single-mindedly devoted itself to that question.

It is possible also that Paul wrote to garner support for his Spanish mission. Though he clearly sought the support of the Roman churches, it is unlikely that such heavy discourse was needed to serve that purpose *only*. But churches divided might bring support for the Spanish mission to more Gentiles into question. Finally, although the theologizing in Romans is profound—some would even say unsurpassed—the letter is not, as Dodd once claimed, a calm, cool, collected summary of Paul's theology, offered as a kind of valedictory at the end of a stormy apostolic career. If that were the case, the absence of a single reference in this letter to the cross, a dominant theme of the recently scribed Corinthian letters, is puzzling indeed.[32]

---

32. Among an entire shelf of excellent commentaries on Romans, those by Leander Keck and Joseph Fitzmyer stand out. See Joseph Fitzmyer, *Romans: A New Translation and Introduction and Commentary* (New York: Doubleday & Co., 1992). More recent and more accessible is that of Leander E. Keck, *Romans*, Abingdon New Testament Commentaries (Nashville: Abingdon Press, 2005), and the monumental Hermeneia commentary by Robert Jewett, *Romans, A Commentary* (Minneapolis: Fortress Press, 2007), whose bibliography is massive. Also recent, substantive, and

Response of Paul

Unlike Paul's other letters, Romans was written to a church he had neither founded nor visited. It named no adversary and attacked no opponent. Yet, like other Pauline epistles, Romans is a genuine letter, not a treatise on systematic theology. Although its depth of insight is great, it has the structure of a letter, breathes the warmth of a letter, deals with a real situation, and functions like a letter as a substitute for absence. Written on the heels of Paul's heated exchanges with the Corinthian and Galatian churches, Romans echoes many of the concerns of those letters (e.g., references to Adam and Christ, the law, Abraham, the love commandment, the faithfulness of Jesus Christ, salvation for Gentiles, God's righteousness, the offering, election, and emphases on judgment and vindication).

But Romans is also quite definitely distinct from Paul's other epistles and is by no means simply a reflective summary of the wisdom gleaned from Paul's turbulent dealings with other churches. In this letter Paul mentions neither Judaizers (Galatians), nor enthusiasts (1 Corinthians), nor itinerant Jewish Christian apostles (2 Corinthians and Philippians), nor the cross and the Eucharist, and, excepting 16:1–24, it makes no reference to the church. When Paul wrote, the Roman churches were troubled, but they were not "sectarian." As Paul said, "I myself feel confident about you, my brothers and sisters, that you yourselves are full of goodness, filled with all knowledge, and able to instruct one another" (5:14). About some things, Paul wrote to strengthen and be strengthened by them (1:11–12). He hoped to reconcile a church divided, to build a base from which to launch his Spanish mission (15:24, 28), to defend his gospel to the Gentiles, and to respond to criticisms threatening the future of his ministry (see 2 Corinthians and Galatians).

Since he had never visited Rome, the situation was delicate. The Gentile majority might resent his intrusion. The Jewish faction, after hearing the rumor that Paul was a dangerous and even reckless innovator, might understandably have been less than overjoyed at the prospect of a visit from this pariah from the east. In the discussion below, we shall note how carefully Paul addressed that Roman situation. He opened the salutation with a defense of his apostolic credentials (deemed specious by some) and the truth of his gospel for *all* (Jew and Greek). In spite of the vituperation heaped on Paul by his critics in the east, he offered no apology: "I am not ashamed of the gospel; for

helpful to specialist and nonspecialist, see Arland J. Hultgren, *Paul's Letter to the Romans, A Commentary* (Grand Rapids: Eerdmans, 2011). Also a favorite for many is the commentary of James D. G. Dunn, *Romans*, Word Biblical Commentary, 2 vols. (Dallas: Word Books, 1988).

it is the power of God for *all* those believing, Jew and Greek" (AE). Then Paul mentally composed the thematic head of the letter, "for in it [i.e., the gospel] the righteousness of God is being revealed out of the faithfulness [of Christ] unto faith [in Christ] and whoever is righteous out of faith shall live" (1:17 AT). Paul needed an endorsement of this basic premise if his mission were to gain support in Rome, the empire's center (15:22–24). For him, God's righteousness denoted no quality of divine being but rather a divine *action* through Messiah Jesus to reclaim a crooked world, to raise up the fallen, and to offer liberation from the "powers that be," manifest in and through the faithfulness of Christ (3:21–22).

Paul wrote that the coming of Christ exposed the historical failure of both Jews and Gentiles either to do the will of God or to render the thanks due. Therefore, boasting by Jew and arrogance by Gentile were both excluded, for "all have sinned and fallen short of the glory of God." Since all "have sinned and fallen short" (3:23 AT), all without exception stand in equal need of the means of grace offered through the faithfulness of Christ (3:21–24). Thus Paul's gospel included, but transcended, individual salvation and assumed cosmic proportions in the announcement of redemption from the tyranny of the cosmic, demonic, enslaving, and alienating powers of Sin and Death and offered a remedy for their human bondage, brokenness, and alienation.

In 4:1–22 Paul invoked Abraham as a model for his inclusive gospel. In Galatia, his Judaizing opponents appealed to the example of Abraham's circumcision (Gen. 17:9–14) to refute Paul's welcome of Gentile males into God's elect without circumcision. But here an apocalyptically driven Paul offered the Abraham story as support for his inclusive gospel; see Genesis 15:1–6, where Abraham received and believed in the promises of God *before* receiving circumcision. In Abraham's faith or trust in God, reckoned to him as "righteousness" while he was still a Gentile (i.e., before circumcision), Paul claimed a precedent for his Gentile gospel and showed that his gospel did not overthrow the law (3:31) but secured its deeper meaning. (Note that the proclamation of "righteousness by faith" was no substitute of one work ["faith" or belief] for another ["works by the law"]. Abraham's trust did not make him righteous. Rather, his faith was the trusting acceptance of the efficacy of God's gracious, righteous work.)

Later, in 5:12–21, Paul responded to the query as to how one man's act of righteousness, namely, that of Jesus, could redound to others. In response, he argued from the first Adam to the last; just as through the disobedience of Adam others who sinned shared his fate, namely, death (Gen. 2:15–3:24), so now through "one man's act of righteousness" justification and life became available for all (Rom. 5:18). Paul's summary—where "sin increased, grace abounded all the more" (5:20) inspired a slanderous jibe: "Should we continue in sin in order that grace may abound?" (6:1; 3:8). Paul was keenly sensitive to the malicious charge that his Gentile gospel turned immorality into a pathway to grace. (Recall that, in Corinth and Philippi at least, some had understood salvation by grace outside the law to mean that all things were lawful. In those cities certain libertines seemed to anticipate Herod's caricature of grace found in W. H. Auden's *For the Time Being: A Christmas Oratorio:* "I like committing crimes. God likes forgiving them. Really the world is admirably arranged."[33])

Drawing on three metaphors—baptism, slavery, and marriage—Paul pointedly asked how anyone sharing the life of the new age could continue behaving like a member of the old. Baptism represented more than the initiation into the new creation, liberation from Master Sin, and symbolic participation in the death of Christ with no preconditions whatsoever. Being raised up with Christ carried a requirement to walk in "newness of life" (6:4). Being liberated from the tyranny of slavery to Sin's grip freed one to submit to the righteousness of God and to resist Sin's imperialism (6:12–23). How, Paul wondered, could a believer who had died to sin continue in its bondage (6:1–14)? Paul also pointed to the way the death of a husband freed the spouse to remarry and "bear fruit" (children) in a new relationship. Similarly, those who had died to the law, Paul asserted, were free from the law of marriage to join with and bear fruit for Christ in another relationship (7:1–6).

Drawing on these images, Paul aimed to correct the impression that his gospel encouraged immorality. He then rose to respond to the question posed by his last metaphor, namely, death to the law freeing the spouse to remarry: "Is the law [therefore] sinful?" (7:7). It was not bad Torah that brought sin and death, Paul bristled (7:12, 16, 21–23; 8:2), but rather the crooked human heart. Calling God's gift (Torah, law) "evil" questioned divine nature and implied a sacred being whose will was so dark and nature so sinister as to offer malevolent gifts to children. Paul submitted that it was the creature's crooked heart that twisted the law into a grotesque caricature that brought death. The law may forbid one to "covet [desire]" (7:7), he argued, but human nature most desires the forbidden. The fault is not in the law or the God who gave it but in the creature itself. Thus it is the *misuse* of the law, not the law itself, that "brings death" (7:13).

Two problems face the reader in (7:13–25): (1) the ambiguity of the term "flesh" (e.g., "nothing good dwells in my . . . flesh"); and (2) uncertainty about how Paul employed the term "I." As an Israelite, Paul would have been unable to attribute evil to "flesh" per se, for even if it was humankind's Achilles' heel,

---

33. See W. H. Auden, *Collected Poems*, ed. Edward Mendelson (NewYork: Random House, 1976), 303.

flesh itself was morally neutral. Through the flesh and its desires, humanity was vulnerable to King Sin (sing).

After gaining a foothold, the evil impulse (Heb. *yetzer*) that took up residence in the flesh could corrupt the whole person. It was possible for the flesh to be corrupted, but the flesh was not in and of itself a corrupting element. Paul referred to this corrupted element when he said "nothing good dwells within me, that is in my flesh," (7:18), but when he did so, he meant not that the physical was evil, but that the person had fallen victim to the power of Sin. When Paul spoke of those who lived "according to the flesh" (8:12), he referred to those whose flesh was taken captive by that demonic power.

The second problem concerns Paul's use of the term "I" in 7:7–25. His use of the first person singular, coupled with the past tense and the apparent parallel he drew between himself and Adam (man) of Genesis, suggest that Paul was speaking autobiographically and thus referring to his own personal experience. It is more likely, however, that Paul used the first person singular to refer not to his personal experience but representatively to all human beings. For example, note 1 Corinthians 13, where the Greek emphatic "I" (*egō*) is not employed, but the first person singular is clearly used. Therefore, this Romans passage probably should not be read as an allusion to Paul's inability to keep the law in its entirety, for earlier, in Philippians 3:4–6, he suggested, on the contrary, that he once was blameless before the law.

The "law of the Spirit," (Rom. 8:1–2), Paul believed, offered a remedy from enslaving powers and freed one from the law [principle] of sin and death; here the term "death" recalled Genesis 2:17, where disobedience led to death. That liberation frees one, he claimed, to walk "after [NRSV 'according to'] the Spirit" (8:4). Paul's theologizing here is one of hope, enabling him to see God working "*in all things*" (8:28 AE). While honestly acknowledging human mortality and weakness, frustration and fear, and trauma and distress, Paul asserted that believers in all of earth's vicissitudes were "more than conquerors through him who loved us" (8:38).

Then follows Paul's tightly reasoned climax to the first part of the letter. In the face of the accusation, perhaps inspired by the position Paul took on law (Torah) in Galatians, he had to defend his Gentile gospel and respond to the accusing question, were God's promises to Israel trustworthy? Only here in the authentic letters did Paul respond to this hostile accusation that his Gentile gospel impugned God's fairness.

With deep pain Paul recognized the rejection of Messiah Jesus by most Jews, and he began with a poignant pathos: "I have great sorrow and unceasing anguish in my heart" for my people (9:2). Echoing Moses' prayer that God would substitute his life for the sin of a wayward people (Exod. 32:30–32), Paul cried out, "I could wish that I myself were accursed and cut off from

Christ for the sake of my own people" (9:3). Avoiding a spiritualization of Israel's election, Paul praised God for Israel's special privileges: the glory, the covenants, the law, the worship and the promises, *and* the Messiah "according to the flesh" (9:4–5). Instead of qualifying that history, Paul praised God for it (9:5). It will soon be obvious to the reader who carefully works through his complicated and passionate reasoning that he inserted his Gentile converts into that narrative.

After this introduction, Paul recalled the story of election to affirm God's freedom to choose Gentiles and emphatically denied that the "word of God has failed" or that the divine promises were unreliable (9:6). Paul then argued that God's goodness required a freedom to choose Gentiles qua Gentiles in the elect. But paradoxically, he asserted, God's temporary rejection of Jews was no contradiction of the long-term divine promises to Israel, and divine election, even if arbitrary, was neither unjust nor transitory (9:14–29). *All* (Jew and Gentile) who turn to God will experience salvation (10:12–13). Finally, their rejection of the apocalyptic gospel was not final (11:1–32). If the temporary rejection of the Jews led to the inclusion of Gentiles (11:7–32)—Paul's normal order, Jew first and then also the Gentile, would be reversed to allow Gentiles to go first—that, he expected, would provoke the Jews to jealousy, leading to their salvation. Then God's strange and cunning game plan would have worked. In the end, Paul emphatically asserted, "all Israel will be saved" (11:26), and "the gifts and calling of God are irrevocable" (11:29 AT).

Elsewhere I have argued that the unbearable tension of this argument was resolved through a racing metaphor (*Myth*, 129–31) that offered a radical and countercultural solution: winners in competition did not, as cultural dogma dictated, require losers; God's inclusion of Gentiles in the elect required neither the rejection of Israel nor the repudiation of promises made. The solution to this great dilemma was, Paul exclaimed, hidden in some divine mystery that surpassed human understanding (11:25). In the inspiration of that moment he launched into a soaring benediction:

> O the depth of the riches and wisdom and knowledge of God! How unsearchable are his judgments and inscrutable his ways!
> "For who has known the mind of the Lord?
>   Or who has been his counselor?"
> "Or who has given a gift to him, to receive a gift in return?"
> For out of him and through him and to him are all things. To him be glory forever. Amen.
>
> *(11:32–36)*

In this brief summary of chapters 9–11 we glimpse tensions so great that they extend Paul's logic to the breaking point. The radical solution that he proposed reconfigured the world in a dramatic way for both Jew and Gentile. This reconfiguration was no abstract exercise but came through Paul's creative reinterpretation of the election tradition. Paul's seminal mind thus offered a solution that affirmed the validity of God's promises to Israel while extending the scope of those promises. The summary of Paul's argument in his own words runs: "As regards the gospel they [the Israelites] are enemies of God for your [i.e., you Gentiles'] sake; but as regards election they are beloved, for the sake of the ancestors; for the gifts and the calling of God are irrevocable" (11:28–29).

Despite its radical depth, Paul's solution did not long go unchallenged, and he would probably have been heartbroken had he lived to see the later separation. His floundering and much maligned Gentile mission succeeded beyond his expectation, and in a century the Gentile majority abandoned his conviction of the importance of its ties to Israel. By the second century Justin argued that Jewish Christians would be excluded from salvation (*Dialogue with Trypho* 47), and Jerome later ridiculed Jewish Christians who wished "to be both Jews and Christians . . . and are neither" (*Selected Letters* 112.13). While Paul's construction in Romans 9–11 was innovative or even brilliant, his attempt to admit difference without ascribing otherness was more difficult to sustain than to assert.

Paul was also alive to the charge that his gospel of salvation apart from the law encouraged immorality. He had already argued in Romans 6–8 that the freedom secured by the gospel provided no license for misconduct. Now in Romans 12–15 he extended that argument.[34] He admonished all addressees to present their bodies as "a living sacrifice, holy and acceptable to God," as their daily "spiritual worship" (12:1). He urged all with special gifts to use them to build up the church (12:3–8; cf. 1 Cor. 12); he exhorted all to genuine love, to perseverance in suffering, to generosity to outsiders, to nonretaliation (12:9–21), to respect for governing authorities (13:1–10), and to the reconciliation of the "weak" and the "strong" (14:1–15:21).

Paul's preoccupation with the outsider segued into his discussion of the believers' relationship to "governing authorities." The influence Romans 13 has had on the Christian view of the state through the centuries requires our attention. In spite of the sometime charge that this passage from Paul's pen encouraged the acceptance of Hitler's rule by Christians, its appearance here forces us to ask how this discussion related to Paul's wider epistolary purposes. Paul had already declared Jesus as the head of the new

---

34. Victor Furnish, *Theology and Ethics in Paul* (Nashville: Abingdon Press, 1968), has correctly shown that the ethical instruction in Paul's letters is hardly restricted to the closing "paraenetic" sections of the letters.

humanity (5:18) and proclaimed him Lord *(Kyrios)* for the believer (5:15–16 and 10:9).

He was painfully aware that eschatological enthusiasm had led believers elsewhere to disregard the claims of this world (see discussion of 1 Thessalonians and 1 Corinthians above). Perhaps believers in Rome had heard that Paul's gospel of the new age encouraged believers elsewhere to neglect or even abandon the present, provisional order in favor of God's rule. By withholding taxes and civil service from the "earthly" kingdom, they may have dared to affirm a commitment to a kingdom not of this world (Paul himself wrote the Philippians that their citizenship *(politeuma)* was in heaven, Phil. 3:20). He may have been responding here to the accusation that his gospel encouraged an irresponsible disengagement from this world.

In response, Paul reaffirmed the otherworldly character of his gospel *and* its this-worldly imperative. He exhorted, "Do not be conformed to this world" (Rom. 12:2), and almost simultaneously added, "Be subject to the governing authorities" (13:1), and "pay taxes to whom taxes are due" (13:7). There was no need for Paul to launch a campaign to reform the government. Why should he?

His conviction was that "the day of the Lord was at hand" (13:12) and that the "form *(schēma)* of this world" was passing away (1 Cor. 7:31) and would bring revolutionary change. The nearness of the end, however, far from canceling out civic duty, gave it cosmic significance. As the grand assize neared, Paul held, the opportunity for witness became more limited and the need for it more urgent; therefore, believers were to seize the day to witness. Although the state provided an orderly context for travel and witness, Paul's intention was to urge the use of the civic realm to give love concrete expression for neighbor, broadly defined to include "authorities" (13:3), persecutors (12:17), and all others—outsiders as well as the proximate "other" or offending, hostile "insider" (14:1–15:13). In the fifties, when Paul wrote this letter, Christ believers had not yet been targeted for systematic persecution. One must wonder what Paul might have said had he lived to see the brutal and localized persecution of Christians by Nero only a decade later.

In 14:1–15:13 Paul turned to deal with peace within the community of the faithful: "Welcome one another . . . as Christ has welcomed you," he admonished (15:7). He urged mutual respect and tolerance of difference between the "weak" and the "strong." He pleaded for the acceptance of those who were different, for example, those with dietary scruples and those without them, those with power and those without it.

The close of the letter allows the western horizon of Paul's mission to break into view: "I will set out by way of you to Spain" (15:28). With the

Caesarea Maritima Marble Columns
(Courtesy of Calvin J. Roetzel; used by permission)

mission in the east completed (15:19), with the offering project for the "poor among the saints" collected and the delivery delegation gathered to carry the collection (15:25–27), Paul's mind raced ahead from Corinth to Jerusalem, then back to Rome and beyond to Spain. As spring neared and the sea calmed, allowing the journey's launch, Paul grew ever more anxious and begged the Roman churches to pray for the success of the mission. His hopes for the success of the mission mingled with fears that it would fail. Paul had every right to be anxious. His last encounter with Peter in Antioch was angry. The people of James who followed him like a truth squad out to correct his gospel incited his wrath (Gal. 2:12). His relationship with the synagogue was a tortured one; he reported five times receiving forty lashes less one from synagogue authorities (2 Cor. 11:24). Moreover, gift giving in Paul's Roman world was very complex and complicated. Should the gift not be deemed acceptable, the rejection would symbolize a repudiation of solidarity of Jewish believers with Gentile gift bearers. A rejection would heap shame and humiliation on Gentile converts presenting it.

After Paul dictated Romans, his voice fell silent. The letters themselves offer no information on how the offering was received. The much-later Acts account (ca. 120) suggests that the pilgrimage to Jerusalem did not end as Paul had hoped for, worked for, suffered for, and eventually died for (Acts 21:17–40). The attempt by Paul and one or some of his Gentile converts to enter the temple, Acts claims, was judged to be provocative and led to an accusation of a desecration of the holy place (Acts 21:28). That in turn provoked Paul's arrest and dispatch to Rome for trial.

But using Acts as a source requires care.[35] It was a later document, tends to blame Jews for the death of Jesus and the stoning of Stephen (7:59), and claims a Roman citizenship for Paul that the letters nowhere report. It is significant that even Acts sets Paul on the way to Rome for trial but interrupts the travelogue before he was tried. So from Acts we do not know how the story ends. That was to come in a late-second-century legendary account, *The Acts of Paul and Thecla*,[36] that placed Paul's trial and execution in Rome under Nero.

So perhaps it is best that we are left to conjure an ending consistent with Paul's gospel. He did indeed harbor a dream that one day God's elect Israel and Gentile converts would join to celebrate the world that the offering symbolized and Paul envisioned, a world in which there would be neither "Jew nor Greek" among the elect (Gal. 3:28). But Paul's apocalyptic vision sketched by the letters (e.g., 2 Cor. 9) envisioned an unfinished world "groaning" for fulfillment (Rom. 8:22).

In any case, when Paul's ship moored for the last time, he left behind a rich legacy to be debated in the second century. Although his letters focus on contextual issues and thus have an ad hoc character, they bear witness to a fierce struggle to secure the legitimacy of a Gentile mission that did not negate Israel's special privileges (Rom. 11:29). The multiple challenges Paul faced in the churches presented him with occasions for fresh theologizing. In Galatians and Romans, Paul was pushed to the limit to articulate a vision that would hold the church together and be faithful to his gospel. The letter fragments in 2 Corinthians reveal what a dynamic and creative thinker he was, in his offering of a revolutionary vision of the marks (power in weakness) of apostolic legitimacy. And nowhere more than in 1 Corinthians does a clear picture emerge of the diplomatic and pastoral skills he needed to hold a fractious church together.

While Paul found much in the churches that was repugnant—immorality, religious puffery, arrogance, greed, and simple selfishness—he preached a gospel that spoke of God's embrace of this lumpish lot *being saved* in Christ (i.e., a process). Through bitter struggles with rival apostles and errant churches, Paul's understanding of life in Christ, the Spirit's work, and the nature of apostleship received varying and sometimes brilliant interpretations

35. Parts of Luke's account give rise to considerable skepticism, however. Most especially, the emphasis in Acts on Paul's Roman citizenship cannot be taken without question. See Calvin Roetzel, *Paul: The Man and the Myth* (Minneapolis: Fortress Press, 1999), 19–22.

36. Edgar Hennecke, *New Testament Apocrypha* (Philadelphia: Westminster Press, 1963–66), 2:253–57.

and reinterpretations. But the second-century Christian thinkers focused less on his theologizing than on his miracle working, celibacy, and martyrdom.

Finally, if chapter 16 were a part of the original letter to Rome, then came Paul's greetings. There Paul greeted twenty-six people, ten of whom were important women in the church (16:1–23). The list includes such notables as Phoebe, a deacon, who may have delivered and interpreted the letter to the Roman churches (16:1), and Junia, the only woman the New Testament called an apostle (16:7). Is she now an apostolic presence in Rome? Then there was the couple, Prisca and Aquila, who had been coworkers of Paul but may now have relocated.[37] Although few if any scholars deny the Pauline authorship of Romans 16, at this stage there is no scholarly consensus as to whether this chapter was a part of the original letter.

Outline of Romans

1. Address and Salutation		1:1–7
2. Thanksgiving		1:8–12
3. Autobiographical Introduction		1:13–17
4. God's Wrath Now Being Revealed		1:18–3:20
a.	Judgment on Gentiles	1:18–2:16
b.	Judgment on Jews	2:17–3:20
5. God's Righteousness Revealed		3:21–5:21
a.	Through faithfulness of Christ	3:21–31
b.	Through Abraham, patron of Gentiles	4:1–25
c.	Through Christ for all	5:1–11
d.	Bringing acquittal, life, grace	5:12–21
6. Defense of the Ethical Dimension of His Gospel		6:1–8:39
a.	Three metaphors with ethical implications	
(1)	Baptism	6:1–14
(2)	Slavery	6:15–23
(3)	Marriage	7:1–6
b.	Is the law sin? "Absolutely not!"	7:7–25
c.	Law of the Spirit	8:1–39
7. Reliability of God's Promises		9:1–11:36
a.	Israel's special privileges	9:1–5
b.	God's freedom to choose	9:6–13
c.	Divine justice or not?	9:14–18
d.	Divine fairness or not?	9:19–33
e.	God not arbitrary	10:1–21
f.	God has not rejected Israel	11:1–10
g.	God's game plan for including Gentiles	11:11–36

---

37. See the late and important work of Susan Mathew, *Women in the Greetings of Romans 16:1–16: A Study of Mutuality and Women's Ministry in the Letter to the Romans* (London: T. & T. Clark, 2013).

CONCLUSION

We have come to the end of our discussion of the letters as conversations. We have confined our treatment to the undisputed Pauline letters, for in those letters it is easier to see that we are dealing with real letters, highly personal in nature, intensely particular in their discussion of problems, and essentially *con*versational in talking *with* not *at* others. I hope that reading the letters as conversation will help the reader appreciate their dynamic and interactive character and their theological depth and insight and will assist in reading them as real conversations about matters of singular importance rather than as static deposits of theological truth waiting to be mined for their treasure.

6

Paul and His Myths

To the person on the street, the term "myth" is synonymous with "fiction" or "untruth." Because the old stories about gods, devils, witches, and talking donkeys and snakes seem quaint, they are shelved, assigned a place with other relics from humanity's infancy. But could it be that myths from the archaic past do not reflect primeval ignorance and superstition so much as they reveal the heights and depths the human spirit reaches when it wrestles with questions about life and death, love and hate, fate and freedom, truth and falsehood? Could it be that myth and legend mirror not what really happened in the ancestral period but rather the soul's response of a people to what happened? Even if unhistorical, could myth be, like art for Picasso, "a lie that makes us realize the truth"? As important as it is to know "what really happened," do we also need to know how men and women responded to those happenings? Increasingly, anthropologists, historians of religion, and biblical scholars are turning their scrutiny to myth and legend because mythological materials provide a living window on women and men of an earlier time expressing their inmost imaginings. Such expressions often sensitize a people to the profundity and high originality of those peoples of old.

To avoid misunderstanding, we must distinguish myth from metaphor. The term "pig" is a graphic expression when applied to a male chauvinist, but it is hardly myth. When Paul calls himself a boxer who pummels his body into submission, he is using metaphor; when he recites the eucharistic formula, "This is my body," he is drawing on myth. Metaphor is descriptive and figurative language about an event, whereas mythological language is an event itself, transporting participants into a zone of sacred time and/or space. The breaking of the bread is more than picture language about Jesus' execution; it is an avenue

149

through which a worshiper may mythically enter the presence of the Redeemer figure and become what Bonhoeffer called, "a contemporary disciple."[1]

No definition of myth will entirely satisfy. Myth has been called a means of comprehending reality and of being apprehended by it, but this description is vague and too general. Henri Frankfort described myth as "a form of poetry which transcends poetry in that it proclaims a truth; a form of reasoning which transcends reasoning in that it wants to bring about the truth it proclaims; a form of action, of ritual behavior, which does not find its fulfillment in the act but must proclaim and elaborate a poetic form of truth."[2]

Although Frankfort's statement is helpful and evocative, it is more a poem about a poem than it is a useful definition of myth. G. van der Leeuw called myth "a spoken word, possessing decisive power in its repetition."[3] Although myth, like all forms of communication, is tied to the word, can its power be restricted to the word? The three statements above are sufficient to show the difficulty of defining myth. Because of this difficulty, most writers discuss instead myth's character and function, an approach that we will follow here.

THE WORLD VIEWED MYTHOLOGICALLY

In the first century, the relationship of both peasant and philosopher to the natural world was closely personal. Where we see a landscape of things stiff and mute, they saw a world redundant with life. Where we see an object passively waiting for our hands to put *it, this thing* to use, they saw a *Thou* actively forcing itself on human consciousness. Where we see an order defined by abstract laws, they saw both order and chaos as vehicles of will and intent. When the cloud rumbled or the wind roared, it happened because the clouds or wind decided to rumble or roar, or because their master commanded them: "Rumble!" or "Roar!"

The apostle Paul's experience of the nonhuman world was likewise a personal one. In Romans 8:22 he wrote of the world's participation in the final woes attending the birth of the new age and of the new creation. The earth's share, so Paul held, in human wretchedness went back to the dawn of creation, when as an innocent bystander it was forced to bear a part of the pain that followed Adam's disobedience. Earthquakes and storms, plagues and drought,

---

1. Before the great German martyr theologian Dietrich Bonhoeffer appropriated this term, it was on the lips of Søren Kierkegaard, *Philosophical Fragments*, trans. David F. Swenson (Princeton, NJ: Princeton University Press, 1962), 68.

2. Henri Frankfort, *Before Philosophy* (Baltimore: Penguin Books, 1963), 16.

3. Geradus van der Leeuw, *Religion in Essence and Manifestation*, trans. J. E. Turner (New York: Macmillan Co., 1938), 413.

snakes and disease, and pain and death were seen as signs of the futility and decay that nature suffered because its destiny was unwittingly linked from the very beginning with the destiny of humankind. In this view the creation shared not only the agony but also the ecstasy of the creature. For God acted in Christ, so Paul held, to redeem not only the wayward creature but also the burdened creation.

As its redemption neared, Paul believed, the creation stood on tiptoe waiting to share in the liberation of the human and nonhuman world (Rom. 8:19–21). All through the ages the creation has worn the image of its Creator. In spite of its distorted nature, the image of the Creator's power and deity has remained recognizable. Notwithstanding humankind's efforts to deface the image, the marks of God's power and deity have never been, he asserted, completely erased (Rom. 1:20). The Gentiles, he held, have always been able to recognize the fingerprints of the Creator on the creation (see Rom. 1:20–21).

Thus the creation, like the creature, suffered an alienation and dislocation that reached back to the primeval period, and nature, like human beings, continued to bear the image of its Maker, even if in a twisted form. We see that the alienation and hope that creature and creation shared made them kin. In spite of this feeling of kinship, however, the world also seemed alien to Paul. He spoke of breaking through the barriers that restricted his existence either by ascending to the third heaven (2 Cor. 12:2) or by being delivered from the struggles that attend life in the world (2 Cor. 5:8; 12:1–10). He saw his life unfolding in a world dominated by Satan (2 Cor. 4:4), and he perceived the unsteady footing of that world. "The present form of this world," he dictated, "is passing away" (1 Cor. 7:31). So Paul did not feel at home in the world as it was but looked forward to the time when the original divine order would be restored and all fear and dread between humanity and the world would be removed. As Paul thought, "When anyone is united to Christ, there is a new world; the old order has gone, and a new order has already begun" (2 Cor. 5:17 NEB).

MYTH AND CULT

In the secular West we tend to view time as an ever-flowing stream that bears its daughters and sons away. But in the cult of Paul's day, time stood still. It stopped and even reversed course as the celebrant mythically recited the acts of God or shared through the cult in the sacred deeds of an earlier day. (The term "cult" as used here refers to corporate worship or religious rites rather than to a fringe group or sect.)

In the celebration of the Passover today, for example, one can witness Jewish families that are indistinguishable from their neighbors in the clothes they wear, the jobs they hold, or the cars they drive. Yet in recalling the deliverance of the Hebrews from Egypt thousands of years ago, they speak as if they are somehow present in the events of the second millennium BCE. Most will never have been to Egypt. Yet in drinking the wine and eating the unleavened bread, they imaginatively or mythically share in the slavery and liberation of the Hebrews in ancient Egypt:

> We were Pharaoh's slaves in Egypt: [they recite] and the Lord our God brought us out therefrom with a mighty hand and an outstretched arm. Now if the Holy One, blessed be He, had not brought our fathers forth from Egypt, then we, and our children, and our children's children, would [still] be slaves to Pharaoh in Egypt.[4]

While to the outsider it may sound strange for an American Jew to speak solemnly of sweating in Pharaoh's quarry long ago, to the insider who views that bondage through the eyes of myth, the liberation that was effected then is experienced mythically once more. Through the cultic act, the worshiper participates in what is real for all time. While the key occurrences of both Judaism and Christianity are historical, for those within the traditions these events possess a vitality that goes beyond the facts of the events themselves. The past was never a "dead past."

As Jacob Neusner well said, "If we, too, the living, have been redeemed: then the observer no longer witnesses only historical men in historical time, but an eternal return to sacred time."[5] The great events that happened once upon a time continue to direct the course of the world and are experienced as current. Through the cult, the worshiper not only shares in the benefits of the primeval time but also finds an organizing center for the current disordered world.

In other instances, the old shepherd ritualistically jumps over his staff three times; the little girl, Mary, regularly calls for her four "friends" (stuffed animals) and her drink before going to sleep; the Inuit woman routinely bows her head to offer thanks both before and after eating her diet of raw fish on the dirt floor of her hut. All are celebrating a tiny slice of life, and for each one, these ritualistic gestures provide a structure for what otherwise would be an incoherent mass of activity.

In myth also an order is imposed. The order is not just any order but the order deemed true, the only order that is fundamentally real. In the Hebrew

4. *The Haggadah of Passover*, trans. Cecil Roth (London: Soncino Press, 1934), 11–12.

5. Jacob Neusner, *The Way of Torah: An Introduction to Judaism* (Belmont, CA: Dickenson Publishing Co., 1970), 17. Neusner develops these ideas at some length; see esp. chap. 1.

experience of the exile we see how even the terrors of history were integrated into a divine order and were thus made bearable because they were meaningful.

In 597 BCE the Babylonian army uprooted the Hebrews from Palestine and exiled them to Mesopotamia. Eventually the temple was destroyed, the daily sacrifice interrupted, and Jerusalem left in shambles. Babylonian troops were garrisoned in the "promised land" while the Hebrews were forcibly settled on the banks of the River Chebar near Babylon (in modern Iraq). There they raised their poignant cry, "How could we sing the LORD's song in a foreign land?" (Ps. 137:4). YHWH had promised them via Abraham "the holy land." Now Babylon had robbed Israel of that divine possession. That historical event raised the problem of theodicy (i.e., questioning God's justice) in the sharpest possible way. Was a god who would allow this to happen credible anymore? Had YHWH simply forsaken the people or reneged on the promise made to Abraham? Since Israel's existence had been defined by its relationship to YHWH, what would happen if the covenant were broken? Would Israel languish and die at the feet of its captors, or would it survive to stand at their grave?

Although a people may be powerless, it is hardly without power. In mythic ritual the Hebrews found strength in the celebration of the Sabbath to face and survive those historical terrors. The Babylonians could occupy the land, destroy the city, reduce the temple to ashes, desecrate the sacred objects, and exile its people; but they could not burn or destroy the Sabbath. On the Sabbath the Hebrews recalled how YHWH had created the world out of formlessness and chaos, or out of "waste and void" (Heb. *tohu we vohu*) and how the Creator had crowned the creation with the Sabbath itself (Gen. 1:1–2:4a). Thus on each Sabbath the Hebrews celebrated an order that was real for all time, an order as old and fundamental as the creation itself, an order that affirmed God's triumph over chaos. Empires might come and go, but this order would always remain. Each celebration of the Sabbath affirmed the confidence that the God who in the beginning had brought order out of chaos would conquer captivity's historical chaos as well. So the Sabbath ritual was a deep source of strength and hope.

In Paul's letters also we see how the liturgy of the church served as a bridge between the past and the present. In all of the early Christian churches baptism served as the rite of initiation, and a sacred communal meal was eaten regularly—although how regularly we do not know. In both of these sacred rites the church shared in God's redemption of the world. Strangely enough, for Paul the death and resurrection of Jesus, rather than his teachings, formed the glowing center of emphasis. In passing through the water (baptism) and in eating the bread and drinking the wine, the rites forged a bond with the crucified Jesus. In baptism the identification with Jesus was so complete that Paul spoke of being united with Christ in a death like his and looking forward to a share in a resurrection like his, of being baptized into his death (Rom. 6:3, 5), or even of being crucified with Christ (Rom. 6:6).

The immersion of the initiate in water simulated burial with Jesus; the emergence of the initiate from the water recapitulated Christ's resurrection. Through this rite the saving significance of the death *and* resurrection of Jesus was experienced or anticipated within the community, and the believer was linked with that which was deemed real for all time. As the spiritual says, in baptism the initiate asked, "Were you there when they crucified my Lord?" At the literal level, the answer is absolutely obvious: "No, I was not there." But at the mythic level a different answer is possible: "Yes, I was there."

Eliade's observation that "every ritual has a divine model"[6] applies to the Eucharist as well as to baptism. In 1 Corinthians 11:23–26 the eating of the bread and the drinking of the wine commemorate Jesus' last meal with his disciples. And the connection of this commemorative meal with the cross was thought to be so close that repetition of it spontaneously brought to mind Jesus' death. For example, Paul's recitation of the received eucharistic tradition placed the worshiper in a sphere of audacious power. Throughout the passage Jesus' death was emphasized to put the worshiper in the presence of Jesus' betrayal, torture, and death. Bread was broken, simulating the breaking of Jesus' body, and red wine was offered as a "new covenant in [the] blood." Finally, to underscore this motif, Paul added the exhortation, "as often as you eat this bread and drink the cup, you proclaim the Lord's *death* until he comes" (1 Cor. 11:26 AE). The proclamation of "the Lord's death" extended beyond a verbal announcement to suggest a mythic *participation* in the death.

In 1 Corinthians 10:1–13, however, Paul countered the Corinthian belief that the Eucharist was magical. He reminded the church that just as its life as the sacramental community was prefigured in Israel's wilderness wandering, so also its punishment for the abuse of its status was anticipated in the judgment of Israel. Israel's status as the "sacramental" community did not exempt it from retribution. Its murmuring brought capital punishment. Immorality and idolatry brought the fall of 23,000 on a single day. Tempting the Lord brought destruction by snakes. Likewise, Paul warned, being in a sacramental community exempted no one from God's judgment or condemnation. While to the modern reader such punishment appears to have been unnecessarily

---

6. Mircea Eliade, *The Myth of the Eternal Return*, trans. Willard R. Trask (New York: Pantheon Books, 1954), 21.

harsh, Paul appropriated that tradition because he assumed that the Corinthians shared his view of the power of the mythic realm celebrated in the ritual.

After citing the example of Israel and warning the Corinthians to "flee from the worship of idols," Paul offered, "The cup of blessing that we bless, is it not a participation (*koinōnia*) in the blood of Christ? The bread that we break, is it not a participation (*koinōnia*) in the body of Christ?" (1 Cor. 10:16 AT, AE). Today the word "koinonia" is used to denote everything from sensitivity groups to church campgrounds. When translated "fellowship," as is common, "koinonia" is taken to mean a spirit of jovial camaraderie. My one-time teacher, Ernst Käsemann, proposed that the word be rendered "falling into a sphere of domination."[7]

Because this eating of the bread (flesh) and drinking of the wine (blood) placed the worshiper in the zone of the sacred, Paul urged the Corinthians to purify themselves, lest they profane the "body." Even perfunctory obeisance to demonic powers, as in the pagan sacrificial meals or modern secular worship, was incompatible with this mythic participation. Because some believers persisted in attending the pagan sacrificial meals, however, and neglected to rid themselves of the taint of such unholy alliances, Paul held that illness and even death had entered the community. This sickness and death was not from natural causes but from the judging presence of the Lord in the cultic meal (1 Cor. 11:30). The radicality of Paul's instruction is most obvious in the way he fixed on the death of Jesus as the locus of God's redeeming activity. In mythic participation in this death and resurrection, the believer already mythically tasted victory over the destructive, negative, and sinister elements in the world and already enjoyed a foretaste of the reconciliation, love, and rejuvenation of the new creation.

Intimations of that promised reality came through participation mythically in an event in the past. But the promise contained in that past event awaited the future for its maturation. Thus the past, brought mythically into the present, became the basis of the future hope.

DEATH AS MODEL

Jesus' death functioned in Paul's writings not only as an earnest of God's future triumph but also as a model for action in the world of Paul's converts. In other words, Jesus' death was experienced not only in the cult but also in the daily round of work and play, eating and drinking, buying and selling, making love

---

7. Ernst Käsemann, "The Pauline Doctrine of the Lord's Supper," in *Essays in New Testament Themes* (London: SCM Press, 1964), 124.

and social interaction. Paul connected his own activity with the death of Jesus. Shipwreck, beatings, imprisonments, conflict, and strife all served as intimations of that death. Looking at the scars left by the "slings and arrows of outrageous fortune" (Shakespeare, *Hamlet, III.1*), Paul spoke of "carrying in . . . [his] body the death of Jesus" (2 Cor. 4:10). Scars etched on his back suffered in Jesus' service he called "marks of Jesus" (Gal. 6:17), an obvious allusion to the marks etched on Jesus' body by the beatings he suffered before his death and to the puncture wounds of crucifixion.

Since the hunger, thirst, nakedness, homelessness, persecution, and slander Paul endured duplicated the suffering of Jesus, and since it was received in service to the Lord, Paul felt that his suffering shared in God's redemptive work. Even the hurt and pain inflicted by the world was shouldered for the sake of that same world. Drawing on his own experience, Paul urged the Corinthians to follow him and share "in Christ's sufferings" (2 Cor. 1:5 RSV).

Many Corinthian converts, however, believed, as we noted above, that they had already overcome the world, that they were already "rich," already "filled," and already ruling (1 Cor. 4:8) and therefore had no need to share the world's incompleteness or futility and grief. Confident of their salvation, they celebrated their liberation from, not participation in, suffering. By citing his own humiliation and deprivation and calling on his converts to "be imitators of me," Paul undermined the claims of the Corinthians. He reminded them that neither their redemption nor the redemption of the world was complete. When Paul wrote, "I decided to know nothing among you except Jesus Christ, and him crucified" (1 Cor. 2:2), he stripped the Corinthians of their pretensions and brought them down to earth to view the reality of the world's hurt and the power of the cross (see 1 Cor. 1:17–25). As in 1 Thessalonians, so also in 1 Corinthians, Paul mythically made suffering into a symbol of honor: "You became imitators of us and of the Lord, for you received the word in much affliction" (1 Thess. 1:6 RSV).

In contrast, those who rejected Paul's example and indulged themselves he dubbed "enemies of the cross of Christ" (Phil. 3:17–18). It was not that sex and food were evil but that an obsession with them made it impossible to accept either the suffering or the power that accompanied the way of the cross. It is possible that the sexual excesses and gluttony at Philippi were fruits of an accommodation of the gospel to old pagan ways, but most scholars believe they sprang from a perversion of religious freedom. In Paul's view, God had been revealed in the cross. Now the transforming power of that moment was to be apprehended anew as it was remembered in both liturgy and the commonplace.

THE POWERS THAT BE

Although science ostensibly has freed us from superstition and fear, demons, monsters, and wormlike and larval beasts live on in our collective fantasy. Goblins and witches come out on All Hallows E'en (Halloween, or evening before All Saints' Day), crepe paper dragons snake their way down city streets in popular parades, monster movies and Star Trek serials punctuate weekly television calendars, and bizarre mutant creatures stalk the pages of science fiction. Despite our scientific better judgment, our fascination with these mythic beings persists. That fascination, however, surfaces sporadically, mostly in our moments of corporate play or our personal dreams. For Paul, however, contact with such powers was real, insistent, and dreadful. Satan, the superhuman rulers of this world-age, the elemental spirits of the universe, the principalities and powers, the beasts at Ephesus, Death, Sin, and pagan deities all lived and contended for dominion and the loyalty of the world Paul inhabited.

Satan, for example, Paul held as an uncanny force, preying on the unsuspecting (1 Cor. 7:5), seeking advantage over all humans (2 Cor. 2:11), and stalking those excommunicated from the realm of the rule of Christ (1 Cor. 5:5). Likewise, Death for Paul was a personalized power that paid wages to its recruits and hosted an army that would be completely vanquished only at the eschaton (1 Cor. 15:26, 54–55). Those hostile powers that crucified Christ made false claims for their wisdom (1 Cor. 2:6–8). Moreover, in pagan cultic feasts, demons offered believers food and drink and sought to wean them from the table of Christ (1 Cor. 10:20–22). Both angels (even evil ones) and principalities, which included but transcended political power structures, vied for the loyalty of the believer (Rom. 8:38–39).

In Paul's view, therefore, those in Christ lived in a contested realm. In this field of forces at war there were no safe zones to which the uncommitted might flee; there was no arena thought free from the claim or dominion of some power. We see, therefore, why the term "Lord" was such a pregnant term for Paul. Informing the term was the belief that in the death and resurrection of Jesus, God had begun the final conquest of these hostile powers. The final moment when God would place all things in subjection, Paul promised, was imminent (1 Cor. 15:24–25). In the meantime, the fiery conflict between God and the hostile powers continued. Those once held captive were now being released from the clutches of the "powers that be," but they still looked to a future when the complete triumph of God's righteousness or Jesus' lordship would be consummated.

The modern reader may find such views of personalized evil strange, dangerous, or offensive. However, our memory of Nazism and our continuing witness of racism make references to demonic forces comprehensible. Though Paul's references to apocalyptic terrors may appear surrealistic, we shall miss the power of individual passages and misunderstand the letters as a whole if we are insensitive to the way these mythological images informed Paul's thought and that of his readers. Life for some was simply empty; for others it was absurdly oppressed, and many felt helpless in the grip of forces too great for anyone to resist or comprehend. Paul's gospel spoke to the first of help and to the second of rescue (i.e., salvation) from that ugly web, and thus he nerved women and men for their daily lives and for the final intense life-and-death struggle.

THE LAST ADAM

Discussing Paul's use of the Adam symbol, Richard Rubenstein wrote: "Almost two thousand years before the depth psychology that his religious imagination helped to make possible, Paul of Tarsus gave expression to mankind's yearning for a new and flawless beginning that could finally end the cycle of anxiety, repression, desire, and craving—the inevitable concomitants of the human pilgrimage."[8]

Whatever one may think of Rubenstein's effort to link Paul with depth psychology, his observation was correct that the Adamic myth played a major role in Paul's thought. Paul could have joined Hamlet in saying, "The time is out of joint." In the apostle's view, this disjointed state represented a degeneration from a flawless beginning. The cosmic decline began when Adam revolted against the Creator's prohibition: "You shall not eat of the fruit of the tree that is in the middle of the garden . . . or you shall die" (Gen. 3:3; cf. 2:17). Before the fall, he believed, man and woman lived in a state of innocence, unshamed by nakedness, strangers to want, freely taking from nature's breast without sweat or toil, and untroubled by anxiety over death. A friend of the animals, Adam was neither hunter nor hunted. Barely inferior to the gods, he shared in the creation by naming the animals and ruling the world without enmity or strife. As her Hebrew name suggests, Eve ("she who makes alive") had the capacity to bring life into the world.

But because of their disobedience, the Genesis writer held, Adam and Eve were exiled from the garden to a life marked by toil and want, fratricide and fear, death and pain. Ever since, Paul held, creature and creation have shared Adam's frustration and futility and have suffered under the dominion of

8. Richard L. Rubenstein, *My Brother Paul* (New York: Harper & Row, 1972), 173.

demonic powers (a later Hebraic concept). Even though Paul nowhere fully articulated this scenario, he took it for granted. For although the Hebrew Scriptures and the Gospels rarely mention the Adamic myth, it occupied a prominent place in the letters. Three passages will receive our attention here: Romans 5:12–5:21; 1 Corinthians 15; and Philippians 2:6–2:11.

Romans 5:12–5:21a

The belief was widespread in first-century Jewish thought that the original state that the world enjoyed would be restored in the end time. Paul obviously shared that view, but for him God's agent of this restoration was the Christ whom he alternately called the "second Adam," "the last Adam," and "the Adam who is to come." In Romans 5:12–5:21 Paul contrasted this last Adam with the first. The two Adams were alike in that the action of each influenced the destiny of all humankind; they were different in that through the last Adam's act of righteousness came acquittal, whereas through the disobedience of the first Adam "many were made sinners" (Rom. 5:19). Through the last Adam came life (5:18), whereas through the first Adam came death (5:21). Although Paul described Jesus as the antitype of Adam, he was uncomfortable with his comparison, for in Jesus grace abounded more to humanity's good than Adam's disobedience redounded to humanity's loss.

   While Paul did write that sin entered the human context through Adam, he did not create or endorse the doctrine of *original sin*. He believed, as did every rabbi of his day, that sin was universal and that Adam was its genesis but that it was perpetuated through repeated acts of disobedience, not by seminal transmission. With few exceptions—for example, Enoch and Elijah, who were not known to die and thus were judged sinless—all become their own Adam. Paul here addressed those who wondered how it was possible for Jesus' acts of obedience and righteousness to benefit others. Those who comprehend what it is to be one with the first Adam, Paul argued, should have no difficulty understanding how one can be united with the last.

1 Corinthians 15

In 1 Corinthians 15 Paul answered skeptics about the resurrection of the dead and even those who claimed to be already in a resurrected state. To many from a Greek tradition, the whole concept of the resurrection of the body was totally repulsive. Apparently it was unclear to the Corinthians how or if the resurrection of Jesus applied to them. Paul argued that God's raising of Jesus was the "first fruit" of the end time and thus anticipated the imminent end, when in the spirit of Jewish apocalyptic thinking believers would be raised (1 Thess. 4:13–17). Paul responded to those who wonder how a believer can be "in Christ" with an example that would have been familiar to any convert having a casual acquaintance with synagogue discussions or the Scriptures. He noted that "as through (*dia*) a man came death, so through (*dia*) a man has come also the resurrection of the dead. For as in Adam all die, so [also] in (*en*) Christ shall all be made alive" (1 Cor. 15:21–22 RSV adapted).

To be "in Adam" for Paul meant to participate in the destiny of Adam, in whom the mortality rate was almost 100 percent, whereas to be "in Christ" meant to share in the life of the new creation. As Robin Scroggs put it, "Christ for Paul is not just an example of but the medium through which one shares in the resurrected life."[9]

The resurrection was to be for Paul a bodily resurrection. In 1 Corinthians 15:35–38 Paul probably addressed Greek Christians who found the whole idea of a resurrection of the body crude and ridiculous. Conventional Greek piety and the major philosophical movements denigrated the body as a living prison. Salvation meant release from the body, not perpetuation of it. In the rhetorical questions of 15:35 we may have an echo of their scorn: "How are the dead raised? With what kind of body do they come?" Coming from a Hebraic tradition in which one did not just *have* a body as a piece of portable plumbing, but in a deep sense *was* a body, Paul responded to the mocking question by distinguishing between different kinds of bodies: human bodies and animal bodies, fish bodies and bird bodies, heavenly bodies and earthly bodies, sea bodies and landed bodies (15:3–40).

In the classic Hebraic sense, "body" was a synonym for the self. Thus Paul compared and contrasted the present earthly self with the future heavenly one. The form and substance that the self now has will perish, he noted, but the heavenly body will last forever (1 Cor. 15:42). Likewise, the first and last Adam belong to different spheres: As the Hebrew *adamah* suggests, the first man was "earth man." The second Adam is from heaven (1 Cor. 15:47). This contrast of "the earth man," who was perishable, with the heavenly man, who was "a life-giving spirit," made his point (15:45). Both are bodies—one earthly, the other heavenly. This torturous route led Paul to affirm that "just as we have borne the image of the man of dust [Adam], we will also bear the image of the man of heaven [Jesus]" (15:49).

9. Robin Scroggs, *The Last Adam* (Philadelphia: Fortress Press, 1966), 84.

Philippians 2:6–11

In Philippians 2:6–11 Paul quoted a Christian hymn in which many scholars see a contrast of Jesus with Adam. Although the hymn nowhere explicitly mentions Adam, a contrast between Jesus and Adam seems implicit. The first strophe of the hymn refers to Jesus, who, "though he was in the form of God, did not regard equality with God as something to be exploited (or 'snatched at')." The mention of "form" (Gk. *morphē*) evidently refers to the image of God, which both Jesus and Adam (Gen. 1:26) bore. Unlike the first Adam, however, the last did not try to usurp the place of God (see Gen. 3:5) but instead took the role of a slave. Whereas Adam sought to exalt himself, this Christ humbled himself; whereas Adam rebelled against the Creator, Jesus was obedient unto death.

The conduct of the last Adam was a model of selflessness, obedience, innocence, and sacrifice that Paul exhorted his converts to emulate: "Let this mind be in you, which was also in Christ Jesus" (Phil. 2:5 KJV). We see, therefore, that the second Adam is not only the agent of redemption, reversing the decline of the cosmos, redefining hardship and death, but also the model of the true Adam before the fall. In this presentation, Christ retains untarnished the image of God, and he will rule as Adam was meant to rule until all things are placed under him (1 Cor. 15:24–28). The last Adam, thus conceived, served as both the medium and the model of restored humanity. Thus to use Romans 5:12, or Philippians 2:5, or 1 Corinthians 15:24–28 to argue that Paul espoused the doctrine of original sin is weak.

Our discussion of the function of myth in Paul is far from exhaustive and is intended to show only how, for Paul, even the distant past was not a dead past, nor the future an unreal one; rather, past and future met and embraced through myth in the present. I hope, however, the treatment will show how mythic materials grow and change. Observing the way myth and symbol receive energetic and creative use in the letters provides a clue to Paul's primary concerns. Our purpose has also been to go beyond investigation of what happened ("external history") and learn how Paul and his converts experienced those happenings ("internal history"). H. Richard Niebuhr first used this distinction between internal and external history and offered a succinct summary:

> To speak of history in this fashion is to try to think with poets rather than with scientists. That is what we mean, for poets think of persons, purposes and destinies. It is just their Jobs and Hamlets that are not dreamt of in philosophies which rule out from the company of true being whatever cannot be numbered or included in an impersonal pattern. . . . Hence we may call internal history dramatic and

its truth dramatic truth, though drama in this case does not mean fiction.[10]

I hope that I am in agreement when I use myth where Niebuhr uses drama, for through myth also we see how events are apprehended from within the community, how history is a lived experience, and how persons interpret the way events shape their destiny. In the cult the believer was in Christ and Christ was in the believer. In the daily life of the Christian the sacrifice of Christ was replicated. In the attack on the demonic powers, the paradise once lost was being regained. In his ascent to the third heaven, Paul was breaking the confines of this world and experiencing what defied articulation (see 2 Cor. 12:1–6).

The only way to speak of it would be mythically, and since the church frequently spoke of such events, it had to be careful. In speaking mythically, the church constantly risked being called (and indeed becoming) a fringe group interested only in subjective, individualistic experiences. It avoided that by insisting that any experience of what happened be judged by the church's memory of what indeed did happen. Moreover, recollection had to be corporate, to weed out the faulty or the fanciful. In this sense the mythological experience of the tradition is different from the private experience of a mystic, and thus Paul spoke not just of his own experience of history but of the experience he shared in and with the Christian community.

10. H. Richard Niebuhr, *The Meaning of Revelation* (New York: Macmillan Co., 1941), 71–72.

7

New Testament Interpreters of Paul

Within the New Testament there are almost as many disputed (six) as undisputed (seven) letters of Paul. That persons would write under the name of other significant figures shocked no one in the ancient world. Within the Old Testament itself, pseudonymous writings like Daniel, the "books of Moses," Second and Third Isaiah, and some of the Psalms appear, and in the period between the testaments, they flourished.[1] In the New Testament as well, the use of pseudonyms was a common literary device (e.g., epistles written under the names of such greats as Peter, James, Jude, and John were hardly scribed by them). While such practices opened the door to forgeries in the second and third centuries CE, literary abuse of the method did little to discredit or discourage writing under a pseudonym in the late first century.

While many factors influenced the adoption and use of a pseudonym, two things played a role: (1) the desire to locate oneself within a tradition linked to an iconic figure, and (2) the attempt to gain credibility, authority, and acceptance for a later interpretation. As the earliest canonical writings for instructing the Christian church, Paul's letters offered teaching that was readily adaptable to meet later challenges. Two generations after his death a collection of Paul's letters was known to the author of *1 Clement*, and the existence of that collection provided an example to be imitated and a metric by which to measure the veracity of other traditions.

Moreover, since Paul was the most apt and eloquent defender of the Gentile mission, the selection of his name became a practical choice under which to write. It was hardly the appeal of Paul's name alone that inspired imitation;

1. R. H. Charles, *The Apocrypha and Pseudepigrapha of the Old Testament* (Oxford: Clarendon Press, 1963–64), vol. 2.

the adoption of his ideas, practical theology, language, and emphases also exerted influence. In the late second century, after Paul's legacy had been vigorously contested and revised by Ignatius, Marcion, Irenaeus, Tertullian, and others, the inclusion of his letters in the canon remained a burning issue. By then (ca. 200 CE), he was such an influential figure and had assumed such importance for the church that the rather unusual step was taken to include his occasional letters in a collection of the church's Scriptures. Although some letters ascribed to Paul were not included (e.g., the Letter to the Laodiceans), thirteen were finally included. That decision dictates the need here to deal with letters attributed to Paul but probably written by a later church leader.

So let us turn now to selected New Testament writings attributed to Paul but of disputed authorship. Generations before Paul's day many Jewish writers practiced pseudepigraphy, attributing their writings to Moses, Abraham, Enoch, and other venerable figures.

COLOSSIANS

The Question of Authorship

Of the deuteropauline letters, Colossians and 2 Thessalonians make the strongest claim to authenticity. But as far back as 1839 the German scholar Mayerhoff questioned the Pauline authorship of Colossians. Reservations about its authenticity have persisted into our own time. The unusual language, style, and theology of the letter are the principal reasons for continuing skepticism about its authenticity. While none is decisive by itself, these reasons, when taken together, make a compelling case against attributing Pauline authorship to Colossians.

Linguistic Evidence

One can easily cite the appearance of language unusual for Paul, the absence of favorite Pauline words and expressions, and the presence of certain stylistic features that are rare or missing altogether in the undisputed letters. In Colossians one finds thirty-three words that occur nowhere else in the New Testament and fifteen words that are used by other New Testament writers but fail to appear in the undisputed letters.

In addition, Colossians contains a number of unusual expressions that Paul never used elsewhere. References to the "blood of his cross" (1:20), "evil deeds" (1:21), "forgiveness of sins" (1:14), and "*the* faith" (2:7 AE) appear in Colossians but are missing in the undisputed letters. Likewise, the contrast of the visible and invisible in 1:16 was mentioned nowhere else by Paul.

While an argument from silence is hardly decisive, it is strange that the author of Colossians does not use such characteristic Pauline words as "salvation," "righteousness," and "justification." Such omissions, in light of the legalistic tendencies of the addressees, are striking. Moreover, given Paul's construction of believing cells as surrogate families, the absence of such favorite Pauline words as "my brothers [and sisters]" is peculiar.

Style

If the presence of non-Pauline language and the absence of favorite Pauline expressions raise questions about the Pauline authorship of Colossians, its style causes further doubt. Even a casual reading of the letter will detect a redundant style. Expressions such as *"praying* for you and *asking"* (1:9), *"endure* everything with *patience"* (1:11), "firmly *established* and *steadfast"* (1:23 AT), "the *ages* and *generations"* (1:26), *"teach* and *admonish"* (3:16), and *"psalms, hymns,* and spiritual *songs"* (3:16 AE) are common in Colossians but less pronounced in the undisputed letters. Moreover, there is a greater tendency in Colossians to string together dependent clauses and phrases into long, rambling sentences. Note, for example, that the thanksgiving beginning in 1:3 continues without interruption for five verses (1:3–8). The long thanksgiving in Romans as a part of a prolonged theme of the apologetic letter is much easier to understand.

In assessing the evidence cited here, few would quarrel with the observation that significant differences exist between Colossians and the undisputed Pauline letters. The disagreement arises over the assessment of the importance of those differences. Those inclined toward assigning the letter to Paul would argue that the differences can be explained by factors unique to the composition of Colossians itself. The peculiarities of language and style can be attributed to the hymnic style of the letter,[2] evoked by circumstances unique to Colossians, created by an aging, mellow, contemplative apostle waiting in prison for his trial, or caused by a secretary (or amanuensis) taking liberties with the apostle's dictation.

But it is difficult to understand how a hymnic style would account for the omissions noted earlier or how an altered context could effect the stylistic changes here present. Moreover, even while Paul's thinking indisputably changed over time, there is little evidence in Paul's later letters (e.g., 2 Corinthians 9 and Romans) of a mellowing process. Finally, if the scribe was responsible for the significant shifts in style and language in the letter, then the writer has in some sense become the author. In any case, while it is

---

2. Werner Georg Kümmel, *Introduction to the New Testament* (Nashville: Abingdon Press, 1966), 241.

important, linguistic and stylistic evidence alone is less than decisive when considering the question of authorship. So usually, as here, the linguistic argument is linked with theological evidence.

Theology

At many points the theology of Colossians agrees with that of the undisputed letters, but in its concepts of apostleship, Christology, and eschatology there are significant differences.[3] In Colossians Paul appears as the apostle who through his preaching *and suffering* took the gospel "to every creature under heaven" (1:23). Although Paul did present himself as the apostle to the Gentiles who shared in the suffering of Christ (e.g., 2 Cor. 11:21b–12:10), nowhere in his undisputed letters did he speak of his suffering as vicarious. In Colossians, on the other hand, the apostle gladly suffers, he told his hearers, "for your sake" (1:24). Thus the vicarious suffering of the apostle for others complements the suffering of Christ (cf. esp. Rom. 3:24–26).

In the undisputed letters, Paul sought to elicit and nurture faith in Jesus as Messiah, but the apprehension of the new life, Paul held, was always partial in nature. In 1 Corinthians especially, Paul scoffs at those who claim to be mature (1 Cor. 3:1–4). In Colossians, on the other hand, Paul appears as the apostle whose message was offered "in all wisdom" (Col. 1:28) and served to make everyone "perfect" (*telios*) in Christ. In the Hellenistic world such *telioi* ("perfect ones") were those deemed worthy of divine illumination and truth.

Finally and most importantly, the apocalyptic urgency of the undisputed letters is largely absent from Colossians. The Colossians apostle no longer wrote in the shadow of the end time. So while in some respects the understanding of apostleship in Colossians resembles that of the undisputed letters (e.g., as a mission to the Gentiles), in its view of the suffering of the apostle, its understanding of the apostolic preaching as wisdom for the perfect, and its diminished sense of apocalyptic urgency, Colossians differs significantly from the undisputed letters.

Moreover, the Colossian view of Christ, like that of his view of apostleship, is unusual for a Pauline letter. Instead of the body of Christ, as in 1 Corinthians 12:12–27, the author viewed the church as the trunk of the body with Christ as the head. The Colossians author also viewed Christ as a cosmic

---

3. Eduard Lohse, *Colossians and Philemon: A Commentary on the Epistles to the Colossians and to Philemon*, trans. William R. Poehlmann and Robert J. Karris (Philadelphia: Fortress Press, 1971), 81. Lohse has pointed out how the author of Colossians integrates major motifs from the genuine letters. Especially noteworthy are the similarities of epistolary style, their view of Paul as the apostle to the Gentiles, the use of traditional ethical materials, the understanding of wisdom materials, and the significance of the suffering of the apostle.

figure whose universal rule was *already* expressed within the church. Such an emphasis on ecclesiology postdates Paul, and most scholars assign it to Hellenistic philosophy.

The above emphases distinguish Colossians from the undisputed Pauline letters. However, the most radical difference between this letter and the undisputed letters is its understanding of eschatology. In the undisputed letters, Paul's belief in the imminent return of Christ profoundly informed his thinking. He viewed the harassment, beatings, misfortunes, and imprisonment that he suffered for the gospel as apocalyptic "woes" that, like birth pains, announced the imminent arrival of the end time. In 1 Corinthians 7:31–32 Paul discouraged normal, wholesome human attachments to a marriage partner in light of the imminent apocalyptic trauma. He encouraged support for civil authority (Rom. 13:11–12) because it would restrain the evil powers loosed in the last days, for he exclaimed, "the night is far gone, the day is at hand."

The believers who now taste salvation, Paul adamantly held, would experience it fully in the near future (1 Thess. 4:17). The offering that assumed such a prominent place in 1 and 2 Corinthians, Galatians, and Romans and carried powerful eschatological significance of the solidarity of Jew and Gentile in God's final resolution (2 Cor. 9) must be viewed against an apocalyptic horizon. The apostle prosecuted his mission and the offering with feverish intensity to complete it before history's finale. Paul's view of the end was central to his understanding of the church, his instruction for believers, and his personal sense of mission; and the ethical imperative he advocated for his converts breathed an apocalyptic air.

In Colossians, on the other hand, the mood of expectation is subdued. No longer does the prospect of the imminent end of the age influence the perception of all human relationships. Rather than the full experience of salvation being a future prospect, the author believed that already God "*has rescued* us [past tense] from the power of darkness" (1:13 AE), a theological concept almost impossible to ascribe to Paul. The mystery hidden for ages, the author of Colossians held, has "now *been revealed* [past tense again] to his saints" (1:26 AE). The author reminded readers: "When you *were buried* with him in baptism, you *were also raised* with him" (2:12 AE), and "you *were dead* in trespasses . . . God *made you alive*" (2:13 AE). The author assured those "*once estranged*" that they were "*now reconciled*" (1:22 AE). The emphasized words of these quotations, with their stress on salvation already achieved, can scarcely be made to harmonize with Paul's understanding of salvation as a work in progress. The full experience of salvation, reserved for the future in the undisputed letters, now moves into the present or even the past. The future dimension almost disappears.

In this shift of emphasis from the future to the present, the concept of hope also changes. Where hope sprang from faith in the undisputed Pauline letters and was linked with the anticipation of the end of the age (a temporal category), hope in Colossians was stored up in the heavenly realms. Thus in Colossians a spatial category replaced a temporal one, and a symbol of anticipation was replaced by a hope deemed a sign of assurance.

While it is possible that these theological departures from the outlook of the undisputed letters can be explained by changes in the thinking of Paul, for we know that Paul's thinking did change, that seems improbable here. It is more reasonable to assume that the alterations in language, style, and theology were the work of a later interpreter or school of interpreters who sought to interpret the Pauline tradition for a new situation. By the way the author integrated major theological motifs and literary devices from the undisputed letters, we know the author was acquainted with the traditions and letters of Paul. But the deviation in language, style, and outlook suggests the author belonged to a time perhaps twenty years after Paul's death.

The Context of the Letter

Like the undisputed letters of Paul, Colossians gives the impression of being a real letter, that is, a real conversation between its author and believers in a concrete situation. And as in the study of the undisputed letters, we must search the letter itself for clues to the context of that conversation. Even though their identity is debated, we learn from Colossians that "false teachers" were present, and the letter offers hints regarding the substance of a "philosophy" (2:8) that was hardly a system of clear, logical thought or speculation but rather a special religious tradition, a revealed knowledge or way of life through which the ultimate ground and secret meaning of the universe was grasped.

The "Philosophy" of the Opponents

Fixed on the cosmic powers or "elemental spirits of the universe" (2:8), the scope of that philosophy was expansive. Rather than merely material elements such as air, earth, fire, and water, those "elemental spirits" were divine beings controlling the entire world and requiring special devotion. That angel worship (2:18), linked to obeisance to the elemental spirits or "principalities and powers" (2:15 RSV), offered a vision of the heavenly *plērōma* ("divine fullness" or mystery) that assured one's place among the perfect ones (*teleioi*).

The author graphically characterized those possessed by divine power as "vainly puffed up by the mind of the flesh" (2:18 AT). Ascetic or world denying by nature (2:18), they passed judgments on the basis of "food and drink" and on the observance of "festivals, new moons, or Sabbaths" (2:16). The world-denying commands, "Do not handle, do not taste, do not touch" (2:21), promoted a certain "self-imposed piety, humility, and severe treatment of the body" (2:23), which simultaneously encouraged a contradictory over-indulgence (3:5). Is it possible that through their asceticism, these believers hoped to strip "off the body of the flesh," a spiritualized, mythic form of cir-cumcision (2:11)? Was their prodigal self-indulgence a demonstration of their defiance of the world and the values of the culture? Perhaps, but we cannot be certain.

The cosmic speculation linked with world denial suggests a gnostic back-ground to many. The reference to the observance of new moons and Sabbaths and the submission to regulations or *dogmata* (2:20), coupled with the worship of cosmic forces, an appeal to visions, asceticism, and indulgence led Günther Bornkamm to assert that there is "no doubt that the heresy was a variety of Jewish Gnosticism."[4]

Others, however, see the teaching as an expression of Hellenistic Jewish piety or neo-Pythagorean spirituality.[5] An emerging consensus views the philosophy as a syncretistic form of Hellenistic Judaism open to popular religious piety. Certain features of this piety (such as cosmic speculation and asceticism) tend toward a gnostic speculation that later received a bewildering array of forms. However that teaching is understood, it is significant for our study that its main contours are not in dispute.[6]

Response to the "Philosophy"

To confront this teaching, the author summoned a collection of known Pauline letters. The Paul of this letter is sketched as a powerful figure with a universal vision. He is said to bring the gospel "to every creature under heaven" (1:23). As an apostle to the Gentiles (1:5–8, 24–29; not "nations," as in NRSV), this world-renowned figure attended to this little church in the remote Lycus River valley in Asia Minor. He shared the limelight with none

4. Günther Bornkamm, "The Heresy of Colossians," in *Conflict at Colossae: A Problem in the Interpretation of Early Christianity Illustrated by Selected Modern Studies*, ed. and trans. Fred O. Francis and Wayne A. Meeks (Missoula, MT: Scholars Press, 1973), 130.

5. Fred O. Francis, "Humility and Angel Worship in Col. 2:18," in *Conflict at Colossae*, 163–195, and Eduard Schweizer, *Der Brief an die Kolosser* (Zurich: Benziger Verlag, 1976), 104.

6. Wayne A. Meeks and Fred O. Francis, "Epilogue," in *Conflict at Colossae*, 209–18.

of the inner circle in Jerusalem and suffered on behalf of the churches and ministered with "divine" credentials (1:25).

By appealing to Paul, our author hoped to secure a hearing for his teaching and to gain a certification for the correctness of his interpretation. This attempt to establish the validity of his teaching was especially important if he were to refute the false teaching. Unfortunately, we have nothing from the "teachers," who doubtless could have found, and may have found, support in Paul's letters for their philosophy. In response to the cosmic speculation and veneration of the elemental spirits, our author subordinated all powers to a cosmic Christ, or head of the church exercising dominion over all principalities and powers. He, and no other, the author wrote, is Lord over the "cosmic forces" (*stoicheia*; "elemental spirits of the universe," 2:8 NRSV) worshiped by the Colossians.

As the "head of all rule and authority," he, the author held, is the *plērōma* or divine fullness (2:10). He disarms and subjugates the celestial powers worshiped by the Colossians (2:15). Through him and his reconciliation, the whole cosmos is brought back into the divine order. In *Christ*, the author added, "the fullness of God was pleased to dwell" (1:19). In Christ is found a circumcision "made without hands" (2:11). In Christ is the resurrection realized here and now (2:12). Through Christ are the aliens reconciled (1:22). So in this way our author set the teaching of Paul over against Colossian "philosophy and empty deceit" (2:8) and contradicted those who delude and beguile the innocent (2:4). Their ascetic commands he called "human commands and teachings" (2:22). Moreover, from a practical point of view, these regulations, our writer said, are ineffective in restraining indulgence (2:23).

In contrast to those who were "puffed up" (2:18) or arrogant, he admonished believers to "clothe yourselves with love" for the sake of church unity and to teach each other "in all wisdom" (3:14, 16). In contrast to the regulations that are essentially world denying ("Do not handle, do not touch," etc.), our author juxtaposed a set of rules adopted from Hellenistic Jewish ethics that were world-affirming: "Husbands, love your wives. Children, obey your parents. . . . Fathers, do not provoke your children" (the so-called household rules or *Haustafeln*, 3:18–4:1).

Although the author has access to some of Paul's letters, it is interesting what he ignored. This small collection of household rules reaffirmed a social hierarchy that required a subordination of women (3:18). He included, "Wives be subject to your husbands," which at times Paul repudiated (cf. Gal. 3:28; Rom. 16:1, 7; 1 Cor. 11:5). The requirement that women be subordinate has caused some to wonder if the rhetoric here used to fix women in their lower place might have been a reaction to some of the more liberal tendencies in Paul.

Unfortunately, we have no further word to or from the church at Colossae. It was eclipsed in importance by Laodicea and ultimately failed to survive one of the many earthquakes that regularly devastated the Lycus valley. So we are left, as is the case so often in New Testament, not knowing how the struggle ended. While we do not know what happened to the church, we do know that the letter survived and very soon profoundly influenced another writing assigned to Paul, namely, the letter to the Ephesians, which we shall next discuss.

Outline of Colossians

1. Address, Salutation, and Thanksgiving	1:1–11
2. Body of Letter: Theological Foundation for Ethics	1:12–2:23
a. Christ hymn and application	1:12–23
b. Apostle's message, divine mystery	1:24–2:5
c. Relationship of cosmic Christ to church	2:6–23
3. Paraenesis or Ethical Instruction	3:1–4:6
a. Theme: "Seek the things that are above"	3:1–4
b. Avoid things "below"	3:5–11
c. Specific things "above" to seek	3:12–17
d. Household rules	3:18–4:1
e. Concluding paraenesis	4:2–6
4. Parousia of Tychicus	4:7–9
5. Final greetings and conclusion	4:10–18

EPHESIANS

Ephesians and Colossians are literary siblings if not twins. Almost one-third of Colossians appears in Ephesians, and approximately one-half of Ephesian's sentences borrow language from Colossians. Although Ephesians shares more of the undisputed Pauline epistles' language than does any other New Testament epistle, with the exception of 2 Thessalonians, the close literary relationship to Colossians strongly suggests dependence. In the household rules taken from Colossians 3:18–4:1, for example, the author of Ephesians changes, expands, and sharpens the Colossian source to fit a new situation. Where Colossians asks wives to "be subject to your husbands, as is fitting in the Lord" (3:18 AE), Ephesians has the more demanding "as you are to the Lord" (5:22 AE). Given the completely different understanding of such key words as "mystery" and "stewardship" in these letters (cf. Col. 1:25–28; 2:2 and Eph. 1:9; 3:3–6, and 5:32), it is unlikely that they came from the same hand. What is more probable is that when Ephesians was penned, the author knew a collection of Pauline letters that included Colossians.

The Question of Authorship

If Colossians is judged to be deuteropauline and the author of Ephesians relied on Colossians, then it follows that Ephesians was also a deuteropauline writing. To answer this question, however, we must also consider linguistic and theological issues that come into play. Even if direct dependence is asserted, however, it is important to take note of the ways the author of Ephesians changes, expands, and sharpens whatever sources he appropriated to address a different situation.

Language and Style

The language and style of Ephesians are unusual for a Pauline letter. Nowhere else in the epistles is there as much interest in the saintliness of the apostle (thirteen references). Note also that nowhere in the undisputed letters did Paul refer to himself as a "holy one" or saint (*hagios*). Instead of the self-reference as the "least of the apostles" (1 Cor. 15:9), Ephesians has Paul as "the very least of all the *saints*" (Eph. 3:8). Ephesian references to "the heavens" (pl., five times), "the beloved" (referring to Christ, 1:6), "flesh and blood" (6:12), "commonwealth" (2:12), "holiness" (*hosiotēs*, 4:24), "debauchery" (*asōtia*, 5:18), "compassionate" (*eusplanchnos*, 4:32), and "favor one with" (*charitoō*, 1:6) appear nowhere in the undisputed letters. The absence of this language in the undisputed letters of Paul plus its presence in later post-Pauline writings both within and outside the New Testament strongly argues for placing Ephesians in the postapostolic period after 80 CE.

Note that Ephesians also shows stylistic idiosyncrasies. Long, complex sentences abound in the Greek of Ephesians (e.g., 1:3–10; 1:15–23; 3:14–19). The heaping up of synonyms is frequent—for example, the "energy of his great strength" (1:19 AT), the "aeon of this world" (2:12 AT), and "prayer and supplication" (6:18). While Paul also did build long, convoluted sentences and multiplied synonyms, even a casual reading of Ephesians will spot excesses that surpass those of Paul.

Theology of the Letter

More than the vocabulary and style, the theology of the letter argues for an author other than Paul. In at least three important areas the outlook of Ephesians differs from that of the undisputed letters: (1) its eschatology, (2) its view of the church (ecclesiology), and (3) its understanding of apostleship. As our discussion of Colossians noted, the feverish expectation of the imminent end of the age that informed the undisputed letters is muted here. The tension between the now and the not yet, so natural to Paul, is absent in Ephesians. The approaching end and impending judgment are alluded to only in the most general way (1:4). Ephesians lacks the urgency that drove the apostolic mission of the undisputed letters and expresses no interest in the *parousia* (coming) of Christ. Spatial categories replace the temporal dimension Paul expressed about the past (e.g., salvation history in Rom. 9–11). Christ appears in Ephesians as the head of the cosmos "far above all rule and authority and power and dominion" (1:21). Those "far off" have been "brought near" (2:13). Believers are given the power to comprehend "the breadth and length and height and depth" (3:18). In these three statements about Christ, salvation of the Gentiles, and the understanding of the believers, space rather than time is the controlling category.

The letter's emphasis on the church is its integrating center. Against 1 Corinthians, which speaks of the church as the body of Christ, Ephesians presents the church as a sphere for the activity of a cosmic Christ who exponentially expands the boundaries of the church. Now the church universal or cosmic, rather than the church local, receives emphasis. The great Christ mystery is no longer God's gracious use of an ignominious cross to embrace both Jew and Gentile but rather an emphasis on the church universal. Founded on "the apostles and prophets" (2:20), this church becomes the seat of the cosmic Christ and differs markedly from the struggling, messy local congregations of the undisputed letters. While the term *ekklēsia* can refer to the wider community in the genuine letters, a subtle shift has occurred. Whereas the undisputed letters view the church in light of Paul's Christology, Käsemann was quite correct that in Ephesians "Christology . . . is interpreted almost exclusively by ecclesiology [not the reverse]."[7]

Understanding of Apostleship

Finally, the understanding of apostleship in Ephesians differs significantly from that of the undisputed Pauline letters. The undisputed letters emphatically assert that the mission of the apostle was to proclaim the gospel to the Gentiles (e.g., Gal. 1:16; 2:7), but Ephesians presents the apostles as the foundation of the church (2:20), even while affirming the unity of Jew and Gentile in the church (3:2–6). This shift of emphasis reflects a situation that developed after Paul, when the Gentile church was no longer a struggling minority but was large enough to control the direction of the Christ movement. The author may have already recognized the dangers embedded in this

---

7. Ernst Käsemann, "Das Interpretationsproblem des Epheserbriefes," *Theologische Literaturzeitung* 86 (1961): 3.

development and been moved to reaffirm the unity of Jew and Gentile.[8] We see, therefore, that the author's language, style of writing, eschatology, view of the church, and understanding of apostleship place this letter in the deuteropauline category.

The Context of the Letter

As we saw in chapter 4, the undisputed epistles of Paul are real letters addressing real people in real situations. In each letter we noted a concrete situation evoking the letter. Ephesians, on the other hand, only grudgingly yields clues to its purpose. Thus attempts to reconstruct the setting of the letter have been disappointing. Paul Sampley may be correct that the "purposes of its author are hidden from the modern reader."[9] But before we surrender our quest, let us offer some possibilities.

The Problems Evoking the Letter

Ephesians resembles a religious tract more than a letter, and the general nature of the instruction has invited a number of theses about its purpose. More than a generation ago Goodspeed argued that Ephesians was written as a summary of Pauline theology to serve as a cover letter for a collection of the Pauline epistles.[10] While such a thesis would explain the general nature of the letter, it would not explain the absence of references to prominent motifs that appear in the undisputed letters (e.g., the *parousia* and the cross). Moreover, if Ephesians ever stood at the head of a collection of Pauline letters, all evidence for such a position has been lost.

Nils Dahl, a distinguished Pauline scholar, once suggested that Ephesians was written to instruct new Gentile converts on the meaning of baptism.[11] With some plausibility Chadwick thought the letter addressed a crisis created by the success of Gentile Christianity and its drift away from its moorings in the Jewish tradition.[12] Others have seen in Ephesians an attempt to counter

8. See Calvin Roetzel, "Jewish Christian–Gentile Christian Relations, A Discussion of Ephesians 2:15a," in *Zeitschrift für die neutestamentliche Wissenschaft* 74 (1983): 81–89.

9. See J. Paul Sampley, "The Letter to the Ephesians," in *Ephesians, Colossians, 2 Thessalonians, the Pastoral Epistles*, ed. J. Paul Sampley et al. (Philadelphia: Fortress Press, 1978), 10.

10. Edgar Johnson Goodspeed, *The Key to Ephesians* (Chicago: University of Chicago Press, 1956).

11. Nils A. Dahl, "Adresse und Prooemium des Epheserbrief," *Theologische Zeitschrift* 7 (1951): 261–64.

12. H. Chadwick, "Die Absicht des Epheserbrief," *Zeitschrift für die neutestamentliche Wissenschaft* 51 (1960): 145–53.

the influence of Gnosticism or a popular religion of the day. A very old thesis that enjoys little favor today was that Ephesians was a Pauline defense against rivals from Johannine and Petrine circles. This short list of hypotheses reveals the confusion that persists about the purpose of this letter. Perhaps the difficulty lies in the attempt of scholars to find a single purpose behind the writing, when in a postapostolic work, no less than in a writing of our own day, a letter, an essay, or a tract may serve multiple purposes.

Adaptations of two of the proposals mentioned above continue to be attractive to scholars: (1) that our author wrote to urge the Gentile Christian majority to accept a Jewish Christian minority and to affirm its ties with the ancient Hebrew traditions and (2) that the ethical admonitions correct libertine tendencies stemming from gnostic influence or from a popular religion of the day (e.g., mystery cults, neo-Pythagorean philosophy, folk religion). Let us now look at each in turn.

1. During and after the Roman-Jewish War (66–70 CE) that left Jerusalem in ruins, tensions increased between Jews and followers of Christ. Before the war, as we know from Paul's letters, it was possible to believe that Jesus was the Messiah and remain active in the synagogue. By the time John's Gospel appeared in the nineties, harsh exchanges between church and synagogue were so intense that belief in Jesus as the Messiah could trigger expulsion from the synagogue. And still later, Luke's Acts of the Apostles ends with a sharp distinction between Jew and Gentile and the curt announcement, "Let it be known to you then that this salvation of God has been sent to the Gentiles; they will listen" (Acts 28:28 RSV).

While it is risky to generalize from these two examples, one can easily imagine a scenario in Asia Minor that exacerbated tensions between Jew and Gentile believers and under Paul's name might at least in part explain the origin of Ephesians. Gentile converts, viewed as Jewish sectarian messianists until the war, might have dissociated themselves from the nationalistic cause of the Zealots, if for no other reason than to avoid Roman reprisals. Thus there would be in both Jewish messianist and Gentile Christian circles an emphasis on a particularity apart from a Jewish tradition dominated by a radical, revolutionary posture.

While understandable, such a posture would have made it increasingly difficult to confess Jesus as the Messiah and continue living as a Jew. The pressure, whether subtle or overt from the Gentile majority, would be to encourage either assimilation or withdrawal into a Jewish Christian sect. The threat of a rupture between Jewish and Gentile followers was real. The danger of isolation from or even repudiation of the Jewish tradition in the Gentile church was ever present. This imagined scenario is plausible, if hypothetical at this point; but later in the second century, with Marcion, a "heretic," and Justin, a Christian apologist, the veil is drawn aside to allow us to view tensions that eventually lead to the rupture of Jewish and Gentile factions.[13] In any case, such an ugly divorce would have come after Paul's death in the sixties and, had he lived to see it, would have broken his heart. If what I propose is credible, then it would appear that the author of Ephesians, a diligent student of Paul, was alarmed by this emerging split and attempted to speak to the crisis.

2. More than a decade ago, scholars observed that both the language of the author and the outlook of the addressees showed some gnostic coloration. Given the protognostic desire to escape the prison of the body to ascend to a higher realm, the command of the author to "put off your old nature . . . and put on the new nature" (4:22, 24 RSV) rings true to the gnostic or pre-gnostic outlook. The libertine inclinations, added to the temptation "to practice every kind of impurity" (4:19), resemble later gnostic traits. But whether the ideology ("every wind of doctrine," 4:14) that informed these tendencies came from organized gnostic circles or from the mysteries, popular religions, or folk piety tinged with Gnosticism is difficult to establish with any certainty.

Although the exact contours of the conceptual landscape are unclear, apparently a concrete situation did provoke this document.

The Response to the Problems

In this response to the concrete situation, the author tapped one or more undisputed letters of Paul and the deuteropauline Colossians. Moreover, paraenetic materials showing a family resemblance to some Qumran scrolls may have shaped the thinking of the writer as well. The later instructions or "household rules" derive from Hellenistic Jewish circles (via Colossians), and the writer's perception of Christ, as the head of the cosmos and in sexual union with the church, betrays both gnostic, Hellenistic, and even Hellenistic Jewish traits. Working out of those materials the author affirmed a unity that derived from Christ, in whom the whole cosmos found unity and purpose, and in a faintly Platonic sense, the author proclaimed the mystery of the unity of the church as a cosmic, divine mystery. Thus we can see how in Christ's reconciliation of the cosmos the author found a model that joined Jew and Gentile in one community.

In the undisputed letters Paul repeatedly argued for the right of Gentiles to be included in the church qua Gentiles without first converting to Judaism (see Rom. 9–11 and Gal. 1–3). In spite of his protestation, the

---

13. See Daniel Boyarin, "The IOUDAIOI in John and the Prehistory of 'Judaism,'" in *Pauline Conversations in Context: Essays in Honor of Calvin J. Roetzel*, ed. Janice Capel Anderson, Philip Sellew, and Claudia Setzer (Sheffield: Sheffield Academic Press, 2002).

Jerusalem church continued to exert a powerful influence on Paul. But with the war and a growth of the Gentile church that Paul could hardly have imagined, the symbiotic relationship between Gentile and Jewish factions of the church, or even between the gospel of Christ and the Jewish traditions, could no longer be taken for granted. Since Paul had argued for the inclusiveness of the church and since he had come to a position of respect and honor (at least in some circles), the use of his name and teaching seemed entirely apt.

Under these altered circumstances, the author of Ephesians used Paul's name to argue for the inclusion of Jewish believers in the community without assimilation to the views of the Gentile majority. While Paul had argued for the inclusion of Gentiles as Gentiles, the author of Ephesians argued for the inclusion of Jewish believers as Jewish believers.

The appeal to the suffering of the apostle for the church was intended to inspire a willingness to follow the instruction in the letter out of gratitude to the "apostle." Paul appears as "a prisoner for Christ Jesus for the sake of you Gentiles" (3:1) and as a "prisoner in the Lord" who encourages the recipients "to lead a life worthy of the calling to which you have been called" (4:1). In 3:13 the hearers are asked to "not lose heart over my sufferings for you." While in the undisputed letters (esp. 2 Corinthians) the emphasis on suffering is stronger, only in the deuteropauline letters does the suffering have a vicarious dimension; it is "*for you*." One can easily imagine how reverence for Paul and careful observance of instructions from him would be fostered by the awareness that the apostle was suffering for the readers."

In the undisputed letters Paul argued that his call and apostolic commission legitimated his gospel to the Gentiles (Gal. 1:15–16; Rom. 1:5). Although the apostolic call remained as an important part of Ephesians, it was understood differently. No longer in a puzzling way did the cross reveal God's nature or the numinous divine presence, but rather it signaled the inclusion of Jews and Gentiles in one church as a "mystery." Since the unity derived from the Christ in whom the whole cosmos found a unity and purpose, in a faintly Platonic sense the mystery of unity of the church shared in that divine, cosmic mystery. Thus, in Christ's reconciliation of the cosmos the author found a model for reconciliation of Jew and Gentile.

The presentation of the apostle as the "least of all the *saints*" (3:8), who belongs to the "holy apostles" of God through whom Gentiles become fellow heirs (3:5), the author rhetorically affirmed the importance of this message and invoked the name of a now-revered apostle Paul to lend authority to this tractate. This elevated reverence for Paul would have surely secured a hearing for an attempt to deal with a crisis that threatened to fracture the church and to cut it loose from its spiritual moorings. Quite appropriately he appealed to Paul to encourage tolerance of and respect for Jewish followers of Christ qua Jews and to discourage participation in the popular religions of the day. He urged the church to resist erroneous doctrine (4:14) and to shun immorality or libertine behavior. Most scholars agree that the paraenetic material comes from many sources, but our author shaped that traditional instruction to emphasize the importance of unity, order, and mutual respect. In a characteristically Pauline fashion, the closing reaffirmed the major concern of the letter. There the church was urged to reaffirm its support for Paul (through prayer) and the mystery (i.e., the unity of the church) (6:18–20).

Outline of Ephesians

1. Address, Salutation	1:1–2
2. The Mystery of the Inclusion of the Gentiles	1:3–3:21
a. Praise to God for including "us" (Jews)	1:3–14
b. Thanksgiving for including "you" (Gentiles)	1:15–23
c. Salvation of Gentiles	2:1–10
d. Union of Israel and Gentiles	2:11–22
e. Mystery of union of Jew and Gentile	3:1–21
3. Paraenesis: Exhortation to Unity of Spirit in Peace	4:1–6:20
a. Unity grounded in faith and love	4:1–16
b. Put off old nature	4:17–5:20
c. Household rules	5:21–6:9
(1) Husbands and wives	5:21–33
(2) Children and parents	6:1–4
(3) Slaves and masters	6:5–9
d. Encouragement to be strong	6:10–20
4. Conclusion	6:21–24

2 THESSALONIANS

The Question of Authorship

This letter has few pages but many problems. In addition to the question of authorship stand questions of the identity and function of the *katechōn* ("restrainer" or "oppressor," 2:7), the literary relationship to 1 Thessalonians, the purpose of the letter, and its context. All of these literary challenges are stubborn, intractable problems facing the interpreter. Although included here in our discussion of deuteropauline letters, 2 Thessalonians has received strong support for inclusion among the authentic letters. Persuasive arguments can be marshaled both for and against its authenticity, but it is included here because its authenticity is in doubt.

The case against Pauline authorship includes the linguistic, literary, and theological arguments seen elsewhere. First, the language and style of this letter differ from the undisputed letters in significant ways. Nowhere else does Paul speak of being made "worthy of the kingdom of God" through suffering (1:5), or of the "restrainer" (or "oppressor," 2:7), or of "good hope" (2:16), "eternal comfort" (2:16), "good resolve" (1:11), or of being "shaken in mind" (2:2). Nowhere else does Paul speak of his readers as those whom God chose to "believe the truth" (2:12d–13).

While such language would sound strange coming from Paul's lips, elsewhere the vocabulary of 2 Thessalonians echoes that of 1 Thessalonians. For example, the salutation of 2 Thessalonians is nearly identical to that of 1 Thessalonians, and the thanksgiving in 2 Thessalonians 1:3–4 closely parallels that of 1 Thessalonians 1:2–3. Similarly, the expression "brothers and sisters, we ask and urge you" in the first letter (1 Thess. 4:1) resembles "we beg you, brothers and sisters" of the second (2 Thess. 2:1). The expression, the "Gentiles who do not know God" (1 Thess. 4:5) is nearly identical to "those [unbelievers] who do not know God" (2 Thess. 1:8), and "Finally, brothers and sisters" (1 Thess. 4:1) is repeated exactly in 2 Thessalonians 3:1. The references to the "labor and toil" of Paul and his coworkers and that they worked "night and day" of 1 Thessalonians 2:9 are almost exactly duplicated in 2 Thessalonians 3:8.

While the language in 2 Thessalonians agrees rather closely with that of 1 Thessalonians in places, scholars dispute the significance of those agreements. Some argue that if Paul wrote 2 Thessalonians either shortly before or soon after 1 Thessalonians, their verbal agreement is hardly surprising. But such a temporal proximity would make their differences harder to explain. Others notice that most of the parallels appear in the letter opening and closing, traditionally the most stereotyped parts of the letter. These would thus be the epistolary sections easiest to duplicate. So we see that the linguistic arguments tend to cancel each other out. The issue of authorship, therefore, must be decided on other grounds.

Second, taking up the literary question, the unusual form of the letter poses more of a problem for Pauline authorship. The thanksgiving especially has been singled out for scrutiny. All of the undisputed letters save Galatians have a thanksgiving, and, except for that in 2 Corinthians, all of the other letters have one thanksgiving, except for 1 Thessalonians, which has two. Birger Pearson has made a compelling case that the second thanksgiving (2:13–16) was added later to tie early persecution to the destruction of Jerusalem by the Roman onslaught in 70 CE.[14] The break in the material, the unusual language,

14. Birger A. Pearson, "1 Thessalonians 2:13–16: A Deutero-Pauline Interpolation," *Harvard Theological Review* 64 (1971): 79–94.

and the veiled allusion to the destruction of Jerusalem support the argument that the second thanksgiving was added after Paul's death. The second
thanksgiving was inserted, he held, to reflect the developing tensions between
nonmessianist Jews and Christ believers after the war. Second Thessalonians
took over that unusual thanksgiving and duplicated its form (e.g., 1:3–12 and
2:13–17). It was probably then that a later writer, using the edited version of
1 Thessalonians with two thanksgivings, imitated its form and some of its content. If such were the case, then Paul could not have written 2 Thessalonians.

One other small clue points to an author other than Paul. In 2:2 the
author urges his hearers not to be disturbed by letters "purporting to
be from us" (RSV). Given Paul's status as a persona non grata in many
regions, it would have been strange to have a pseudonymous letter circu-
lating in his name. From what we know of pseudepigraphy elsewhere, the
names of venerated figure from the past (e.g., Moses, Enoch, Abraham,
and in the New Testament, Peter, Paul, James, and John) were used to gain
credibility for a view or to offer instruction. We have no known instance of
a pseudonymous letter being written in the name of a *living* person. From a
practical point of view we can see why. It would be risky for a person to
adopt the name of a contemporary, when the risk of being exposed or corrected would be rather high. Moreover, a special problem intrudes when
one argues, as some do, that Paul wrote the second letter only a few weeks
after scribing the first.

While such an argument would explain the similarity of the letters, it is
difficult to see how in only a few weeks after the writing of the first letter
a pseudonymous writing could appear bearing the apostle's name. Moreover, the conclusion of the letter, "I, Paul, write this greeting with my own
hand" (3:17), appears to be a brazen attempt to establish the credibility of
the letter against the claim of rivals in the post-Pauline period, when deuteropauline letters were appearing. In any case the claim ascribed to Paul
to write 2 Thessalonians "with my own hand" is hardly proof of the letter's
authenticity.

Third, the theological outlook of 2 Thessalonians differs from that of the
first letter in important ways. In the first letter Paul expects that some of his
readers will still be alive at the *parousia* of Christ (4:17). That emphasis on the
imminent return persists throughout the undisputed letters of Paul. Even in
one of Paul's last letters (Romans), Paul announced that the end "is nearer
to us now than when we became believers; the night is far gone, the day is
near" (Rom. 13:11–12). It seems strange then that 2 Thessalonians offered
an apocalyptic timetable that explained the delay of the end. Before the "day
of the Lord" (2 Thess. 2:2) the believers were told they would witness the

appearance of the "restrainer" (2:7), a "man of lawlessness" (2:3), and a period of apostasy from the faith (2:2–12).

Although the end of the age still lingered on the horizon in 2 Thessalonians, the delay that timetable imposed is unique in Paul's letters. Gerhard Krodel has noted how the use of the apocalyptic timetable there functioned differently than that of the eschatological allusions in the Corinthian letters.[15] Before the *parousia* of Jesus there must come first the apostasy of believers, the arrival of the Rebel, and the disappearance of the Restrainer. Presupposed by this timetable is a delay. In 1 Thessalonians, on the other hand, Paul used an imminent eschatology to counter the discouragement of his addressees.

In addition to the altered eschatological strategy in 2 Thessalonians, other prominent Pauline emphases are subdued. The Pauline view of the cross, resurrection, and the Spirit played a diminished role in 2 Thessalonians. Instead of asking his hearers to imitate his suffering as their share of the cross, "Paul" invited his addressees to copy his work ethic, that is, to earn their bread, as does he, by sweat and toil (3:7–13). For these reasons, therefore, we incline to view 2 Thessalonians as a letter from the generation after Paul's death. In spite of these reasons for caution in judging the authenticity of 2 Thessalonians, however, no scholarly consensus exists on this question. Fortunately, the problem the epistle addresses is much clearer than the identity of the author. It is to that issue that we now turn.

The Context of the Letter

Second Thessalonians addressed two problems: eschatological enthusiasm and persecution. The suffering that some endured (1:5) they understood as a sign that the end had already come. Some were disturbed and others alarmed by a bogus Pauline letter announcing that "the day of the Lord is already here" (2:2). Moreover, "wicked" people allegedly preyed on this anxious congregation, deceiving some and exploiting others (3:2). This period of feverish expectation of the world's end, created by a bogus letter and by false teachers, led some to quit work and wait for the end (3:6). They idled away their time and sponged off of the workers (3:11–12). Their claim to liberation from work's sweat and grime disturbed the exploited in the church (3:11).

15. See Gerhard Krodel, "2 Thessalonians," in Sampley et al., eds., *Ephesians, Colossians, 2 Thessalonians, the Pastoral Epistles*, 80.

In response our author promised relief and/or rest to terror's victims. Also the author offered consolation and hope to those tortured and harassed and confidently predicted the demise of the faceless oppressors. Recalling the *lex talionis* that exacted "an eye for an eye, and a tooth for a tooth," that is, making punishment fit the crime, the author predicted affliction for those afflicting the church (1:6) and rejection for those rejecting the gospel (1:8). This interpreter assured the oppressed that he, the "apostle," was praying for them, exhorted them to persist in good resolve (1:11), in order that "Jesus may be glorified in you" (1:12), promised God's comfort for those who remained calm and resolute in persecution (2:1), and exhorted them all to hold fast "to the traditions" (2:15, a strikingly un-Pauline phrase). The author promised that the Lord would strengthen them for their struggle and guard them from evil (3:3).

By establishing an apocalyptic timetable, the author sought to modify the intense apocalyptic enthusiasm threatening the church and warned those who claimed that "the day of the Lord" had come (2:2) to remember that the "day" will arrive only after the apocalyptic rebellion, after a period of apostasy, after the judgment of *"the man of lawlessness"* (2:3 AE), and after the exposure of his signs and wonders as false (2:9). Although the identity and function of the "restrainer" (*katechōn*, 2:7) was probably known to the readers, his identity remains concealed from us in a Jewish apocalyptic haze. The precise role this figure would play in history's final apocalyptic drama is also a mystery.

Through the skillful use of these traditions, however, the author sought to modify the enthusiastic eschatology of his readers. By speaking of the delay of the "end" and the apocalyptic reversal of the position of the oppressor and oppressed on that day, he offered encouragement and consolation to the persecuted and exhorted the idle to work. The apostle's toil and labor while he preached the gospel offered an example worthy of imitation (3:7–12). The letter urged the church to shun all idle busybodies and, by publicly shaming them, to reclaim them for the church (3:6, 11, 14–15).

This author certainly knew 1 Thessalonians, for he drew on it and its Jewish apocalyptic tradition to address both the persecuted and the enthusiasts. Thus, by relying on 1 Thessalonians and the apostle's example and name, he offered comfort, encouragement, and correction. Although his use of a metric timetable marking the path to the end differed from that of the apostle Paul, the author correctly understood Paul's resistance to the excesses of religious enthusiasm, his emphasis on "work with the hands," and his suspension of the believer in an energy field between the now and the not yet.

1 TIMOTHY, 2 TIMOTHY, AND TITUS (THE PASTORALS)

The Question of Authorship

Since they were ostensibly written from a "pastor" [Paul] to "pastors," some 350 years ago these letters came to be known as the "pastorals." For much of the time since, it has been simply taken for granted that these letters, written under his name, were by Paul. In the early nineteenth century, however, biblical critics took notice that the language, style, and content of these letters radically differed from authentic Pauline letters. With very few exceptions, scholars today agree that Paul did not write the Pastorals. While their absence from an early manuscript (P[46]) may be discounted because part of the papyrus that might have held them appears to be missing, it is more difficult to explain why the second-century Marcion omits the Pastorals from his collection of Paul's letters (ca. 150 CE).

One could object that the antignostic polemic in the Pastorals was so offensive to Marcion that he rejected them, but it is harder to explain why they were eventually tacked on as an appendix to the letter collection in the church's first canon of Scriptures. That subordinate position suggests that though they were included, that acceptance was tentative. The church could not say no to the Pastorals, but it was unable to utter a resounding yes. Origen, the venerable church father of the third century, reputedly said, "God only knows who wrote the pastorals; Paul did not."

As with the other deuteropauline letters, the more compelling arguments against Pauline authorship of the Pastorals are linguistic and theological. Excluding proper names, about 20 percent of the vocabulary appears nowhere else in the New Testament, and approximately 30 percent of the language of the Pastorals is altogether absent from the undisputed letters. More decisive, however, than the quantity of unusual words is their distinctive character. The vocabulary of the Pastorals more reminds one of a Hellenistic-Jewish philosophical treatise than a Pauline letter. Such words as "piety" (*eusebeia*, 2 Tim. 3:5, Titus 1:1), "irreligious" (*anosios*, 2 Tim. 3:2), "way of life" (*agōgē*, 2 Tim. 3:10), "truth" (*alētheia*, 2 Tim. 2:15), "in accordance with piety," "loving good" (*philagathos*, Titus 1:8), "temperate" (*sōphron*, Titus 1:8), "self-controlled" (*enkratēs*, Titus 1:8; all ATs) are more characteristic of the popular Hellenistic writings of the day than of the letters of Paul.

Moreover, some of the vocabulary that is integral to the undisputed letters appears nowhere in the Pastorals. Such words as "uncircumcised" (fourteen times), "to die" (thirty-five times), "to proclaim the good news" (*euangelizestai*) (eighteen times), "spiritual" (eighteen times), and "body" (fifty-nine times), though important to Paul, appear nowhere in the Pastorals. While an argument from silence is suspect if used alone, when taken with the other positive evidence cited above, it raises insurmountable objections to Pauline authorship.

While statistical evidence is valuable, seldom is it decisive by itself in deciding questions of authorship. A comparison of the outlook of the Pastorals with that of the genuine letters is more instructive. First, the understanding of the church in the Pastorals is markedly different from that of the undisputed letters. The institutional forms we see in the Pastorals are clearly more developed. Through the laying on of hands "Paul" ordained Timothy to a ministerial task (2 Tim. 1:6), and Timothy in turn was to pass on the apostolic charisma (2 Tim. 2:1–2). Thus the church received an ordained clergy that claimed apostolic authority authorizing it to maintain "sound teaching." In that apostolic chain Timothy and Titus were empowered to appoint "elders" to govern the church and proclaim the word. They also were to choose deacons who were sober, unselfish, married only once, and good managers (1 Tim. 3:8–13). Those deacons, once installed, were to manage the church and to administer charity; the elders were to govern and to preach. The Pastorals charge leaders to protect "sound teaching" from false interpretation or compromise and to guarantee institutional health. The genuine letters met both internal and external threats with vigorous and often heated rhetoric. The Pastorals, however, offer little independent argumentation. The mission of their church was expansive and its posture defensive.

The emphasis of the Pastorals departs significantly from that of the undisputed letters. For Paul, church leadership was charismatic or Spirit-endowed; for the Pastor, the leadership was institutional. For Paul, "faith" was usually understood in an active sense (e.g., trust in God, acceptance of God's work in Messiah Jesus); for the Pastor, "faith" was a body of Christian truth to be guarded and defended. For Paul, the church was the body of Christ; for the Pastorals, the church was a fortress that defended its treasured "deposit" (1 Tim. 6:20; 2 Tim. 1:12, 14). For Paul, error was corrected by forceful debate; for the Pastor, the correction came through a calm comparison with truth. For Paul, the imminent return of Christ suffused all of his thought; for the Pastor, the second coming played an insignificant role. We see, therefore, that in their understanding of the church and its organization, purpose, and function, Paul and the Pastor were poles apart.

The ethical instruction of the Pastorals also differs wildly from that of the undisputed Pauline letters. Martin Dibelius, an influential German scholar, once referred to the paraenesis of the Pastorals as a bourgeois ethic.[16] That is, the deeds and rules prescribed in the Pastorals encourage a type of piety that was indistinguishable from that of the popular cultural ethos of the day. When Paul borrowed ethical material from Hellenized circles, he normally placed his own stamp upon it. The Pastor, on the other hand, hardly exerted such a masterful reshaping of his material.

Most importantly, the Pastorals depart significantly from their model in reaffirming a gendered hierarchy. In describing the role women exercise in the church, Paul spoke approvingly of the ministry of women. He noted with appreciation the contribution of female coworker Prisca; the important charismatic role of female prophets in the interpretation of Scripture in Corinth; the important leadership role of Mary, a servant of the Roman churches (Rom. 16:1, 3, 6). Only he in the entire New Testament recognized a female as an apostle (Rom. 16:7: Junia, not the masculine Junias of the RSV).[17] In Galatians Paul cited with approval a baptismal formula that announced that in Christ there is "no longer Jew or Greek, there is no longer slave or free, there is *no longer male and female*" (Gal. 3:28 AE). In the Pastorals, on the other hand, the accepted cultural norms prevail and still are oft cited as if they were Pauline.

Although the Pastor assigned some role to widows *over sixty*, he forbade a woman to teach or "to have authority over a man"; rather, the woman was

16. For one of the better commentaries and introductions to the Pastorals, see Martin Dibelius and Hans Conzelmann, *The Pastoral Epistles*, trans. Philip Buttolph and Adela Yarbro, Hermeneia (Philadelphia: Fortress Press, 1972), 22–25, 39–41. For an excellent, accessible, and more recent treatment, see Jouette M. Bassler, *1 Timothy, 2 Timothy, Titus*, Abingdon New Testament Commentaries (Nashville: Abingdon Press, 1996).

17. The definitive word on the textual veracity of Paul's reference to Junia as a female apostle has been offered by the preeminent textual critic Eldon Jay Epp, *Junia the First Woman Apostle* (Minneapolis: Augsburg Fortress, 2005).

"to keep silent." She was to earn salvation by bearing children, "*provided* [she continued] in faith and love and holiness, with modesty" (1 Tim. 2:12, 15 AE). It is hardly possible to harmonize the Pastor's thinking about women of faith with that of Paul's undisputed letters. Many contemporary church institutions still appeal to the Pastorals as if they were Pauline, to authorize their subordination of women.

But as noted above, the Pastorals should hardly be ascribed to Paul. In their own time the Pastorals played an important role. Some kind of institutional order was needed, and a structure in the emerging Jesus movement was necessary. Given the delay of Jesus' *parousia*, the threat posed by the "heretic" Marcion, the ascendancy of gnostic teaching, and episodic persecution and harassment, some adjustment of Pauline theology was deemed necessary. To that development we now turn.

Context of the Pastorals

Generations after Paul, the context of the church and the society that framed his ministry had changed dramatically. During his lifetime, Paul fought tenaciously and heroically to sustain, defend, and advance a Gentile mission whose long-term success was by no means certain. But by the early second century, the Gentile population of the Jesus movement was becoming dominant. That movement was by no means unified or assured of its future structure or theological vision. Inevitably, the problems Paul faced and addressed were later replaced by other challenges requiring institutional responses that Paul was hardly required to fashion. Paul's imminent expectation of the end in the face of its delay required some adjustment. The Pastorals obviously were crafted to face challenges Paul never knew.

The Problem within the Community

Although the Pastor refrained from aggressive confrontation with the false teacher, his contrast of sound doctrine with erroneous teaching offers an interesting picture of the teaching or "heresy" he opposed. Subscribing to Jewish "myths," "genealogies," and "commandments of those who reject the truth" (1 Tim. 1:4; Titus 1:14), the Pastor's opponents also engaged in certain ascetic practices. They repudiated marriage and avoided certain foods (1 Tim. 4:3). In claiming a present experience of the resurrection (2 Tim. 2:11), they effectively removed the eschatological reservation at the core of Paul's theology (2 Tim. 2:18).[18] They claimed "knowledge" (*gnōsis*, 1 Tim. 6:20; Titus

18. See notes 16 and 20 for suggested readings.

1:16) and possibly claimed the total freedom of expression by men *and women* in the service of worship. The emphasis on asceticism, aeon speculation, a realized eschatology, a higher salvific knowledge, and a libertine behavior linked with law observance suggests that this version of the Christ movement was a form of Jewish Gnosticism. The "false teachers" had enjoyed some success with the naive and unstable (2 Tim. 3:6–7; Titus 1:11); they had enriched themselves at the expense of the credulous.

In the paragraphs below, we shall note the Pastor's assured response to these challenges.

The Pastor's Response

The Pastor juxtaposed his reading of Paul's letters to those of his adversaries. His corrective had two facets. First, he sought authority for his interpretation of his "teaching" against that of the "errorists" by invoking the name of their hero—the once much maligned but now revered and rehabilitated apostle (especially by Marcion and Valentinus). He also adopted and wrote in Paul's name. By selecting and interweaving selected traditions from Paul, whom he presented as a patriarchal figure whose ministry was linked with the church's origin, he offered a corrective to false teaching.

Second, by appropriating those chosen and trusted by Paul, namely, Timothy and Titus, the Pastor claimed authority for commissioning deacons and elders to guide the church and legitimized them with this historical linkage. The Pastorals had "Paul" write Timothy, a coworker and a "loyal child in the faith" (1 Tim. 1:2), and Titus, "my loyal child in the faith we share" (Titus 1:4), and authorize them to "appoint elders" (Titus 1:5) and "deacons" (1 Tim. 3:8–13). Thus, through Paul's students in ministry, the Pastor cleverly forged a historical link with Paul that said "mine is better than yours." In the dispute with the later gnostics, this chain of authority evidently proved useful. Although the link with the apostle was forced, there was a certain aptness in the appeal, because Paul had opposed gnostic tendencies in Corinth. Though his strategy would have been different, Paul might have agreed with the Pastor on the seriousness of the threats posed by the rival teachers.

In addition to his appeal to authority through Paul, the Pastor also provided a substantive alternative to the rival emphasis on asceticism, aeon speculation ("myths"), realized eschatology, and superior knowledge (*gnōsis*). Instead of seeking to discredit the views of the "false teachers" through direct confrontation, the Pastor simply contrasted their "silly myths" with his "sound doctrine." A "knowledge of the truth" (Titus 1:1), "sound doctrine" (Titus 1:9), and what was "sound in *the* faith" (Titus 1:13 AE), or "teaching" (1 Tim. 4:16) was contrasted with the *gnōsis* of the adversaries. The "sound words of our Lord Jesus Christ and the teaching that [was] in accordance with godliness" (1 Tim. 6:3) were compared to the claims of those swollen with conceit (1 Tim. 6:4). The "good confession" (1 Tim. 6:12) belonged to those who "rightly [handle] the word of truth" (2 Tim. 2:15) and confuted those who engaged in "wrangling over words" (2 Tim. 2:14) or who engaged in "profane chatter" (2 Tim. 2:16).

Thus not only did the Pastor avoid a pitched battle with his adversaries; he also advised his addressees to refrain from any direct challenge to the "false teachers." He urged them instead to abstain from "stupid and senseless controversies" (2 Tim. 2:23, thus dignifying their "godless and silly myths" by refuting them directly) and to correct their "opponents with gentleness" (2 Tim. 2:25), hoping for their repentance. One feature that shone through all of his response was the Pastor's remarkable confidence that this soft approach to the errors of those "of corrupt mind" (2 Tim. 3:8) would be recognized by all and would lead to reform.

In his attempt to counter the ascetic tendencies of the gnostics, the Pastor suggested that all foods were to be received with thanksgiving (1 Tim. 4:3). Against those who forbade marriage,[19] the Pastor recommended it for young widows and presumably for the unmarried as well. Against those who claimed to have already experienced the resurrection, he held up a pale copy of traditional Pauline eschatology that assigned "the last days" and the resurrection to the future. Appealing to Pauline teaching, the Pastor said, "If we have died with him, *we will* also live with him" (2 Tim. 2:11 AE). Finally, it seems possible, if not probable, that the traditionally subordinate position assigned to women in the Pastorals was a reaction against alternatives in vogue elsewhere in the Marcionite church and among the gnostics.[20]

We saw in our discussion of the Corinthian correspondence that religious enthusiasts promised an existence transcending sexuality to those fully experiencing salvation in the present. In their glorified state some Corinthians held that all distinctions between men and women were erased. Agreeing with Paul, and following his celibate model, they could say that in Christ "there is no longer male and female" (Gal. 3:28). Gnostics known to the Pastor shared a similar viewpoint. The Pastor attempted to refute such claims by imposing on women the traditional social restrictions that the gnostics had abandoned in the name of liberation.[21]

19. See Calvin Roetzel, "Paul in the Second Century," in *The Cambridge Companion to St. Paul* (Cambridge: Cambridge University Press, 2003), 227–41.

20. See reference in footnote 19.

21. It is interesting that those who oppose the ordination of women or who seek to assign women a subordinate role most often appeal to the Pastorals rather than the undisputed Pauline letters.

The Pastor commanded women to avoid alluring attire and to "learn in silence with full submission" (1 Tim. 2:11). They were forbidden to teach (as they did in Corinth) or to exercise authority over men, as Phoebe and Junia would have done, and they were to earn their salvation by bearing children, that is, the church was to grow by propagation as well as evangelism (1 Tim. 2:12–15).

It is tempting to suggest that these letters lack the vitality and interest of the undisputed Pauline letters. The Pastor's static view of faith and his demeaning view of women offend modern sensibilities. He could be faulted for his bourgeois ethic, which has significantly impacted Pauline interpretation over the centuries. One could easily point to the Pastor's lack of intellectual rigor and theological creativity. But however harshly we judge his ideology, in retrospect we know that the ideology of the gainsayers was formidable. Had Gnosticism or the teaching of Marcion dictated the future and theology of the church,[22] the history of the whole Western world would have been very different. Had Gnosticism triumphed, the church as we know it would hardly be recognizable.

In summary, our survey of the deuteropauline letters has recognized various interpretations of the Pauline tradition designed for later contexts. The Gentile mission had succeeded so well that the Gentile church was in a position to determine its own agenda, to create its own theological idiom, and to chart its own course, heedless of the views of the Jerusalem circle or the sensibilities of a shrinking Jewish Christian membership. The Roman-Jewish War had exacerbated tensions between Jews and non-Jews, and those tensions threatened the relationship of Jewish to Gentile believers. The growing theological disputes and animosity between synagogue and church were waving them steadily toward a decisive rupture. The loss of confidence in traditional religious forms, combined with a growing disenchantment with social institutions, was to spark off a vast array of world-denying movements (Gnosticism being the most notable among them). The *parousia*, or return of Jesus, so eagerly expected by Paul, had not come, even though Jerusalem lay in ruins and Roman Christians had suffered severe persecution under Nero.

None of these events was foreseen or addressed by Paul. It is a tribute to him, nevertheless, that in his teaching, personality, and example, others in a vastly different age found instruction and encouragement, consolation and hope. Given the benefit of our perspective, we can see certain differences

22. J. D. Quinn, *The Letter to Titus* (New York: Doubleday, 1990), and John Knox, *Marcion and the New Testament: An Essay in Early Christian History* (Chicago: University of Chicago Press, 1942), both held Marcion to be the object of the mild polemic in the Pastorals.

or even contradictions when comparing the deuteropauline letters with the undisputed epistles of Paul. But the very use of the Pauline tradition is proof that the deuteropauline authors chose to associate themselves with the tradition of an apostle who, in spite of being viewed as a pariah in some circles, was also seen as a prodigy in others. They chose to associate themselves with the traditions of the prodigy in order to complement it, rather than contradict it.[23]

Outline of 1 Timothy

1. Address and Salutation	1:1–2
2. The Theology of the Opponents	1:3–20
3. Instruction for Prayer and Worship	2:1–15
4. Requirements for Bishops and Deacons	3:1–16
5. The Ethics of the Opponents	4:1–10
6. Instructions for Directing the Church	4:11–6:19
7. Letter Ending	6:20–21

Outline of 2 Timothy

1. Address, Salutation, and Thanksgiving	1:1–5
2. Advice to Timothy	1:6–4:5
a. Do not be ashamed	1:6–14
(Example: Onesiphorus)	1:15–18
b. Be strong in suffering	2:1–7
(Example: Paul)	2:8–13
c. Strategy to be used against the "heresy"	2:14–4:5
(1) Avoid godless chatter; rightly handle the word of truth	2:14–19
(2) Shun passion and controversy; seek love and peace	2:20–26
(3) Struggle with false prophets; follow Paul's example in teaching, endurance, and love	3:1–17
(4) Preach the word; endure suffering	4:1–5
3. Paul's Situation	4:6–18
a. Imminent martyrdom	4:6–8
b. Final instructions for Timothy	4:9–15
c. Paul's trial and rescue	4:16–18
4. Letter Closing	4:19–22

23. From Luke's extended treatment of Paul's mission in Acts, the collection of Paul's letters noted in 2 Pet. 3:16, and the imitation of his epistolary style in Colossians and Ephesians, it is clear that Paul, who was unwelcome in many quarters during his lifetime, was widely hailed in Asia Minor and Greece after his death.

Outline of Titus

8

Currents and Crosscurrents

Controversy swirled around Paul in death and life. During his Gentile mission, heated exchanges with antagonists punctuated his letters. Conflict with public officials, arrest, and incarceration interrupted his ministry. Harassment and beatings at the hands of his synagogue critics sapped his energies and aggravated his spirit. And even after death cut short his mission, Paul's power to provoke continued. More than a century after his burial, he still infuriated some Jewish Christians. One circle of believers tagged him with the unflattering epithet "Simon Magus," a notorious demonic magician whom Christian apocryphal materials castigated.[1] Some later accused Paul of diverting Christianity away from Jesus' teachings into a stagnant dogmatic backwater.[2] Paul is still anathema to some who view him as a male chauvinist.

Although Paul has always had his detractors, he also has had his defenders. If the test of profound and seminal thinking was its ability to generate debate, then certainly Paul's thought has met that test. His letters meant enough to merit collection and preservation. His vigorous and imaginative interpretation of the gospel spawned a family of letter imitations. The writers of those imitations (Colossians, Ephesians, 2 Thessalonians, 1 and 2 Timothy, and Titus) were so impressed by Paul that they adopted his name to legitimate their teaching. The shadow of the apostle also fell across Acts, Hebrews, possibly the Gospel of Mark and other, noncanonical Christian writings. The *Acts of Paul and Thecla* of the late second century was considered canonical in

---

1. Edgar Hennecke, *New Testament Apocrypha*, ed. Wilhelm Schneemelcher (Philadelphia: Westminster Press, 1964), 2:122.
2. This unfortunate juxtaposition of Paul and Jesus is discussed below.

the Syrian church. Allusions to Paul and quotations from his letters abound in writings of the early church. Pivotal exegetes like Augustine and Luther found in Paul the lens through which they read all Scripture. We see, therefore, Paul's power to provoke and excite endured and still remains.

In the following pages we shall sketch key topics of the continuing dialogue with and about Paul. Viewing the currents and crosscurrents in the history of Pauline interpretation should help us gain a better appreciation of the subtlety or even profundity of Paul, as well as locating passages in his letters that continue to challenge, excite, and frustrate. Although there is no magic formula that will guarantee easy mastery of these ancient documents, the recognition of passages that have provoked and inspired may assist in our attempt to divine the substance of Paul's thought.

We shall focus on five issues that have dominated Pauline interpretation. In chronological order, they are (1) Gnosticism: the problem of evil in the world; (2) Pelagianism: the problem of sin; (3) the relationship of Paul to Jesus; (4) the relationship of Paul to his background; and (5) Paul and women.

GNOSTICISM: THE PROBLEM OF EVIL IN THE WORLD

The feud over the proper relationship of the Christ believer to the world smoldered for almost a century and then erupted in blazing fury in the second century. The first-century author of Colossians already attacked those in the church who scorned the world below and favored the world above. The worship of angels (Col. 2:18), the elevation of visionary experiences, and the promise of an apotheosis for those who acquired divine or cosmic knowledge (2:18, 20) all unveiled the otherworldly preoccupation of those marginal groups. Their special disdain for this world manifested itself in such prohibitions as "Do not handle, do not taste, do not touch" (2:21). That reckless abandon joined an ascetic emphasis that treated the material world with disgust and accused those bound to this world of "fornication, impurity, passion, evil desire, and greed" (3:5). A strange logic held that world denial and physical indulgence together. World rejection demonstrated deliverance from the world, and worldly indulgence manifested one's triumph over it. Some Christ gnostics felt obligated to transgress all moral strictures that earthlings imposed, to claim a place in a higher order.

In the second century the Pastorals (1 and 2 Timothy and Titus), written under Paul's name, were summoned to authorize the thought of gnostic opponents. In 1 Timothy, for example, those who had "missed the mark as regards the faith" (6:21) claimed knowledge (Gk. *gnōsis*). More than just intellectual apprehension, that *gnōsis* became synonymous with salvation for "heretics"[3] who claimed an enlightenment (2 Tim. 2:18) that bestowed a euphoric sense of triumph over the evil world. Even though those opponents were called "Jews" (Titus 1:10), they rejected the Jewish belief in the creation's fundamental goodness (1 Tim. 4:4). Their adherence to "godless and silly myths" (1 Tim. 4:7 RSV) and their use of "endless genealogies" (1 Tim. 1:4) invoked a hierarchy of angelic mediators to bridge the gulf between the good God and the evil world. Against that gnostic appeal to Paul's letters for support, the Pastorals offered a counterweight.

Second-century Gnosticism almost conquered under Paul's banner.[4] Although Gnosticism was multifaceted, it echoed Paul's writings with regularity. Gnostic sects everywhere disdained the material world and things of the flesh, and that disdain spilled over onto the world's Creator. If the earth is evil, they reasoned, its architect must also be evil. Christian Gnosticism, consequently, often contrasted the creator God of the Old Testament with the God revealed in Christ. The world's creator or "god of this world" (2 Cor. 4:4) they deemed diabolical and the direct opposite of the good and gracious God of the highest heaven. Salvation, naturally enough, they understood as liberation from this earthly prison and as rescue from it and its worldly flesh.

The gnostic myth held that through some tragic failure a spark of the divine was planted in some (but not all) persons. With the memory of that divine origin erased, humanity sank into an ignorant stupor until the high merciful God sent Christ to awaken the memory of the "spiritual" in those fallen into ignorance of their divine origin. More than an instant of mental recall, however, that epiphany forged a union with the heavenly self through which came experiences of transcendence. In dreams, visions, tongues speaking, and heavenly journeys (see 2 Cor. 12:1–6) came intimations of the fullness of their celestial home. The gnostic *Gospel of Philip* later described that process: "Those who say that the Lord died first and (then) rose up are in error, for he rose up first (then) died. If one does not first attain the resurrection, will he not die?" (*Gospel of Philip* 56:15–19).[5]

3. As noted above, the term "heretics" in this early period hardly referred to a person who was doctrinally perverse and, therefore, to be damned, but, rather, to one of a different religious opinion.

4. See Elaine Pagels, *The Gnostic Paul: Gnostic Exegesis of the Pauline Letters* (Philadelphia: Trinity Press Int., 1992).

5. James M. Robinson, ed., *The Nag Hammadi Library* (New York: Harper & Row, 1977), 134. See also a "Life of Rabbula," composed by a colleague of the bishop and cited in Walter Bauer, *Orthodoxy and Heresy in Earliest Christianity*, 2nd ed., ed. Robert A Kraft and Gerhard Krodel (Philadelphia: Fortress Press, 1971), 26–27, and Calvin Roetzel, "Paul in the Second Century," in *The Cambridge Companion to St. Paul* (Cambridge: Cambridge University Press, 2003), 227–41.

Moreover, since the physical body shared the taint of this depraved world, the very idea of the resurrection of that body was repugnant. Absorption with celestial things—divine mysteries, esoteric wisdom, manifestations of the power of the Spirit, and libertine demonstrations of freedom from the body—balanced the imprisonment in this fallen world. As "spiritual" beings, gnostics worshiped the *spiritual* Christ and conveniently ignored or even cursed the *earthly* Jesus.[6]

Marcion was a key second-century figure at the center of raging controversy about Paul. Whether he was a gnostic, strictly speaking, is questionable; certainly his outlook shared features of the gnostic vision and, perhaps mistakenly, was associated with the movement. Although he was excommunicated from the Roman church in 144 CE, the movement that he founded dominated Syria until the beginning of the fifth century. So-called orthodoxy prevailed over the Marcionite church only after Bishop Rabbula (411–35) of the state church promoted the destruction of its churches and confiscation of its property. Thereafter, the zealous bishop "gently" persuaded Marcionites to give up their "error," be "baptized," and submit to the "truth."[7]

Interestingly enough, Paul's letters, along with the Gospel of Luke, formed the heart of Marcion's Bible, which he called the "New Testament" as opposed to the "Old Testament" (also his term). It may seem strange that the gnostics were so fond of Paul, until one notices that certain statements of Paul, isolated from their immediate and broader context, seem to buttress gnostic claims. For example, in 1 Corinthians 9:26–27 we read, "I punish my body and enslave it"; Paul spoke of the body as an enemy to be beaten into submission. Elsewhere Paul spoke pejoratively of the flesh (e.g., "nothing good dwells . . . in my flesh," Rom. 7:18) and begged for deliverance from "this body of death" (Rom. 7:24). Romans 8:23 also resonated with the gnostics; they read Paul's view that we "ourselves, who have the first fruits of the Spirit, groan inwardly while we wait for adoption, the redemption *of* our bodies," as "redemption *from* our bodies" (AE). Since they despised the body, the gnostics could easily join Paul in saying, "Flesh and blood cannot inherit the kingdom of God" (1 Cor. 15:50).

In other passages too the gnostics claimed that Paul advocated views they cherished. They were preoccupied with "spiritual things" and with divine mysteries. Paul also, they discovered, spoke of "what no eye has seen, nor ear heard, nor the human heart conceived" (1 Cor. 2:9). Moreover, Paul boasted of a vision in which he was "caught up into Paradise and heard

6. Birger A. Pearson, "Did the Gnostics Curse Jesus?" *Journal of Biblical Literature* 86 (1967): 301–5.

7. Ibid.

things that are not to be told, that no mortal is permitted or able to repeat" (2 Cor. 12:3–4). They too aspired to fly to the third heaven to receive special visions and to taste the ambrosial food and drink. They found Paul's division of people into the "spiritual (*pneumatikoi*)" and the "fleshly (*sarkikoi*)" (1 Cor. 3:1) quite useful.

The gnostics also found support in Paul for the radical dualism between the world above and the world below. In 2 Corinthians 4:4 Paul referred to the "god of this world [who] has blinded the minds of the unbelievers." While Paul was probably referring there to Satan, the gnostics read the passage to mean the "creator God." They concluded from this reference that it was the evil God, YHWH/Elohim, who "blinded the minds" of humanity so that mere mortals could no longer remember the true, extramundane, changeless God or even their own celestial origin. The stubborn insistence of the gnostics that YHWH was the evil "god of this [evil] world" clashed with the classic Hebrew view that YHWH was just and merciful and that the creation was good. The Jew delighted in the pride that YHWH took in this handiwork: "God saw everything that he had made, and indeed, it was very good" (Gen. 1:31). The gnostic rejection of the Old Testament as the revelation of a base, pretender God, in favor of Christian writings about a gracious higher God, drove a wedge between Hebrew Scriptures and Christian tradition.

This threat of divorce sharply posed the question of the relationship between Jewish and gnostic Christ traditions. Early in the second century the church fathers[8] took up their cudgels against the gnostic position. Central to their attack was the conviction that the Hebrew Scriptures and Christian writings belonged together. They vehemently denounced as a grotesque caricature the gnostic teaching that YHWH was wicked. They argued instead that the God of the creation and Israel was the same God revealed in Jesus Christ. They tirelessly maintained that there was no basis in Paul for the dualism of the gnostics. Third-century Origen persistently objected that there was no evidence in Paul's letters to support the view that matter per se was evil. Irenaeus, a second-century bishop of Lugdunum (Lyons), attempted to rob the gnostics of their base of support in Paul. He knew of the gnostic use of Paul's statement that "flesh and blood cannot inherit the kingdom of God" (1 Cor. 15:50), but against that use Iraeneus submitted four reasons for his belief in the resurrection of the physical, fleshly body, all of them drawn from Paul's letters.

Causing the greatest challenge for the Fathers was Paul's interpretation of the law. The gnostics had gathered grist for their mill from passages such as Romans 3:21, where Paul appears to repudiate the law: "But now, apart from

---

8. Church leaders of both east and west whose writings were the chief sources of emergent doctrine and church observance.

law, the righteousness of God has been disclosed." The gnostics read this and similar passages as support for their rejection of the Hebrew Scriptures. The Fathers *were* justifiably puzzled by the ambiguity and shifting emphases in many of Paul's statements about the law. Origen, for example, noted six different ways Paul used the term "law."[9] The Fathers admitted that Paul's characteristic emphasis on grace seemed to relegate law to a subordinate role, yet Paul's own recasting of the law in messianic terms as the "law of the spirit" (Rom. 8:1) and the "law of Christ" (Gal. 6:2) demonstrated his positive assessment of law.[10] Following these cues, the Fathers overcame the most serious objection by reading the letters in the light of, rather than in opposition to, the Jewish tradition.

Their position prevailed, and in time the gnostic threat diminished. Nevertheless, the relationship of God to the world and the church to Judaism were hot issues, not only because those questions were important for understanding Paul, but also because they stood so near the heart of the life of the church until the modern period. Christian theologians still wrestle with the problem of how to be open to the surprises embedded in God's new acts without repudiating the old ones.

PELAGIANISM: THE PROBLEM OF SIN

Even during the controversy between Christian gnostics and the Roman church, other disputes were brewing over the interpretation of Paul. Whereas the gnostics longed for deliverance from the evil world, other believers fixed on the problem of sin and the release from its burden in this world as well as the world to come. Thus salvation from sin—that is, the justification of the unrighteous—held the attention of Christian theologians from the fourth century to the present. The principal figures in that debate were Augustine and Pelagius, both churchmen of the fourth and early fifth centuries. We know Augustine, of course, from his *Confessions* and other writings of the period. The British monk Pelagius, a brilliant theologian and serious biblical exegete, wrote major commentaries on Romans and 1 and 2 Corinthians[11] and shorter ones on all of the other letters in the Pauline corpus.

---

9. Origen, *Contra Celsum*, trans. Henry Chadwick (Cambridge: Cambridge University Press, 1965), 3.42, 4.66.

10. Maurice F. Wiles, *The Divine Apostle* (Cambridge: Cambridge University Press, 1967), 39.

11. Alexander Souter, *Pelagius's Expositions of Thirteen Epistles of St. Paul*, (Cambridge: Cambridge University Press, 1926), vol. 2, gives 120 pages of Latin text for the Romans commentary and 177 pages of commentary on the Corinthian letters.

At issue between Augustine and Pelagius was the understanding of the nature of sin, that is, its origin and remedy. Long before the first ink flowed from his pen against Pelagius (in 412 CE), Augustine had already tagged humanity as a "lump of sin" that could do nothing toward its own salvation.[12] Meanwhile Pelagius was teaching that humanity possessed the ability to live a sinless life but decided not to do so. His exegesis of Romans led him to reject the idea that sin was seminally transmitted. Following Jewish interpretations, Pelagius argued that the transmission of sin from Adam to all humankind was not by propagation but by imitation.[13] In his painstakingly careful exegesis of Romans 5:12, Pelagius found support for the view that human beings are sinners not by birth but by choice.

He concluded that the doctrine of "original sin" held by Augustine was false and contradictory: if "sin is natural, it is not voluntary; if it is voluntary, it is not inborn." These two definitions are as mutually contrary as are necessity and [free] will, Pelagius argued.[14] Pelagius thus raised questions about the scriptural basis of the doctrine of original sin and the anthropology implicit in it. He also asserted that such a view undermined the Christian doctrine of God. How, he asked, could a just God create sinners and then condemn them for sinning? How could a righteous God command, "You shall be holy, for I the LORD your God am holy" (Lev. 19:2), after making the human being congenitally incapable of holiness? How could Jesus command the believer to be perfect, "as your heavenly Father is perfect" (Matt. 5:48), if humanity should be so stained by sin at birth that it would be rendered incapable of perfection?

Pelagius quickly saw the implications of this understanding of Paul for the practice of infant baptism. Since he rejected the doctrine of original sin, he denied that babies were in need of cleansing from sin's stain. Although he endorsed infant baptism, he balked at the suggestion that it was necessary for the infant's salvation.

Given the position of Pelagius, it is easy to understand why he was infuriated by Augustine's prayer, "Grant what You command, and command what You will."[15] Such an attitude, Pelagius argued, would undermine moral striving and sanction the immorality that was pervasive in Rome.[16] Now that it

---

12. J. N. D. Kelly, *Early Christian Doctrines* (London: Adam & Charles Black, 1958), 357.

13. Souter, *Pelagius's Expositions*, 2:45.

14. See Jaroslav Pelikan, *The Christian Tradition: A History of the Development of Doctrine* (Chicago: University of Chicago Press, 1971), 1:1, 315 for his citation and further treatment of this passage.

15. Augustine, *Confessions*, 10:29.

16. Heiko A. Oberman, *Forerunners of the Reformation* (New York: Holt, Reinhart & Winston, 1966), 126.

was socially acceptable to become a Christian, Pelagius feared that the high
ethical imperative in Paul's gospel would soon be fatally compromised.

Not surprisingly, Pelagius and Augustine soon engaged in a public fight.
In 412 CE Augustine began writing to expose the "errors" of his rival. He
attacked both Pelagius's understanding of sin and his doctrine of human
nature. He disputed Pelagius's claim that God, not people, could be blamed
for the existence of sin, if it were imputed at birth. On the contrary, Augustine
objected, God made Adam and Eve free and innocent. It was through their
rebellion, not by God's design, that they and all after them became sinners.
Adam was able to introduce sin into the human context, but he was unable to
remove it. It was inconceivable to Augustine that the disobedient Adam could
produce innocent offspring.

Consequently, in Augustine's view the whole human experiment begun
by God suffered blight through Adam's fatal error. Augustine believed that
Romans 5:12 supported his understanding of sin. Working from a Latin text,
he read this verse to say that "death came to all, *in whom* [i.e., Adam] all
sinned." Also, his Vulgate text inspired him to read the Latin *in quo* as masculine ("in whom"), even though *quo* could be read as neuter ("in which"),
changing the meaning entirely. Apparently unfamiliar with the Greek text,
Augustine took the Latin *in quo* as masculine, giving the passage a different
and false meaning. Pelagius's reading of the Greek (*eph' hō*) as "because" was
not only linguistically more correct; it was more in line with the typical Jewish
reading: "death came to all *because* all sinned" (AE).

Paul obviously was indebted to his Jewish tradition that held that each
person became his or her own Adam by choice, not through propagation.
The apostle did recognize that social context exerted pressure on people to
act selfishly, but he hardly held the view of original sin as we know it. Thus
Paul could grant that there was a cultural or "worldly" bias toward sin, without calling it a necessity. Moreover, both Augustine and Pelagius seemed to
misunderstand Paul's view of sin as a cosmic power, competing with God for
control of the world.

Augustine further argued that Pelagius underestimated the power of sin
and overestimated the human power to conquer it. For once Adam introduced sin into the human context, Paul held, the trap was sprung. Creatures
in the grip of this dark and sinister cosmic power were, like drug addicts,
powerless to free themselves. Deliverance (i.e., salvation) had to come from
outside. Augustine held that this remedy was provided only by God and
of late through Christ. Thus he endorsed infant baptism, because at birth
infants need redemption. To Pelagius's objection that such redemption could
be effected only by faith, and therefore was not available to untutored infants,
Augustine retorted that faith is no human work but a gracious gift of the

Creator. For their salvation all mortals are dependent on God, and there is nothing they can do to redeem themselves.

The charge by Pelagius that total reliance on God sanctioned moral indifference brought an angry reply from Augustine. Like the ancient rabbis, he placed statements about God's grace and human responsibility side by side, without sensing any tension between them. Pelagius saw the Christian life as a cooperative affair: one half of the responsibility belonged to God, who endowed people with the ability to do right; the other half of the responsibility rested on individuals to exercise that ability. On the other hand, appealing to Paul, Augustine viewed the work of divine grace and human response in paradoxical and total terms: all is given by God, yet all is required of human beings.

In the opinion of Augustine, Pelagius's confidence in human achievement took the power to direct history out of the hands of God and placed it in mortal hands. If the creature is the maker of its destiny and has the ability to direct the course of history, the doctrine of the sovereignty of God is needless, or worse. Pelagius's emphasis on human freedom and responsibility virtually eclipsed the traditional stress on divine providence. In response, Augustine resorted to paradox once again to hold the two motifs in balance. Drawing on Paul's discussion of predestination in Romans 9:14–27, he coupled opposing statements: all things are predestined by God; the human is totally free and responsible.

The debate between Pelagius and Augustine raged for six years. Finally, in 418 CE Pelagius was officially condemned by the Synod of Carthage in North Africa and dropped out of sight. The debate continued, however, in spite of the official condemnation, because it was thought to be about a core issue of Christian faith.[17] More than a thousand years later Martin Luther argued that the anti-Pelagian tracts of Augustine still addressed the most urgent doctrinal question of his time. Augustine and Luther clearly were intellectual brothers in their assessment of human depravity and divine grace. Both came to their understanding of the gospel after searing personal struggles, and both found their way out of their distress through Paul's letters. Luther's own tortured autobiography colored the way he read both Paul and Augustine and led him to regard Pelagius's confidence in the ability of human beings to keep God's commandments as vain and naive.

With great poignancy Luther described his collision with Romans 1:17 and its obstinate refusal to surrender its meaning. He was galled by Paul's statement that "the justice of God is being revealed from heaven against all ungodliness and wickedness" (AT), and he was angry at God for exacting justice

17. Ibid., 127.

even if it were through the gospel. For no matter how hard Luther tried, he still failed to fulfill God's just demand. If salvation depended on performing the impossible, Luther groaned, how could one ever be saved? Near despair, he noticed the context of Romans 1:17. With astonishment he read the words, "the just shall live by faith" (KJV). Luther's moment of enlightenment came when he saw that it was through faith not works that one came to a proper relationship with God. This emphasis on God's justification of the sinner held enormous implications for the interpretation of Scripture and gave the interpretation of Paul a critical place in the theological debates that followed.

In assessing these men and the implications of their thought for our understanding of Paul, we should remember that Pelagius, Augustine, and Luther were all committed Christian intellectuals eager to discern and properly interpret the Pauline tradition. Pelagius did raise questions about troublesome passages whose truth could not be decided by some independent arbiter suspended somewhere above the rough-and-tumble of this world. Augustine misread and misunderstood Romans 5:17, but Pelagius failed to appreciate fully the cosmic and mysterious power of Lord Sin (a power, not sins [moral missteps]). So which was the more faithful to Paul?

Without realizing it, most American Christians, Protestant and Catholic, come to the letters with spectacles provided either by Luther, or Augustine, or even Pelagius. Justification by faith, which was at the heart of the thought of all three, has traditionally assumed a dominant place in Western Christianity. This motif stood near the center of Paul's argument in Romans and Galatians. But it is mentioned infrequently or not at all in the other letters. We need to be careful in reading these other letters, lest our preoccupation with the guilt of the individual and God's grace blind us to the great variety and scope of Paul's concerns elsewhere. Some scholars feel that Paul's thought should be viewed in a broader cosmic frame that includes but transcends the emphasis on individual salvation.[18] Others argue that justification by faith was the center of gravity of the whole body of Pauline letters. These unresolved issues continue to make the reading of Paul an exciting and challenging experience.

THE RELATIONSHIP OF PAUL AND JESUS

"Jesus was not a Christian, he was a Jew." So spoke the influential German scholar Julius Wellhausen in 1905. Many would still heartily agree. They would view Jesus as a charismatic Galilean with an uncanny feel for the

18. See Roetzel, *Paul: The Man and the Myth* (Minneapolis: Fortress Press, 1999), 93–134, for a discussion of election in Paul.

essence of true religion. Trusting completely in God, he lived a life free of anxiety and devoid of pretense. He cared little for religious rules or rituals, and he stepped across social barriers to befriend criminals, prostitutes, the poor, the sick, the ritually unclean, and little children. But somehow the primitive and beautiful religion of that Galilean peasant, so it is ofttimes claimed, has been spoiled by interpreters like Paul who obscured Jesus' simple religion with theological overlay, cluttered it with dogmatic assertion, and robbed it of vitality by institutional dogma.

In this scenario it is usually the apostle Paul who is seen as the initial corrupter of this vital, true religion. According to this view, Paul's insistence on the Jesus of the cross totally eclipsed Jesus the teacher in parables. Paul pushed aside the "gentle Jesus, meek and mild" in favor of the vindictive judge coming with God's angels in flaming fire. He forced Jesus' simple announcement, "Your sins are forgiven" (Mark 2:5), into theological speculation about guilt and redemption. This interpretation holds that the history of Christianity would have been entirely different had Paul's influence been limited to a small circle of converts. Paul's interpretation was decisive, however, because his influence was so far flung. As the Johnny Appleseed of early Christianity, he planted his gospel from Antioch to Rome. As the founder of churches, he locked the religion of Jesus in an institutional case. This Paul, many feel, cut Christianity off from its roots in the life and teachings of Jesus the Galilean holy man.

This juxtaposition of Jesus and Paul has a long history. As early as the seventeenth century, John Locke, an English deist, saw such a cleavage. He reached this conclusion after beginning a search for a "reasonable Christianity," free from the "shackles of dogma." He wanted to make a fresh appraisal of the New Testament, independent of the bias of a Christian orthodoxy inspired by Paul. This independent study convinced him that a great chasm ran through the New Testament between the simple gospel of Jesus and the complicated, obscure theology of Paul. The gospel of Jesus, according to Locke, came from the lips of Jesus himself, but the gospel about Jesus was the invention of later interpreters like Paul. The implications of Locke's study were clear. If one is to recover the message of Jesus in its pristine purity, one must strip off all dogmatic distortions, whether of the Church of England, of the Council of Nicaea, or of the apostle Paul himself. The four Gospels must be used as the primary and even exclusive source, if the simple gospel of Jesus is to be reclaimed.

This tendency to divorce the teaching of Jesus from the theology of Paul reached its apogee in the thought of William Wrede (1859–1906),[19] a

19. Wilhelm Wrede, "Paulus," in *Das Paulusbild in der neueren deutschen Forschung*, ed. Karl Heinrich Rengstorf (Darmstad: Wissenschaftliche Buchgesellschaft, 1964),

brilliant German biblical scholar. In his view, Jesus was a simple, pious Galilean peasant whose prophetic insight, moral sensitivity, empathy for the oppressed, and strong sense of the divine presence meant nothing to Paul. Although the apostle remembered Jesus as a real historical figure, the particulars of his earthly life meant little to Paul. Before Paul came, Wrede argued, Christianity was only "an inner Jewish sect," but after Paul we have "a Christian Church."[20] According to Wrede, the religion of Jesus is true Christianity, but the religion of Paul is a fabricated and institutionalized dogma.

More recently Geza Vermes, a reader in Jewish studies at Oxford University, tried once again to untangle the Jesus of history from the Christ of dogma. His study of the Dead Sea Scrolls and the Talmud persuaded him that Jesus was fully understandable only within the framework of first-century Galilean Judaism.[21] He found in northern Palestine a strong interest in the Elijah miracle tradition and in meditation, which would explain Jesus' acceptance there and his mixed reception in Jerusalem.[22]

Religious enthusiasm and ignorance of rabbinic tradition, Vermes concluded, were viewed differently in Galilee and Jerusalem. Placing Jesus in this Galilean setting, Vermes contended that Jesus probably did not claim to be the Jewish Messiah, that he certainly did not claim to be divine, and that he would have been outraged by the incarnation formula "true God from true God, . . . and was made man," as the Nicene Creed affirms. Vermes believed that it was Hellenistic paganism, not Paul, that led Gentile Christianity astray; nevertheless, it was church doctrine that spoiled the simple religion of this pious Galilean peasant and his Jewish followers.

It is difficult to understand why Paul should escape blame, since he enjoyed his greatest success in interpreting the Christian gospel for the Hellenistic mind. Vermes's approach avoided some of the mistakes of former scholars, but the jury is still out on his case. It would seem, however, that the challenge his thesis posed had already been met by two earlier developments in this century: (1) the advent of form criticism and (2) the studies of Albert Schweitzer.

Rudolf Bultmann and Martin Dibelius first taught that the traditions of Jesus circulated orally in certain forms (e.g., parables, sayings, miracle stories, and passion narrative) long before they were assembled and edited by the Gospel

---

94. More recently see the excellent treatment by William Baird, *History of New Testament Research*, vol. 2, *From Jonathan Edwards to Rudolf Bultmann* (Minneapolis: Fortress Press, 2003), 144–51. Also useful is Wayne A. Meeks, *The Writings of St. Paul* (New York: W. W. Norton & Co.), 363–64.

20. Work cited in note 19 above.

21. Geza Vermes, *Jesus the Jew* (London: William Collins Sons & Co., 1973).

22. Note the anachronism of using late Talmudic materials from post–third century CE to decipher a first-century practice.

writers. Through his careful study of the forms and their use of the Gospel writers, Bultmann proved that the church not only kept alive the Jesus materials through the oral tradition, but also shaped and interpreted them to address changing needs in the churches.[23] Gradually scholars have come to accept that the Gospel writers further shaped, edited, and interpreted the materials that they appropriated from the oral stream to speak to their own times.

Exegetes now realize that the Gospel writers were not composing objective historical biographies of Jesus but were writing their own story of Jesus' life with a strong theological emphasis. Mark, for example, underscored the importance of Jesus as the suffering and dying Son of Man. Matthew emphasized Jesus' role as the eschatological teacher. Luke spoke of Jesus as the bearer of the Spirit, the friend of the poor, and the fulfillment of Israel's hopes. Through form criticism we have learned to appreciate the Gospel writers as creative interpreters who left their imprint on their work through their selection, arrangement, and interpretation of the oral tradition. Once it was realized that the Gospel writers as well as Paul had strong ideological interests, the older view that the Jesus of the Gospels was free of dogmatic interpretation was no longer defensible. If any transformation had taken place, it clearly was not the work of Paul alone.

When Albert Schweitzer died in 1965, he was aptly eulogized as one of the great human beings of the twentieth century. As a missionary doctor in what was then known as French Equatorial Africa, a concert organist, and winner of the Nobel Peace Prize, he won the hearts of the Western world. It was his biblical scholarship that in the first place prompted him to give up promising careers in music, theology, philosophy, and a university professorship in order to enroll in medical school and found a hospital in Lambaréné. When Schweitzer went to West Africa in 1913, he carried with him a book-length manuscript on Paul. Fifteen years elapsed before he found time to prepare the manuscript for publication. When his *The Mysticism of Paul the Apostle* appeared, it was revolutionary. Scholars still consider familiarity with that work to be an absolute requirement for an intelligent discussion of scholarship on Paul. (See also Schweitzer's *Quest of the Historical Jesus* [1906], claiming to find the key for understanding the roots of Jesus' preaching and teaching in Jewish apocalyptic thought.)[24]

23. See Rudolf Bultmann, *History of the Synoptic Tradition*, rev. ed., trans. John Marsh (1st ed. in German, 1921; Peabody, MA: Hendrickson Publishers, 1993).

24. For an excellent critical assessment of Schweitzer's work on Jesus, see James M. Robinson's introduction to the 1968 edition of Albert Schweitzer, *The Quest of the Historical Jesus* (New York: Macmillan Co., 1968), xi–xxxiii. See W. D. Davies, *Paul and Rabbinic Judaism*, 1st ed. (London: SPCK, 1955; reissued numerous times), vii–xv, for an incisive treatment on Schweitzer's estimation of Paul.

In his Paul book he argued that the apostle likewise understood Jesus in the light of Jewish apocalypticism. In the first century, Jewish apocalyptic communities often held that God's eschatological rule would soon be ushered in by a period of intense suffering. Jesus, Schweitzer argued, identified his own rejection and death with that final trauma that would provoke God's rule. Paul likewise saw the cross as the pain or woe accompanying the birth of the new age. Schweitzer concluded from this that in their common reliance on Jewish apocalyptic thought and in their understanding of the passion, Paul and Jesus agreed.

Even while recognizing his groundbreaking scholarship, few scholars, if any, now accept Schweitzer's thesis that Jesus provoked his death sentence to force God's final denouement. Nor do they accept his view that the mystical solidarity with or participation in Christ was the core of Paul's thought. But all would agree that Schweitzer opened up new dimensions in the study of the relationship of Paul and Jesus. Whatever faults Schweitzer's work may have had, there is no escaping his essential point that both the character of Jesus' life and ministry and the proclamation of Paul were eschatological through and through, and both must be assessed in the full light of the Jewish apocalyptic thinking of their day.

Unquestionably, however, Paul's letters differ from the Gospels in style and emphasis. Long, involved discussions weave complicated patterns and make complex arguments in the epistles. Short, pithy sayings dart from the lips of Jesus; Paul's letters are heavy with thick abstractions (e.g., the righteousness of God). Authentic Jesus materials such as the parables bear the unmistakable aroma of this earth; the frequent allusions to Jesus' return (*parousia*) in Paul sound unnatural on Jesus' lips. The postresurrection situation and Paul's worldwide mission summon forth themes that were muted or absent altogether in Jesus' ministry. Paul reflected long and deeply on the meaning of the Christ event and the cross. But even though Paul modified the traditions and created new centers of meaning in Christian thought, his theology does not contradict the proclamation of Jesus. His work is an extension and even a reformulation of the meaning of the Christ event, but he and Jesus are no more incompatible than are Bartok and Beethoven.

THE RELATIONSHIP OF PAUL TO HIS NATIVE JUDAISM

Paul's theology is often portrayed as the antithesis not only of the teachings of Jesus but also, paradoxically, of first-century Judaism. When Paul entered the Jesus movement as an apostle, it is often assumed that he repudiated his ancestral religion, recalling it only in order to throw his gospel into bold relief.

In the conversion experienced by Augustine, Luther, and sixteenth-century pietists, it is generally believed, we have a carbon copy of Paul's own spiritual biography.

"Pick it up, read it. Pick it up, read it," Augustine reportedly heard a child singing. When he took up the Bible to read, his eyes fell on Romans 13:13: "not in reveling and drunkenness, not in debauchery and licentiousness, not in quarreling and jealousy. Instead, put on the Lord Jesus Christ, and make no provision for the flesh, to gratify its desires." Augustine reported: "Instantly, as the sentence ended, there was infused in my heart something like the light of full certainty and all of the gloom of doubt vanished away."[25]

So ended Augustine's long, dark night of the soul and his experimental profligacy. His dabbling in philosophy and Manicheism left him empty. His excursion into hedonism was unsatisfying, and with his conversion to Christianity, Augustine felt his period of blind and aimless groping ended. The change in Augustine was dramatic. In a sensitive discussion of his pilgrimage of faith, he contrasted the dissatisfaction and fruitless searching before his conversion with the peace and purpose he felt afterward. Even the birds knew, he said, that he was a Christian.

In many ways Luther's experience paralleled that of Augustine. Restless and dissatisfied, Luther left the study of law and philosophy at the university in Erfurt, Germany, hoping to find peace in the Augustinian monastery. But despite herculean efforts to live a blameless life, he felt condemned, empty, and wanting. Release came for his troubled soul through his discovery of Paul's emphasis on salvation by grace. A total reorientation in his self-understanding and theological outlook occurred. Energies once sapped by anxiety and guilt burst forth in highly creative ways.

The pietists of the late-sixteenth and seventeenth centuries likewise found support in Paul for a strong emphasis on conversion. In Romans 7 and 8 they thought they had found evidence that Paul divided life into two stages, one before conversion and the other after conversion. They read the first-person-singular references in Romans 7 as autobiographical statements that Paul made about his life as an unconverted, frustrated, guilt-ridden Pharisee. They pointed to 7:9, where Paul wrote, "I (*egō*) was once alive apart from the law, but when the commandment came; sin revived and I died." In 7:15 they believed they found a Paul distracted and utterly confused: "1 do not understand my own actions. For I do not do what I want, but I do the very thing I hate." That inward struggle, they believed, finally erupted in a cry of defeat in verse 24: "Wretched man that I am! Who will rescue me from this body of

---

25. Augustine, *Confessions*, 8.12.29.

death?" Then came the exclamation, "Thanks be to God through Jesus Christ our Lord" (7:25).

In this view, chapter 8 then referred to Paul's Christian life after his conversion. After the light of Christ had illumined his night, Paul exclaimed triumphantly: "Who will separate us from the love of Christ? Will hardship, or distress, or persecution, or famine, or nakedness, or peril, or sword? . . . No, in all these things we are more than conquerors through him who loved us" (8:35, 37). The pietistic gush over Paul's conversion was further supported, they believed, by Paul's appeal to his Damascus road experience reported in Acts (9:1–9; 22:6–11; 26:12–18). Upon conversion Paul, the zealous Pharisee, finally acknowledged that his efforts to keep the law had failed. Now he openly admitted what he had tried to conceal by frenetic activity. Now the ethical crisis was overcome in a dramatic conversion by which he found release from an enormous psychological burden of guilt.

The numerator in the experiences of Augustine, Luther, and the pietists was in each case different, but the denominator was the same. All spoke poignantly of a rescue from a dreadful past. All viewed life under grace as the exact opposite of a former life. All found in the letters of Paul the inspiration and direction for a metamorphosis. Given the pattern of their experience, it was natural for them to see in Paul the same rupture they experienced between unbelief and faith. Paul the Jew was called the unbeliever; Paul the emissary of Christ was made the model of faith. Paul the devotee of law was cast as a wayward, guilt-ridden Pharisee; Paul the recipient of grace became the apostle of freedom. Understandably such an assessment tended to drive a wedge between Paul's life in Christ and his life under the law.

Without question most Jews rejected Jesus as Messiah, and Paul, the apostle, endured conflict with the synagogue. Moreover, in Philippians he dismissed his considerable achievements under the law as "dung" (*skyballa*, Phil. 3:8). To the end of his life he expressed remorse for his persecution of followers of Christ before he reversed himself to become an apostle to the Gentiles. And finally, he wrote movingly of the revelation of God's righteousness "apart from law" (Rom. 3:21). All of this would seem to argue for a radical discontinuity between Paul the "Christian" and Paul the Jew.

A growing number of scholars, however, question this reading of Paul. They point out that Paul nowhere suggested either that he found the law intolerable or that he felt conscience-stricken because his frenzied attempts to keep it failed. On the contrary, Philippians 3:6 has Paul say just the opposite, namely, that he was "under the law, blameless." Furthermore, Romans 8:2 hardly meant that Paul held the two eras to be incompatible. Instead, Paul wrote of two laws: "The law of the Spirit of life in Christ Jesus has set you free from the law of sin and death." Whatever life in the Spirit was for Paul, it was not lawless. Did Paul here, as Jeremiah suggested, find that the gap between God's requirement (Mosaic law) and the human tendency to resist had been overcome? If so, he may not be repudiating the law but rather announcing the arrival of the day when the gulf between God's speaking and the human response was overcome. Jeremiah heard the Divine say, "I will put my law within them, and I will write it on their hearts" (Jer. 31:33). For Jeremiah that hardly meant that God's Torah would be repudiated, but that human resistance to the Divine would end. Evidently Paul believed that that time had arrived. In that day God would etch the law of the Spirit on the human heart, and human resistance would vanish, so there would no longer be a chasm between hearing and doing, or divine command and human resistance, but God's people would freely do what God inscribed on the heart.[26]

Also misleading, if not erroneous, was the view that Paul rejected his past when he became an apostle. Until his last letter (Rom. 11:1; 9:4–5) Paul continued to locate himself in the people of Israel (see also 2 Cor. 11:21b–26). He often wrote of the coming of the Messiah (Christ) as the fulfillment of God's promise to the Jews "first." He quoted from the prophets who, he held, anticipated God's new day in Jesus, and he believed that salvation not only emerged from the Jews but would also embrace them in the end time (Rom. 11:26). In addition, Paul's eschatology closely resembles that found in Jewish apocalyptic literature.

In his eager waiting for God's final visitation, as well as in the way he imagined the end to be, Paul was at one with much of first-century Judaism.[27] The difference is to be found in his conviction that in the death and resurrection of Jesus the end had already begun. The time clock read differently, but the numbers on the face were the same. We see, therefore, that although there were differences between the views of Paul and those of his Jewish contemporaries, the distinction was not total. Even Paul's reference to his achievements under the law as "rubbish" (Phil. 3:8) was not so much a repudiation of his past as it was a revaluation of it in light of his encounter with the new age inaugurated by Christ.

Almost daily we are made painfully aware of the separation of Judaism and Christianity. History books are replete with reports of bitter and shameful strife between Jews and Christians. Synagogue members go to their worship on Friday night and Saturday; Christians gather on Sunday. Vandals desecrate Jewish cemeteries and spray paint swastikas on synagogue walls.

---

26. For a fuller discussion, return to chap. 2 above.

27. See Roetzel, *Paul: The Man and the Myth*, 44. For a fuller discussion, see Roetzel, "Paul as Mother: A Metaphor for Jewish-Christian Conversion?" in *Paul, A Jew on the Margins* (Louisville, KY: Westminster John Knox Press, 2003), 9–18.

The memories of *Kristallnacht* and Auschwitz linger and haunt both Jew and Christian. Time and again these ugly acts stain human hands and painfully aggravate divisions and distrust. All of Western history and much of the present experience underscore the difference between these sister faiths. We should be careful, however, when we project these patterns of discrimination, prejudice, and hooliganism back onto Paul. Nowhere does Paul speak of "Christianity" as an entity separate from Judaism. Everywhere he envisions his Gentile mission as a part of God's promise to Israel to include all peoples in a final redeemed human family.

As we read the letters of Paul, therefore, it is best to guard against the too-common assumption that Paul rejected the tradition he once loved. Not only does this dislocation of Paul do violence to his thought; it also distorts our picture of first-century Jewish faith. Indeed, by reversing everything Paul says about his life in Christ, scholars have often fabricated a poor likeness of first-century Judaism. The construction went like this: Paul's gospel was joyful; Judaism was joyless. Paul was liberated from sin and death through grace; Jews earned their deliverance from divine wrath by law observance. Paul worshiped a God of grace; Jews worshiped a severe taskmaster God. Paul was self-giving; Jews were self-righteous religious snobs. But the more we know about first-century Judaism, the better we realize that this reconstruction is an absurd and dangerous parody.

As noted in chapter 2, the scrolls from Qumran have offered a needed corrective.[28] The community attended to God's law and knew itself also as the beneficiary of God's grace. The rule of the community offers a concise and sharp repudiation of the false and vicious historical fiction that law observance and grace were mutually exclusive. As strict observers of the law, their instruction proffered divine grace. Let us listen: "If I stagger because of the sin of flesh, my justification shall be by the righteousness of God which endures forever. . . . He will draw me near by His grace, and by His mercy will he bring my justification" (*The Community Rule* 11:12). The community opposed insincerity and hypocrisy, and its piety, although intense, was hardly joyless (e.g., see the Hymn Scroll). We see, therefore, that reading Paul by the light of the popular total reversals crafted out of Luther and Augustine not only sets Paul adrift from his moorings in the Hebrew religion, but also focuses our attention too narrowly on the salvation of the individual. With our attention riveted to this motif, as important as it is, we sometimes neglect other emphases in the letters.

---

28. See Geza Vermes, *An Introduction to the Complete Dead Sea Scrolls* (Minneapolis: Fortress Press, 1999) and *The Complete Dead Sea Scrolls in English* (New York: Penguin Books, 1998).

Most scholars would readily agree that Paul's theology is multidimensional. Disagreement exists, however, about what really was the dominant motif in Paul's theology. Scholarly opinion has fluctuated from the view that Paul's message was individualistic to the core, to the belief that his gospel was communal throughout.

The works of the late Rudolf Bultmann and Johannes Munck, two important twentieth-century Paul scholars, best pose these alternatives. Bultmann, possibly the most influential biblical scholar of the twentieth century, found the key to Paul's theology in his understanding of the human (i.e., in Paul's anthropology).[29] In formulating Paul's anthropology, Bultmann leaned on existentialist thought for guidance. Paul was aware, he believed, of the one question that forced itself on all humanity: Can a person be open to the future that stretches out ahead? Each person yearns, he believed, to be free enough to be open and honest in each encounter. In spite of this longing for truth in the inward being, however, each person feels that his or her life lacks the integrity, authenticity, and fulfillment that belong to its true nature. The creature begins, therefore, with a deep sense of emptiness. Each person wants authentic existence, but each refuses to believe that such comes only as a gift from God, as a reprieve from self. Each tries to secure authentic life by human efforts, not realizing that self-assertiveness always ends in self-deception and doubt.

This self-reliant/self-assertive spirit manifests itself in many ways, religious as well as secular. To attain to oneness with the cosmos, some perform sedulous religious duties but become self-righteous and alienated from the self and others. Others labor for recognition, cash, authority, children, and power, only to find that in truth they are working solely against a sense of their personal inadequacy. One's best efforts fail to secure what one most yearns for. The authentic existence they seek, however, is elusive. Yet each is unable to accept life from God, because God is out of his or her control. To enjoy freedom, the individual must surrender his or her autonomy, but that risk is great. The more insecure one is, the more one turns in on himself or herself; the more one turns in on the self, the more insecure one is; trapped, one is unable to break out of this vicious circle by one's own efforts.[30]

Liberation from this tangled web, Bultmann claimed, comes through the proclamation of the word of God. In that proclamation God's grace comes to the individual, not as a support of efforts to control one's future, but as a question: "Will you surrender, utterly surrender, to God's dealing?" In response to

---

29. Rudolf Bultmann, *Theology of the New Testament*, trans. Kendrick Grobel (New York: Charles Scribner's Sons, 1951), 1:190–252.

30. Bultmann, *Theology*, 1:285.

that question, one comes to the knowledge that one is loved unconditionally without doing anything to earn that favor. One can become open to a future where risk is possible. This authentic existence is not realized once and for all, but must be continually reexperienced in the question of God and the renewed acceptance of that unconditional love. While this brief summary is appealing in many ways, it so focused on the individual's experience of grace that it neglected the broad corporate themes and historical scope of Paul's theologizing.[31] For this brilliant scholar, decisive history was not world history but individual experience.

Juxtaposed against this understanding of Paul stands the epochal work of Johannes Munck, *Paul and the Salvation of Mankind*.[32] His book opened with a study of Paul's Damascus road experience. In the traditional view, that experience is seen as a release from pent-up frustrations accumulated through Paul's repeated, unsuccessful, and obsessive attempts to keep the law and from guilt heaped up by his compulsive hatred and fanatical persecution of innocent Christians. Like a boil opening to release its poison, so this theory goes, through conversion Paul's life was cleansed of its gangrenous infection. Munck objected that neither Acts nor Paul's letters offer even a hint that Paul's preconversion history groaned under any such heavy psychological burden. Instead, Munck argued, Paul's Damascus road experience conformed rather closely to the pattern of Old Testament prophetic calls. Paul, like Jeremiah and Isaiah, scribed that God "set me apart before I was born" (Gal. 1:15; see also Rom. 1:1; Isa. 49:1; Jer. 1:5). In Galatians 1:15–16, as also in Isaiah and Jeremiah, the call "from the womb" was linked with the mission to the Gentiles. Just as the prophets served under constraint, so Paul was under compulsion to fulfill Christ's commission.

According to Munck, these similarities place Paul among the ranks of the prophets. Like those prophets, he had a peculiar role to play in the history of God's people. Unlike the Old Testament prophets, however, Paul's role was to be acted out during the final scene in God's historical drama. In fact, as the apostle to the Gentiles, Paul was assigned the lead role before the curtain was to fall. The end of the age was delayed, Paul believed, so that the Gentiles could be brought into the community of God's people. In other words, the end of the world stood waiting for the completion of Paul's mission.

---

31. This has been best shown in the approach to Paul by one of his students, Ernst Käsemann, who emphatically and correctly underscored the importance of the cosmic sweep of Paul's vision and emphasis.

32. Johannes Munck, *Paul and the Salvation of Mankind* (Richmond: John Knox Press, 1959). I am certain that, were Munck still alive, he would insist that the term "mankind" included all humanity, without respect to gender, nationality, or status.

Romans 9–11 assumed pivotal significance for Munck's thesis. In traditional Jewry the question was often asked, "What is holding back the coming of the Messiah?" The usual answer was that only when Israel is converted will the messianic age come. Paul's mission to the Gentiles, enunciated in Romans 9–11, therefore, becomes essential for the success of God's plan. The strategy was to use the conversion of the Gentiles to arouse jealousy in the Jews and thus lead them to salvation. Paul's conviction that his role was crucial for the redemption of all humankind lent energy and urgency to his mission.

Munck wedged neatly into this scheme even the offering that Paul collected for the "poor among the saints" in Jerusalem. This act, like the prophetic signs of old, was pregnant with meaning. From Hebrew prophecy, Israel expected that in the messianic age Gentiles would stream to Jerusalem bearing tribute and uttering praises to Israel's God. Therefore, when Paul gathered in Corinth along with a delegation from the Gentile churches to deliver the offering to the "poor among the saints," they claimed a role in an eschatological drama. The offering symbolized the arrival of the messianic age to all, Jews and Gentiles.

In this brief resumé of Munck's thesis we have passed over many stimulating features of his work. Even this short summary, however, shows where he and Bultmann differ. Whereas for Bultmann the dominant emphasis in Paul was the salvation of the individual, for Munck everything in Paul was subordinated to the eschatological mission. The purpose of that mission was not the conversion of the individual but the reassertion of God's dominion over the entire creation.

Whatever the blemishes of his work (and there are many),[33] Munck at least identified the danger of melting Paul's thought down into a single emphasis on the individual and his or her salvation. Perhaps a swing to the opposite extreme is equally unwise. Paul was concerned with the salvation of the individual (1 Cor. 5:5), but never in isolation from wider historical and corporate concerns. Paul's theology does brush in broad cosmic themes (Rom. 8:19ff.), but the individual is not thereby reduced to the status of an insect.

Given our emphasis today on the gospel as a resource for the "inner life," and given our tendency to view matters of faith as private affairs, it is hardly surprising that we look for the individual emphasis in most things we read. I do not wish to speak against the dignity or worth of the individual, but it must be said that such an emphasis, if taken alone, stands in real tension with the outlook of Paul. God's call, for Paul, was more than a summons to enjoy salvation; it was an invitation to participate in a divine narrative that embraced

33. See the stunning review essay of Munck's book by William David Davies, in *New Testament Studies* 2 (1955): 60–72.

the entire human and nonhuman world (cf. Rom. 8), past and present. For the apostle there was no separation between individual fulfillment and group participation. To be in the community of God's people was in and of itself fulfillment on the highest level. So although in a certain sense Paul's message was personal, it was never private, and the individual was first, last, and always a social being.

PAUL AND WOMEN

George Bernard Shaw once called Paul "the eternal enemy of woman."[34] In his view, Paul insisted that the wife "should be rather a slave than a partner, her real function being, not to engage a man's love and loyalty, but on the contrary to release them for God by relieving the man of all preoccupation with sex just as in her capacity of housekeeper and cook she relieves his preoccupation with hunger."[35]

A modern view of Paul suggests that his words were, to say the least, patronizing. The outlook Shaw laid on Paul, however, was drawn from the deuteropauline letters, which portray Paul as a patronizing apostle who, even while urging love and mutual respect, commanded the wife to be submissive to the husband (Eph. 5:21–24). There a fictionalized Paul forbade women to exercise authority over men (1 Tim. 2:12) and decreed that they fulfill the divine purpose by having children and continuing in faith (1 Tim. 2:5). But really were they, as 1 Corinthians 14:34 suggests, to be silent in the churches? And ideally were both men and women in Christ to remain celibate (1 Cor. 7:7)?

Robin Scroggs once issued a savage caveat against this popular caricature.[36] He correctly noted that the support for the view of Paul as a male chauvinist

34. George Bernard Shaw, "The Monstrous Imposition upon Jesus," in *Androcles and the Lion*, as cited in Wayne A. Meeks, ed., *The Writings of St. Paul* (New York: W. W. Norton & Co., 1972), 299.

35. Ibid.

36. See the work of the late Robin Scroggs, "Paul: Chauvinist or Liberationist?" *Christian Century* 89 (1972): 307–9; "Paul and the Eschatological Woman," *Journal of the American Academy of Religion* 40 (1972): 283–303; and responding to critics, "Paul and the Eschatological Woman Revisited," *Journal of the American Academy of Religion* 42 (1974): 532–37. Various authors have commented on one of the more problematic passages in Paul's letters: 1 Cor. 11:2–16: William O. Walker, "The Non-Pauline Character of 1 Corinthians 11:2–16?" *Journal of Biblical Literature* 95 (1976): 615–21; Lamar Cope, "1 Cor. 11:2–16: One Step Further," *JBL* 97(1978): 435–36; G. W. Trompf, "On Attitudes toward Women in Paul and Paulinist Literature: 1 Cor. 11:3–6 and Its Context," *Catholic Biblical Quarterly* 42 (1980): 196–215. However, the removal

comes primarily from the deuteropauline epistles (1 and 2 Timothy, Ephesians, and Colossians). He joined other scholars in arguing that 1 Corinthians 14:33b–36 ("women should be silent in the churches") was inserted by a later hand to harmonize 1 Corinthians with 1 Timothy. Elsewhere in 1 Corinthians Paul assumed women were to be vocal participants in the church as prophets (1 Cor. 11:5). Moreover, Scroggs sided with Hurd[37] and the NRSV translators who place the slogan in 1 Corinthians 7:1 ("It is well for a man not to touch a woman") in quotation marks and thereby suggests that the slogan came not from Paul but from a religiously enthusiastic Corinthian church. According to Scroggs, the celibacy advocated for men *and* women revealed no disdain for women but a response to an apocalyptic emergency. (It was common in Jewish circles to suspend normal sexual activities in times of crisis [e.g., holy war] and for a time before priestly service at the altar.)

First Corinthians 11:2–16 posed more of a problem, however, for Scroggs. There Paul appeared to locate woman in an inferior position in the creation's hierarchy: just as God is the head of Christ, and Christ is the head of man, so also man is the head of woman, and woman is the head of the slave. But Scroggs countered by noting that that apparent hierarchy is actually a reflection on the Genesis creation myth. Since Paul took Christ to be preexistent and therefore an active partner in the creation of the world, God came first, then Christ, who became an agent of creation. Adam thus came from Christ, and the woman from the rib of man. Scroggs made this clever move by taking the Greek word for "head" (*kephalē*) to mean "source." Thus Scroggs was able to propose a novel reading: God is the source of Christ, Christ the source of Adam, and Adam the source of Eve or woman (via the rib).

If one follows Scroggs, then this hierarchy is not a recipe to subordinate woman or to establish male superiority, but a midrash on the creation story of Genesis 2. Scroggs held that Paul here stressed different origins in order to maintain a distinction between men and women in a congregation tending to erode them. In other words, Paul here responded to what he judged to be a scandalous view that in Christ all sexual distinctions disappear when possessed by the Spirit and in the company of angels.[38]

Scroggs concluded that there is no substance to the charge that Paul was an "eternal enemy" of women. On the contrary, he found support in the letters

---

of this passage would hardly alter the basic point of Scroggs, given the exhortation elsewhere on the important role women played in the early church (esp. Rom. 16). J. Murphy-O'Connor has argued that 1 Cor. 11:2–16 makes sense in its present setting, in "Sex and Logic in 1 Cor. 11:2–16," *CBQ* 42 (1980): 482–500.

37. See John C. Hurd, *The Origin of 1 Corinthians* (Macon, GA: Mercer U. Press, 1983) in relevant sections noted above.

38. See Scroggs, "Paul and the Eschatological Woman," 283–303.

for an enlightened or even liberationist view. Scroggs held that Paul proclaimed the complete equality within the community of all people and groups. Distinctions between groups remain. Values and roles built upon such distinctions are destroyed. Every human being is equal before God in Christ and thus before each other. Scroggs also noted that Paul lists women among his coworkers and alludes to a number of women who were active (presumably as leaders) in the church.[39]

Many scholars were delighted that Professor Scroggs was willing to challenge the historical accuracy of the persistent notion of Paul's view of the subordination of women. Few would quarrel with either the spirit or substance of his argument, for Paul is nowhere overtly hostile to women. Nevertheless, Scroggs's argument has met resistance not from the Christian right, but from other Pauline scholars.

Professor Elaine Pagels has expressed reservations about Scroggs's argument.[40] Although Paul did say that slaves are free in Christ, he quite obviously did not challenge the institution of slavery. In a similar way, Paul's affirmation that women are equal did not mean he was challenging "the social structures that perpetuate their subordination."[41] Professor Pagels pointedly challenged Scroggs's interpretation of 1 Corinthians 11:2–16.

In his statement that Christ is the source of man and man the source of woman, she argued that Paul does seem to fall back on the natural order to argue for the subordination of women. Especially troublesome is Paul's statement in 11:7 that man is the glory of God while woman is the glory of man. Pagels argued that Paul viewed "certain incidents or practices in the Corinthian community provoked by the presence of unveiled women believers to be disorderly or even scandalous and that by appealing to the primeval (i.e., divine) order, he hoped to restrict women's activity and thus restore order."[42] It is worth noting that Professor Pagels does not mention Paul's correction of male conduct making men also responsible for the restoration of order. Paul's final summary noting the interdependence of women and men (woman came

---

39. See the relevant discussion above in chap. 4, and Phil. 4:2–3 and Paul's reference to Euodia and Syntyche, who he noted "struggled beside me in the work of the gospel," and Rom. 16 if genuine. Also note 1 Cor. 16:19, which speaks of Aquila and Prisca, who host the church in their house.

40. Elaine Pagels, "Paul and Women: A Response to Recent Discussion," *Journal of the American Academy of Religion* 42 (1974): 538–49.

41. S. Scott Bartchy makes a strong case for this view in his *First-Century Slavery and 1 Corinthians 7:21* (Missoula, MT: Scholars Press, 1973), 161–72. And more recently, Jennifer A. Glancy, *Slavery in Early Christianity* (Minneapolis: Fortress Press, 2006), has offered a much acclaimed, wide-ranging investigation of slavery in early Christianity in antiquity.

42. Pagels, "Paul and Women," 544.

from man via the rib, and man now from woman through live birth, 1 Cor. 11:12) largely goes unnoted by Pagels.

As the scholarly debate over Paul's view of women continues, much remains unresolved. But the discussion has borne good fruit. The conventional picture of Paul as a culture-bound male chauvinist has collapsed under scholarly investigation. In many ways Paul's views were in tension with dominant cultural patterns, both Jewish and non-Jewish. He clearly expected that women would take an active role in the worship and witness of the church. Moreover, the evenhanded way he addressed both men and women in 1 Corinthians 7 is instructive. The equal share of responsibility apportioned suggests that he envisioned at least approximate equality in the partnership. That was revolutionary.

However murky 1 Corinthians 11:2–16 may appear, it seems clear that Paul laid a heavy burden on females *and males* to preserve the order in a fractious church. Some degree of subordination of woman may be taken for granted (esp. in 11:7), but it is often overlooked that Paul's main point was the distinction between the sexes, not the dominance of one over the other. With their claim of membership in an angelic company, did the Corinthian converts claim an existence above sexual distinction? We can hardly be certain.

In any case, Scroggs and Pagels agreed that it is unfair to criticize Paul for not challenging the structures of discrimination against women from an enlightened modern, liberal viewpoint. While it is true that Paul's gospel did relativize social and political structures and may seem to make some look unjust, he did not overtly call for their abolition (e.g., slavery). We cannot conclude from this that Paul either did or did not approve of such social discrimination. Paul may simply have found it unnecessary to challenge discriminatory social structures because to him they were temporary and would soon be gone. For example, in 1 Corinthians 7:31 Paul expressly encouraged his readers to "deal with the world as though they had no dealings with it. For the present form of this world is passing away."

One additional note is useful. Professor David Daube, of Orthodox Jewish heritage himself, once pointed out that Paul's expectation that a woman (in Christ) could consecrate her marriage with an unbelieving husband had no Jewish precedent (see 1 Cor. 7:14).[43] According to Jewish tradition, Daube argued, it was the male and only the male who consecrated the marriage after conversion. Translated, that consecration meant that the marriage contract,

---

43. David Daube, "Pauline Contributions to a Pluralistic Culture: Recreation and Beyond," in *Jesus and Man's Hope*, ed. Donald H. Miller and D. Y. Hadidian (Pittsburgh: Pittsburgh Theological Seminary, 1971), 223–45.

which was temporarily abrogated when the person became a new person with a new name after conversion, would be reconsecrated by the male through sexual intercourse. Paul, however, following Diaspora tradition, gave females the equal right to initiate divorce and in 1 Corinthians 7 allowed the female convert the power to "consecrate" her marriage to an unbelieving husband (v. 14); that is, after becoming a new person in Christ, when contracts abrogated required renewal, the wife could, through sexual intercourse, reconsecrate the abrogated marriage contract.

To return to our main point, even though the Scroggs-Pagels debate was groundbreaking, it occurred over a generation ago and now sounds dated. Since that time, other scholars, such as Fiorenza, Boyarin, Castelli, Wire, Anderson, and Susan Mathew, have offered a more developed and nuanced reading of the issues of power, gender, and metaphor in the Pauline letters. Certain texts from Galatians, 1 Corinthians, and Romans have taken center stage in this ongoing interpretative exercise. Of crucial importance in this discussion has been Galatians 3:28, where Paul says that in Christ, "There is no longer Jew or Greek, there is no longer slave or free, there is no longer male and female." Most agree that, in this fragment of a baptismal confession Paul cited, there was at least an implicit critique of the subordination of women. To my knowledge, no exact parallel to this creedal statement existed elsewhere in the ancient world.

To make being a Jew the primary referent, Paul argued, devalued the adequacy of his gospel. What scholars disagree about is the meaning of the phrase "there is no longer male and female" and the influence it had on Paul's thinking. Originally, Fiorenza argued, the phrase echoed Jesus' critique of "patriarchal marriage," which by definition constructed and promoted a structure of dominance.[44] Paul, however, compromised this radical imperative when he condemned Christian wives to silence in the worshiping church (1 Cor. 14:34–36). Unmarried women, Fiorenza argued, were allowed to speak, if by default they had no husband to ask or to speak for them. Thus Fiorenza saw a contradiction between the baptismal confession, in which all gender distinctions and hierarchies were swept aside, and 1 Corinthians 11:2–16 and 14:34–36, in which discriminatory gender distinctions were apparently reaffirmed and hierarchical structures reinforced.

Moreover, even within 1 Corinthians there is a contradiction. Resisting cultural pressures, Paul allowed women to remain unmarried (1 Cor. 7:34, 38) and thus to enjoy a new level of equality and freedom, but at the same time he subordinated Christian married women to their husbands (11:3) and

---

44. Elisabeth Schüssler Fiorenza, *In Memory of Her: A Feminist Theological Reconstruction of Christian Origins* (New York: Crossroads, 1983), 211.

forbade them to speak in the assembly of "saints" (14:34–36). Thus, Fiorenza suggested, even in the equality in Christ promised in baptism there was an inequality implied. In citing with approval a student's creation of an apocryphal letter from Phoebe, Fiorenza seems to endorse the suggestion that Paul's attempt to put women "in their place" was a vestige of Paul's "rabbinic prejudice."[45]

One of the sharpest critics of Fiorenza has been a distinguished Jewish Pauline scholar, Daniel Boyarin. He criticized Fiorenza for her tacit approval of a view that traces Paul's chauvinism to an attempt to completly "exorcise a demonized Jewish past."[46] While it is easy to agree that such historically "false and prejudicial depictions of Judaism" should have no place in Pauline interpretation, it may be more difficult to find a resolution to the apparent contradiction between the liberation promised in Galatians 3:28 from all hierarchies and structures of inequality and the reimposition of the hierarchies in 1 Corinthians 11.[47] It may be that Boyarin was correct, namely that Paul was simply inconsistent.

While they disagree on much, Boyarin and Fiorenza agreed on the importance of Galatians 3:28 as a key text for understanding Paul. Appearing in bright green letters on the dust jacket of his important book on Paul, this text, Boyarin argued, revealed Paul's "Hellenistic desire for the One, which among other things produced an ideal of a universal human essence, beyond difference and hierarchy. That universal humanity, however, was predicated on the dualism of the flesh and the spirit."[48] In Boyarin's view, Paul did not reject the body (i.e., its particularity as Jew or Greek, male or female), but he did subordinate it to the spirit, which he saw as universal.[49] Translated, this meant that Galatians contains a "theology of the spirit," and 1 Corinthians "a theology of the body." Boyarin argued that these two theologies were complementary, not contradictory. Whereas in the spirit there is no hierarchy, in the body there is a hierarchy.[50] These two opposed readings represented two realities: the "new creation," experienced in the ecstasy of baptism that negates all hierarchies, and the real world, in which there are indeed hierarchies. Thus, Boyarin claimed, there is "no contradiction between Galatians and Corinthians."[51] Paul's solution was a compromise. His gospel broke down all social

---

45. Ibid., 182.
46. Daniel Boyarin, *Paul and the Politics of Identity: A Radical Jew* (Berkeley: University of California Press, 1994), 182.
47. Ibid., 182–83.
48. Ibid., 7.
49. Ibid.
50. Ibid., 185.
51. Ibid., 190.

hierarchies on one level, but he was willing to accept them on another. At one level there was "permanent change in the status of gender at baptism, but insofar as people still live in unredeemed bodies, gender transcendence is not yet fully realized on a social level."[52]

While Boyarin's work is provocative, it raises almost as many questions as it answers. Can we legitimately make such a neat distinction between a theology of the spirit in Galatia and a theology of the body in Corinth? For example, there is considerable evidence against Boyarin's view that Paul unambiguously reinstituted hierarchy in Corinth. Was Paul really instituting a social hierarchy in 11:3, or was he projecting his preexistent Christ (Phil. 2:6) back onto Genesis 2 and thus creating the lineage God, Christ, Adam, Eve? Moreover, in 12:7–13:1 Paul appears to be subverting all hierarchies, even charismatic hierarchies; realizing their silliness and self-contradiction he suggested in a flash of insight, "I will show you a still more excellent way" and then offered his powerful ode to love (*agapē*) (13:1–13), the ultimate eschatological, charismatic gift that relativized all others.

Other questions also push forward. Can we isolate the experience of the transcendence of categories of gender to baptism's ecstatic moment? What role did Paul's eschatology play in his thinking that the age now breaking in was the age of the spirit, which could be experienced at many levels? Do the categories universal versus particular adequately frame the whole of Paul's thought? Does the presentation of Paul as an agile practitioner of realpolitik do justice to his deep conviction that he stood at history's decisive moment, when compromise was impermissible? Boyarin, however, correctly noted the tension in Paul's thinking and the apostle's steadfast effort to keep one foot firmly planted in this world, even as he moved the other into the world to come. That awareness is surely useful in deciphering Paul's understanding of gender.

Of the feminist critics who have sensitized Pauline scholars to issues of power in the relationship between men and women in the ancient world, few have been more adept in bringing those issues to the fore than Elizabeth Castelli and Antoinette Wire. Castelli has argued that Paul emphasized mimesis (imitation) as an artifice of power to control disruptive elements in the churches.[53] For example, in 1 Corinthians 11:1 Paul commanded his converts, "Be imitators of me, as I am of Christ." By identifying with Christ, Castelli noted, Paul secured his own superior position and used that advantage to suppress the dissent of voices such as the

---

52. Ibid., 195.

53. Elizabeth A. Castelli, *Imitating Paul: A Discourse of Power* (Louisville, KY: Westminster John Knox Press 1991).

female prophets.[54] By using a mimetic emphasis Paul discredited other gospels; in his metric there was either his gospel or no gospel at all. In the interest of conformity and unity in the church, rival versions of the truth were suppressed. Although Castelli cautioned that Paul did not actively coerce his converts against their will, "his repression of difference later became a license for brutal reprisals against dissidents in the church and Western institutions."[55]

Antoinette Wire held instead that Paul engaged Corinthian women prophets in conversation *throughout*, not merely in the isolated passages that explicitly named them (1 Cor. 11:5).[56] Partners in the conversation throughout the letter, these female prophets played an important leadership role in the church, and, Wire argued, Paul sought to limit their activity by urging them to surrender their status as prophets, to marry, and to preserve the reputation of the community. (Unmarried ecstatic women, she asserted, were frequently suspected of loose sexual behavior.) Paul, Wire noted, was disturbed by their wisdom theology, spirit possession, their charismatic speech (*glōssolalia*), and their claim to a freedom that allowed them to eat idol meat, to participate in free table fellowship with men, and to reject marriage for celibacy.

While all of 1 Corinthians includes these women prophets in conversation, two passages in particular play key roles in her investigation, 11:2–16 and 14:34–35. While Paul penned the former to control women prophets, he wrote 14:34–35, Wire held, to deny them voice altogether. Wire took the command that "women should be silent" as authentic, and as an address to female prophets. Of course, if 14:34–35 were original, Wire has a point. If, however, as I claim earlier, this passage was most likely a non-Pauline interpolation written to harmonize 1 Corinthians and the role it gave to women with the culturally conformist viewpoint of 1 Timothy 2:11–12, then Wire's argument is seriously weakened.[57] Given the second-century redaction of Pauline texts evident elsewhere, and evidence of tinkering with Gospel texts in the same period (n.b., the multiple endings of Mark), it is hardly useful to appeal to a later manuscript tradition (e.g., P[46]) to adjudicate this case. Finally, how could Paul have possibly cited the example of "all the churches of the saints" in which women are silent, when that was patently false? Carolyn Osiek has shown that Euodia and Syntyche, mentioned in Philippians 4:2–3, were influential women leaders collaborating with Paul, Clement, and other coworkers

54. Ibid., 112.
55. Ibid., 119–36.
56. Antoinette Clark Wire, *The Corinthian Women Prophets: A Reconstruction through Paul's Rhetoric* (Minneapolis: Fortress Press, 1990).
57. Gordon D. Fee, *The First Epistle to the Corinthians* (Grand Rapids: Eerdmans, 1987), 699–708, makes a compelling case for this being a later insertion. While Wire is aware of Fee's evidence, she does not respond to its substance.

and obviously speaking in church.[58] Their disagreements, therefore, according to Osiek, were theologically substantive and not mere "petty quarrels of women." Moreover, the women in the Roman churches were hardly expected to be silent. Phoebe served as a deacon (Rom. 16:1); Prisca (or Priscilla) was probably a member of a female-male missionary team and had risked her life for Paul (Rom. 16:3; Acts 18:2); Junia was a female apostle (Rom. 16:7); Tryphaena and Tryphosa were "workers in the Lord," as was Persis (Rom. 16:12); the mother of Rufus was like a mother to Paul (16:13); and Julia and the sister of Nereus were also worthy of mention. Of the twenty-six names noted in Romans 16, ten were women, and all were assigned important roles and obviously had a voice in the shaping of the mission of the early church.[59]

Although Paul may have sought to suppress voice at times, to deny women specifically a voice in his churches is historically incorrect. Clearly Paul had a history of collaborating with women as well as men in the spread of the gospel. The passages above then flatly contradict that 1 Corinthians 14:34–35 was from Paul's pen and that it sought to silence women's voices in "all the churches." Fee was correct; these verses were not from Paul but were added later to try to make Paul conform to the image of Paul in deuteropauline 1 Timothy.

Where does this discussion leave us? It is likely that Paul was neither a chauvinist nor a liberationist, but something in between. The evidence is contradictory. One cannot dismiss Paul's evenhanded treatment of men and women in 1 Corinthians 7, his references to women as his coworkers (Rom. 16), or his assumption that women would actively prophesy in a service of worship or serve as deacons and apostles. Nor can one convincingly argue that Paul's statement in Galatians 3:28 that in Christ there "is no longer male and female" had little social relevance. There are glimpses of an exciting new order in parts of Paul's letters, and the second century opens a window onto the importance of the role women played in the church (see the *Acts of Paul and Thecla*; note Marcionite women performing priestly functions; observe gnostic and Montanist women of importance, and note the women featured in early martyrologies).

At the same time, however, some degree of subordination seems to be taken for granted in Paul's statement that man is made in "the image and glory of God; but woman is the reflection of man" (1 Cor. 11:7). And even

58. See Carolyn Osiek's commentary on Philippians, in *Searching the Scriptures,* vol. 2, *A Feminist Commentary,* ed. Elisabeth Schüssler Fiorenza (New York: Crossroad, 1994), 246–47.

59. See the recent, excellent work of Susan Mathew, *Women in the Greetings of Romans 16.1–16: A Study of Mutuality and Women's Ministry in the Letter to the Romans* (London: T. & T. Clark, 2013).

Paul and Thecla Grotto Sketch in Ephesus (Courtesy of
www.HolyLandPhotos.org; used by permission)

though Paul applied feminine metaphors such as "nurse" and "mother" to his
own apostolic work (1 Thess. 2:7; Gal. 4:19; 1 Cor. 3:2), they were inversions
of his status as a dominant male. That dominant status comes through in
his use of masculine metaphors to persuade and threaten. In 1 Corinthians
4:14–21, for example, he claimed a father's right to thrash his children when
he came if they did not renounce their arrogant ways, and in 2 Corinthians
10 he assumed the status of a warrior. Castelli correctly noted the power
aspect of Paul's relationship with his churches, and Boyarin also correctly
saw tension in Paul between his acceptance and rejection of hierarchies of
domination.

So in Paul we find a mixture of the subversion and reinforcement of traditional hierarchical patterns. It would be remarkable indeed if the human
Paul did not reflect some of the prejudice, superstition, and bias of his own
time. The question is, how much should we worry about Paul's cultural views?
Does his unconsidered prejudice against women vitiate his views on Jesus and
on other important questions of life? Theologians have long argued that the
gospel is greater than any particular witness to it. (Perhaps that is why we
retain the versions of Matthew, Mark, Luke, and John, rather than one work
entitled "The Gospel.") Moreover, Paul's letters addressed a rather limited

set of circumstances. It seems unfair to denounce him for not anticipating and addressing concerns that the modern era has rightly raised to a high level of consciousness. This is not to say, however, that we can appeal to Paul's apparent acceptance of discrimination in his day to justify discrimination in our own. It was the gospel Paul preached, rather than his limited application of and witness to it, that became definitive for the centuries following.

SUMMARY

We have here sketched only the very broad contours of the history of Pauline interpretation. Hundreds of variations could be written on the five positions outlined here, and other issues could be added. Someone is bound to ask, is Paul worth all of this attention? Millions of hours of devoted labor have gone into the copying, translation, study, and interpretation of his letters. Vast material resources have gone into great church buildings that bear his name, and even cities rest under the rubric he bequeathed. Moreover, the influence he exerted on key individuals such as Augustine, Luther, Wesley, Knox, Hildegard von Bingen, and others has been of enormous historical consequence. One can easily imagine that Paul would be embarrassed by all this attention and surprised if not horrified that his personal, occasional ad hoc letters became Scripture.

Yet the labors on his letters and the place they have assumed seem wholly justified, for he raised hard questions that the church had to face, and he dealt with real questions, most of which still lie near the heart of humankind: Does history have a purpose? Can a broken and alienated world be reconciled? What is the nature of the human and divine justice? Can the whole human and nonhuman world be saved from its futility and grief? How can one live with partialities—partial sight, partial knowing, partial being, and an unfinished narrative? What does it mean to be alive "in Christ" and have "Christ alive" in oneself in an age of disbelief? What did the redemption of the human and nonhuman world mean to Paul? And what are its implications still? What light does a study of Paul shed on our understanding of centuries of Western history for good or ill, and what might we learn from such an understanding about living in the modern age? And what inspiration and instruction do the letters still have for a fractured Christian church struggling to find its voice and way in an increasingly secular world?

Suggested Additional Reading

Chapter 1: Paul and His Hellenistic World

Hellenistic World (Introductory)

Boring, M. Eugene, Klaus Berger, and Carsten Colpe, eds. *Hellenistic Commentary to the New Testament*. Nashville: Abingdon Press, 1995.

Bultmann, Rudolf. *Primitive Christianity in Its Contemporary Setting*. Translated by R. H. Fuller. New York: World Publishing Co., Living Age Books, 1957.

Dodds, E. R. *The Greeks and the Irrational*. Berkeley: University of California Press, 1966.

Hengel, Martin. *Judaism and Hellenism*. Translated by John Bowden. 2 vols. Philadelphia: Fortress Press, 1974.

Meeks, Wayne A. *The First Urban Christians: The Social World of the Apostle Paul*. New Haven, CT: Yale University Press, 1983.

Schürer, Emil. *The History of the Jewish People in the Age of Jesus Christ*. Revised and edited by Geza Vermes, Fergus Millar, and Martin Goodman. 4 vols. Edinburgh: T. & T. Clark, 1973–87.

Tcherikover, Victor. *Hellenistic Civilization and the Jews*. Translated by S. Applebaum. New York: Atheneum Publishers, 1970.

Walbank, F. W., et al., eds. *The Cambridge Ancient History*. Vol. 7, *The Hellenistic World*. 2nd ed. Cambridge: Cambridge University Press, 1984.

Argumentation

Diatribe

Stowers, Stanley K. *The Diatribe and Paul's Letters to the Romans*. Chico, CA: Scholars Press, 1981.

Rhetoric

Marrou, H. I. "Education and Rhetoric." In *The Legacy of Greece: A New Appraisal*, edited by M. I. Finley, 185–201. Oxford: Clarendon Press, 1956.

———. *A History of Education in Antiquity*. London: Sheed & Ward, 1956.

225

Allegory

Barr, James. "Typology and Allegory." In *Old and New in Interpretation: A Study of the Two Testaments*, 103–48. London: SCM Press, 1966.

Hellenistic Religion and Philosophy

General

Burkert, Walter. *Greek Religion*. Translated by John Raffan. Cambridge, MA: Harvard University Press, 1977.

Nilsson, Martin. *Greek Piety*. Oxford: Clarendon Press, 1948.

Teixidor, Javier. *The Pagan God: Popular Religion in the Greco-Roman Near East*. Princeton, NJ: Princeton University Press, 1977.

Mystery Religions

Metzger, Bruce M. "A Classified Bibliography of the Graeco-Roman Religions 1924–1973 with a Supplement 1974–1979." In *Aufstieg und Niedergang der Römischen Welt*, edited by Hildegard Temporini and Wolfgang Haase, part 2, vol. 17/3:1259–1423. Berlin: Walter de Gruyter, 1984.

Reitzenstein, R. *Hellenistic Mystery Religions: Their Basic Ideas and Significance*. Translated by J. E. Steely. Pittsburgh: Pickwick Press, 1978.

The Eleusinian Mystery

Burkert, Walter. *Ancient Mystery Cults*. Cambridge, MA: Harvard University Press, 1987.

Mylonas, George E. *Eleusis and the Eleusinian Mysteries*. Princeton, NJ: Princeton University Press, 2000.

Isis and Osiris Mystery (or Serapis Cult)

Frankfort, Henri. *Ancient Egyptian Religion*. New York: Columbia University Press, 1948.

Heyob, Sharon Kelley. *The Cult of Isis among Women in the Greco-Roman World*. Leiden: E. J. Brill, 1975.

Solmsen, Friedrich. *Isis among the Greeks and Romans*. Cambridge, MA: Harvard University Press, 1979.

Witt, R. E. *Isis in the Graeco-Roman World*. Ithaca, NY: Cornell University Press, 1971.

The Dionysiac Mystery

Houser, Caroline. *Dionysus and His Circle: Ancient through Modern*. Cambridge: Fogg Art Museum, Harvard University, 1979.

Nilsson, Martin. *The Dionysiac Mysteries of the Hellenistic and Roman Age*. Lund: W. K. Gleerup, 1957.

Walter, Friedrich Otto. *Dionysus, Myth and Cult*. Bloomington: Indiana University Press, 1965.

The Healing Cult of Asclepius

Edelstein, E. J., and L. Edelstein. *Asclepius: A Collection and Interpretation of the Testamonies*. 2 vols. Baltimore: John Hopkins Press, 1945.

Kee, Howard C. *Medicine, Miracle and Magic in New Testament Times.* Cambridge: Cambridge University Press, 1986.

Kerenyi, C. *Asclepios: Archetypal Image of the Physician's Existence.* Translated by Ralph Manheim. Princeton, NJ: Princeton University Press, 1959.

Stoicism

Colish, Marcia L. *The Stoic Tradition from Antiquity to the Middle Ages.* Leiden: E. J. Brill, 1985.

Engberg-Pedersen, Troels. *Paul and the Stoics.* Edinburgh: T. & T. Clark, 2000.

Rist, John M. *Stoic Philosophy.* London: Cambridge University Press, 1969.

Cynicism

Attridge, Harold W. "The Philosophical Critique of Religion under the Early Empire." In *Aufstieg und Niedergang der Römischen Welt,* edited by Hildegard Temporini and Wolfgang Haase, part 2, vol. 16/1:45–78. Berlin: Walter de Gruyter, 1984.

Mahlerbe, A. J. *The Cynic Epistles: A Study Edition.* Missoula, MT: Scholars Press, 1977.

Sloterdijk, Peter. *Critique of Cynical Reason.* Translated by Michael Eldred. Minneapolis: University of Minnesota Press, 1987. See pp. 101–6 and 155–68.

Neo-Pythagoreanism

Burkert, Walter. *Lore and Science in Ancient Pythagoreanism.* Translated by Michael Edwin L. Minar Jr. Cambridge, MA: Harvard University Press, 1972.

Philostratus. *The Life of Apollonius of Tyana.* Translated by F. C. Conybeare. Loeb Classical Library. Cambridge: Harvard University Press, 1960.

Thesleff, H. *An Introduction to the Pythagorean Writings of the Hellenistic Period.* Abo [Turku], Finland: Abo Akademi, 1961.

Gnosticism

Pagels, Elaine H. *The Gnostic Paul: Gnostic Exegesis of the Pauline Letters.* Philadelphia: Fortress Press, 1976.

Robinson, James M. ed. *The Nag Hammadi Library in English.* Leiden: E. J. Brill: 1988.

Rudolph, K. *Gnosis: The Nature and History of Gnosticism.* Translated by R. McL. Wilson. San Francisco: Harper & Row, 1983.

The Greek Translation of the Bible (The Septuagint, LXX)

Bickerman, E. *Studies in Jewish and Christian History.* 2 vols. Leiden: E. J. Brill, 1976–80.

Dodd, C. H. *The Bible and the Greeks.* London: Hodder & Stoughton, 1935.

Greenspoon, Leonard. "Septuagint," in *The New Interpreter's Dictionary of the Bible,* edited by Katherine Doob Sakenfield et al., 5:170–77. Nashville: Abingdon Press., 2009.

Jellicoe, S. *Studies in the Septuagint: Origins, Recensions, and Interpretation.* New York: KTAV Publishing House, 1974.

Peters, Melvin K. H. "Septuagint." In *The Anchor Bible Dictionary,* edited by David Noel Freedman et al., 5:1093–1104. New York: Doubleday & Co., 1992.

Chapter 2: Paul and His Jewish World

Baron, Salo W. A. *Social and Religious History of the Jews.* 2 vols. 2nd ed. New York: Columbia University Press, 1952–80.

Green, William Scott. *Approaches to Ancient Judaism.* Vols. 2–4. Chico, CA: Scholars Press, 1980–83.

———. *Approaches to Ancient Judaism.* Vol. 5. Decatur, GA: Scholars Press, 1985.

Hengel, Martin. *Judaism and Hellenism.* 2 vols. Translated by John Bowden. Philadelphia: Fortress Press, 1983.

Safrai, Shemuel, and M. Stern, eds. *The Jewish People in the First Century: Historical and Literary Studies, Torah, Pharisees and Rabbis.* Philadelphia: Fortress Press, 1974.

Schürer, Emil. *The History of the Jewish People in the Age of Jesus Christ.* Revised and edited by G. Vermes, Fergus Millar, and Martin Goodman. 4 vols. Edinburgh: T. & T. Clark, 1973–87.

Smallwood, M. E. *The Jews under Roman Rule: From Pompey to Diocletian.* Leiden: E. J. Brill, 1976.

Talmon, S. "The Emergence of Jewish Sectarianism in the Early Second Temple Period," in *Ancient Israelite Religion: Essays in Honor of Frank Moore Cross,* edited by Patrick D. Miller Jr., Paul Hanson, and S. Dean McBride, 587–616. Philadelphia: Fortress Press, 1987.

Tcherikover, Victor. *Hellenistic Civilization and the Jews.* Translated by S. Applebaum. New York: Atheneum Press, 1970.

Pharisaism

Baeck, L. *The Pharisees, and Other Essays.* New York: Schocken Books, 1966.

Saldarini, A. J. "Pharisees." In *The Anchor Bible Dictionary,* edited by D. N. Freedman et al., 5:289–303. New York: Doubleday & Co. 1992.

Schwartz, S. *Imperialism and Jewish Society from 200 BCE to 640 CE.* Princeton, NJ: Princeton University Press, 2001.

Scripture Interpretation

Carson, D. A., and H. G. M. Williamson, eds. *It Is Written: Scripture Citing Scriptures.* Cambridge: Cambridge University Press, 1988.

Hays, Richard B. *Echoes of Scriptures in the Letters of Paul.* New Haven, CT: Yale University Press, 1989.

Apocalypticism

Charlesworth, James H. *Old Testament Pseudepigrapha.* Vol. 1, *Apocalyptic Literature and Testaments.* Garden City, NY: Doubleday & Co., 1983.

Collins, John J. *The Apocalyptic Imagination: An Introduction to the Jewish Matrix of Christianity.* 2nd ed. New York: Crossroad, 1998.

———. *The Encyclopedia of Apocalypticism.* Vol. 1, *The Origins of Apocalypticism in Judaism and Early Christianity.* Sheffield: Continuum Press, 2002.

Hellholm, David. ed. *Apocalypticism in the Mediterranean World and the Near East.* Tübingen: J. C. B. Mohr (Paul Siebeck), 1983.

Rowland, Christopher. "Apocalypticism." In *The New Interpreter's Dictionary of the Bible,* 1:190–95. Nashville: Abingdon Press, 2006.

———. *The Open Heaven: A Study of Apocalyptic in Judaism and Early Christianity.* New York: Crossroad, 1982.

Vanderkam, James C., and Peter W. Flint. *The Meaning of the Dead Sea Scrolls: Their Significance for Understanding the Bible, Judaism, Jesus, and Christianity*. New York: Harper Collins, 2002.

Vermes, Geza. *The Complete Dead Sea Scrolls in English*. Translated from Hebrew and Aramaic and edited by Geza Vermes. Great Britain: Penguin Press, 1998.

Chapter 3: The Anatomy of the Letters

Aune, David E. *The New Testament in Its Literary Environment*. Philadelphia: Westminster Press, 1987.

Dahl, Nils A. "Letter." In *Interpreter's Dictionary of the Bible, Supplementary Volume*, 538–41. Nashville: Abingdon Press, 1976.

Richard, E. Randolph. "Letter." In *New Interpreter's Dictionary of the Bible*, 3:638 41. Nashville: Abingdon Press, 2008.

Stowers, Stanley K. *Letter Writing in Greco-Roman Antiquity*. Philadelphia: Westminster Press, 1986.

White, John L. "New Testament Epistolary Literature in the Framework of Ancient Epistolography." In *Aufstieg und Niedergang der Römischen Welt*, edited by Hildegard Temporini and Wolfgang Haase, part 3, vol. 25/2:1730–56. Berlin: Walter de Gruyter, 1984.

Chapter 4: Traditions behind the Letters

Betz, Hans Dieter. "A Catalogue of Vices and Virtues." In *Galatians: A Commentary on Paul's Letter to the Churches in Galatia*, 281–83. Philadelphia: Fortress Press, 1979.

Davies, W. D. "Ethics in the New Testament." In *Interpreter's Dictionary of the Bible*, 2:167–76. Nashville: Abingdon Press, 1962.

Furnish, Victor Paul. *The Moral Teaching of Paul*. 3rd ed. revised. Nashville: Abingdon Press, 2009.

Matera, Frank. "Ethics in the New Testament." In *The New Interpreter's Dictionary of the Bible*, 2:328–38. Nashville: Abingdon Press, 2007.

Sampley, J. Paul. *Walking between the Times: Paul's Moral Reasoning*. Minneapolis: Augsburg-Fortress, 1991.

Sanders, Jack T. *New Testament Christological Hymns: Their Historical Religious Background*. Cambridge: Cambridge University Press, 1971.

Schnackenburg, R. *Baptism in the Thought of St. Paul: A Study of Pauline Theology*. Translated by G. R. Beasley-Murray. New York: Herder & Herder, 1964.

Schweitzer, Eduard. *The Lord's Supper according to the New Testament*. Translated by James M. Davis. Philadelphia: Fortress Press, 1967.

Chapter 5: The Letters as Conversations

1 Thessalonians

Donfried, Karl P. "The Cults of Thessalonica and the Thessalonian Correspondence." In *Paul, Thessalonica, and Early Christianity*, 21–48. Grand Rapids: Eerdmans, 2002.

Furnish, Victor Paul. *1 Thessalonians, 2 Thessalonians*. Abingdon New Testament Commentaries. Nashville: Abingdon Press, 2007.

Koester, Helmut. "1 Thessalonians—Experiment in Christian Writing." In *Continuity and Discontinuity in Church History: Essays Presented to George Huntston Williams*, edited by F. F. Church and T. George, 33–44. Leiden: E. J. Brill, 1979.

Krentz, Edgar M. "Thessalonians, First and Second Epistles to the." In *The Anchor Bible Dictionary*, ed. David Noel Freedman et al., 6:515–23. New York: Doubleday, 1992.

1 Corinthians

Barrett, C. K. *A Commentary on the First Epistle to the Corinthians*. New York: Harper & Row, 1968.

Betz, Hans Dieter, and Margaret M. Mitchell. "Corinthians, First Epistle to the." In *Anchor Bible Dictionary*, 1:1139–54. New York: Doubleday, 1992.

Castelli, Elizabeth A. *Imitating Paul: A Discourse of Power*. Louisville, KY: Westminster/John Knox Press, 1991.

Horsley, R. A. *1 Corinthians*. Abingdon New Testament Commentaries. Nashville: Abingdon Press, 1998.

Hurd, J. C. Jr. *The Origin of First Corinthians*. New York: Seabury Press, 1983.

Mitchell, Margaret M. *Paul and the Rhetoric of Reconciliation, An Exegetical Investigation of The Language and Composition of 1 Corinthians*. Tübingen: J. C. B. Mohr, 1991.

Pagels, Elaine H. "Paul and Women: A Response to Recent Discussion." *Journal of the American Academy of Religion* 40 (1972): 538–49.

Scroggs, R. "Paul and the Eschatological Woman." *Journal of the American Academy of Religion* 42 (1972): 283–303.

———. "Paul and the Eschatological Woman Revisited." *Journal of the American Academy of Religion* 44 (1974): 532–37.

Wire, Antoinette Clark. *The Corinthian Women Prophets: A Reconstruction through Paul's Rhetoric*. Minneapolis: Fortress Press, 1990.

2 Corinthians

Furnish, Victor Paul. *II Corinthians*. Garden City, NY: Doubleday & Co. 1984.

Mitchell, Margaret M. "Paul's Letters to Corinth: The Interpretative Intertwining of Literary and Historical Reconstruction." In *Urban Religion in Roman Corinth*, edited by Daniel N. Schowalter and Steven J. Friesen, 307–38. Cambridge, MA: Harvard Theological Studies, 2005.

Roetzel, C. J. *2 Corinthians*. Abingdon New Testament Studies. Nashville: Abingdon Press, 2007.

Galatians

Betz, Hans Dieter. *Galatians*. Philadelphia: Fortress Press, 1979.

———. "The Literary Composition and Function of Paul's Letters to the Galatians." *New Testament Studies* 21 (1974–75): 353–73.

Hays, Richard B. *The Faith of Jesus Christ*. Chico, CA: Scholars Press, 1983.

Williams, Sam K. *Galatians*. Abingdon New Testament Commentaries. Nashville: Abingdon Press, 1997.

Philippians

Furnish, Victor Paul. "The Place and Purpose of Philippians III." *New Testament Studies* 10 (1963–64): 80–98.

Roetzel, Calvin J. "Philippians, Book of." In *Dictionary of Biblical Interpretation*, 280–83. Nashville: Abingdon Press, 1999.

Sellew, Philip. "*Laodiceans* and the Philippians Fragments Hypothesis." *Harvard Theological Review* 87 (1994): 17–28.

Philemon

Petersen, Norman R. *Rediscovering Paul: Philemon and the Sociology of Paul's Narrative World*. Philadelphia: Fortress Press, 1985.

White, J. L. "The Structural Analysis of Philemon: A Point of Departure in the Formal Analysis of the Pauline Letters." *Society of Biblical Literature Seminary Papers* 1 (1971): 1–45.

Winter, S. C. "Paul's Letter to Philemon." *New Testament Studies* 33 (1987): 1–35.

Romans

Badenas, Robert. *Christ the End of the Law: Romans 10:4 in Pauline Perspective*. Sheffield: JSOT Press, 1985.

Bassler, Jouette. *Divine Impartiality: Paul and a Theological Axiom*. Chico, CA: Scholars Press, 1982.

Beker, J. Christiaan. *Paul the Apostle: The Triumph of God in Life and Thought*. Philadelphia: Fortress Press, 1980.

Fitzmyer, Joseph A. *Romans: A New Translation with Introduction and Commentary*. New York: Doubleday & Co., 1992.

Jewett, Robert. *Romans*. Hermeneia. Minneapolis: Fortress Press, 2007.

Käsemann, Ernst. *Commentary on Romans*. Translated by Geoffrey W. Bromiley. Grand Rapids: Eerdmans, 1980.

Keck, Leander E. *Romans*. Abingdon New Testament Commentaries. Nashville: Abingdon Press, 2005.

Stendahl, Krister. "The Apostle Paul and the Introspective Conscience of the West." In *Paul among Jews and Gentiles*. Philadelphia: Fortress Press, 1976.

Stowers, S. K. *A Rereading of Romans, Justice, Jews & Gentile*. New Haven, CT: Yale University Press, 1994.

Chapter 6: Paul and His Myths

Bultmann, Rudolf. *Jesus Christ and Mythology*. New York: Charles Scribner's Sons, 1958.

———. *Kerygma and Myth: A Theological Debate*. Edited by Hans Werner Bartsch. New York: Harper & Row, 1961.

Cassirer, Ernst. *Language and Myth*. Translated by Susanne K. Langer. New York: Harper & Bros., 1946.

———. *The Philosophy of Symbolic Forms*. Vol. 2, *Mythical Thought*. New Haven, CT: Yale University Press, 1955.

Douglas, Mary. "Deciphering a Meal." In *Myth, Symbol, and Culture*, edited by Clifford Geertz. New York: W. W. Norton & Co., 1971.

Eliade, Mircea. *The Myth of the Eternal Return.* Translated by Willard R. Trask. New York: Harcourt Brace & Co., 1959.

———. *Rites and Symbols of Initiation.* New York: Harper & Row, 1965.

Forsyth, Neil. *The Old Enemy: Satan and the Combat Myth.* Princeton, NJ: Princeton University Press, 1987.

Frye, Northrop. *The Great Code: The Bible and Literature.* San Diego: Harcourt Brace Jovanovich, 1983.

Frye, N., L. C. Knights, et al. *Myth and Symbol: Critical Approaches and Application.* Lincoln: University of Nebraska Press, 1963.

Geertz, Clifford. *The Interpretation of Cultures.* New York: Basic Books, 1973.

Harrison, Jane E. *Mythology.* 1924. Reprint. New York: Harcourt, Brace & World, 1963.

Kluckhohn, Clyde. "Myth and Ritual: A General Theory." *Harvard Theological Review* 35 (1942): 45ff.

Leach, Edmund. *Claude Lévi Strauss.* New York: Viking Press, 1970.

———. *Genesis as Myth, and Other Essays.* New York: Grossman Publishers, 1970.

———, ed. *The Structural Study of Myth and Totemism.* London: Tavistock Publications, 1967.

Ricoeur, Paul. "The Adamic Myth and the Eschatological Vision of History." In *The Symbolism of Evil,* 232–78. Boston: Beacon Press, 1982.

Turner, Victor. *The Ritual Process: Structure and Anti-Structure.* Hawthorne, NY: Aldine Publishing Co., 1982.

Wilder, Amos N. *Jesus' Parables and the War of Myths: Essays on Imagination in Scripture.* Philadelphia: Fortress Press, 1982.

Chapter 7: New Testament Interpreters of Paul

Colossians

Dahl, Nils A. "Christ, Creation, and the Church." In *Jesus in the Memory of the Early Church.* Minneapolis: Augsburg Publishing House, 1976.

Dunn, James D. G. "Colossians, Letter to." In *New Interpreter's Dictionary of the Bible,* edited by Katherine D. Sakenfeld et al., 1:702–6. Nashville: Abingdon Press, 2006.

Francis, Fred O., and Wayne A. Meeks, editors and translators. *Conflict at Colossae.* Missoula, MT: Scholars Press, 1973.

Käsemann, Ernst. "A Primitive Christian Baptismal Liturgy." In *Essays on New Testament Themes.* Philadelphia: Fortress Press, 1982.

Wilson, R. McL. *Colossians and Philemon: A Critical and Exegetical Commentary.* Edinburgh: T. & T. Clark, 2005.

Ephesians

Caird, G. B. *Principalities and Powers: A Study of Pauline Theology.* Oxford: Clarendon Press, 1956.

Perkins, Pheme. *Ephesians.* Abingdon New Testament Commentaries. Nashville: Abingdon Press, 1997.

Roetzel, Calvin J. "Jewish Christian-Gentile Christian Relations: A Discussion of Ephesians 2:15a." *Zeitschrift für die neutestamentliche Wissenschaft* 74 (1983): 81–89.

Sampley, J. Paul. *Ephesians, Colossians, 2 Thessalonians, the Pastoral Epistles*. Philadelphia: Fortress Press, 1978.

Schlier, Heinrich. *Principalities and Powers in the New Testament*. New York: Herder & Herder, 1961.

Turner, Max. "Ephesians, Letter to the." In *New Interpreter's Dictionary of the Bible*, edited by Katherine D. Sakenfeld et al., 2:269–76. Nashville: Abingdon Press, 2007.

Wink, Walter. *Naming the Powers: The Language of Power in the New Testament*. Philadelphia: Fortress Press, 1984.

2 Thessalonians

Furnish, Victor P. *1 Thessalonians, 2 Thessalonians*. Abingdon New Testament Commentaries. Nashville: Abingdon Press, 2007.

Krentz, Edgar M. "Through a Prism: The Theology of 2 Thessalonians as a Deutero-Pauline Letters." In *Society of Biblical Literature Seminar Papers*, edited by David J. Lull, 1–7. Atlanta: Scholars Press, 1986.

———. "Thessalonians, First and Second Epistles to the." In *The Anchor Bible Dictionary*, edited by David Noel Freedman et al., 6:515–23. New York: Doubleday, 1992.

1 and 2 Timothy and Titus (The Pastorals)

Barrett, C. K. "Pauline Controversies in the Post-Pauline Period." *New Testament Studies* 20 (1973–74): 229–45.

Bassler, Jouette M. *1 Timothy, 2 Timothy, Titus*. Abingdon New Testament Commentaries. Nashville: Abingdon Press, 1996.

Dibelius, Martin, and Hans Conzelmann. *The Pastoral Epistles*. Translated by Philip Buttolph and Adela Yarbro. Philadelphia: Fortress Press, 1972.

Gealy, Fred D. "The First and Second Epistles to Timothy and the Epistle to Titus, Introduction and Exegesis." In *The Interpreter's Bible*, 6:343–551. Nashville: Abingdon Press, 1955.

Käsemann, Ernst. "Paul and Early Catholicism." In *New Testament Questions of Today*. Philadelphia: Fortress Press, 1972.

Quinn, Jerome D. *The Letter to Titus*. New Haven, CT: Yale University Press, 1990.

Chapter 8: Currents and Crosscurrents

Bauer, Walter. *Orthodoxy and Heresy in Earliest Christianity*. Edited by Robert A. Kraft and Gerhard Krodel. Philadelphia: Fortress Press, 1971.

Boyarin, Daniel. *Paul and the Politics of Identity: A Radical Jew*. Berkeley: University of California Press, 1994.

Brooten, Bernadette J. "Jewish Women's History in the Roman Period: A Task for Christian Theology." In *Christians among Jews and Gentiles*, edited by George W. E. Nickelsburg, 22–30. Philadelphia: Fortress Press, 1986.

Brown, Peter. *The Making of Late Antiquity*. Cambridge: Harvard University Press, 1978.

Castelli, Elizabeth A. *Imitating Paul: A Discourse of Power*. Louisville, KY: Westminster/John Knox Press, 1991.

Fiorenza, Elisabeth Schüssler. *In Memory of Her: A Feminist Theological Reconstruction of Christian Origins*, 205–41. New York: Crossroad, 1988.

Lerner, Gerda. *The Creation of Feminist Consciousness: From the Middle Ages to 1870*. Oxford: Oxford University Press, 1993.

Wiles, Maurice F. *The Divine Apostle*. Cambridge: Cambridge University Press, 1967.

Index

235